Parliaments and Legislatures Series

Samuel C. Patterson
GENERAL ADVISORY EDITOR

Parliaments and Legislatures Series

The aims of this series are to enhance knowledge about the well-established legislative assemblies of North America and western Europe and to publish studies of parliamentary assemblies worldwide—from Russia and the former Soviet bloc nations to Asia, Africa, and Latin America. The series is open to a wide variety of theoretical applications, historical dimensions, data collections, and methodologies.

OTHER BOOKS IN THE SERIES

Cheap Seats: The Democratic Party's Advantage in U.S. House Elections
James E. Campbell

Coalition Government, Subnational Style: Multiparty Politics in Europe's Regional Parliaments
William M. Downs

Creating Parliamentary Government

The Transition to Democracy in Bulgaria

ALBERT P. MELONE

OHIO STATE UNIVERSITY PRESS · Columbus

All photographs courtesy of the Bulgarian News and Telegraph Agency, except for the one on p. 234, which is courtesy of the Constitutional Court of the Republic of Bulgaria.

Library of Congress Cataloging-in-Publication Data

Melone, Albert P.
Creating parliamentary government : the transition to democracy in Bulgaria / Albert P. Melone.
p. cm. — (Parliaments and legislatures series)
Includes bibliographical references (p.) and index.
ISBN 0-8142-0769-3 (cloth : alk. paper). — ISBN 0-8142-0770-7 (pbk. : alk. paper)
1. Bulgaria. Narodno sŭbranie—History. 2. Legislative bodies—Bulgaria—History. 3. Representative government and representation—Bulgaria—History. 4. Democracy—Bulgaria—History. 5. Bulgaria—Politics and government—1990– I. Title. II. Series.
JN9607.M45 1998
320.9499′09′049—dc21 98-16298
CIP

Text design by David C. den Boer.
Type set in Times New Roman and Basilia Haas by Graphic Composition, Inc.
Printed by McNaughton & Gunn, Inc.

The paper used in this publication meets the minimum requirements of the American National Standard for Information Sciences—Permanence of Paper for Printed Library Materials. ANSI Z39.48-1992.

9 8 7 6 5 4 3 2 1

To Peggy Jo Harles Melone, a scion of the Northern Prairie,
for her life-sustaining charm, wit, wisdom, support, and love

Contents

Part III
Consolidation Politics: Parliament and Interinstitutional Conflict

Illustrations

Foreword

We are living in an age in which democratic constitutions and politics are being established, or are emerging, in parts of the world hitherto suffering authoritarian domination. Democracy is one of those rather uncertain political concepts susceptible to varying meanings. In contemporary writing, democracy often means the existence of a culture of civic participation in which free expression and free elections may thrive. Democratization, or democratic consolidation, is too frequently analyzed only in these terms, without giving attention to political institutions, and especially to legislative or parliamentary institutions.

Yet, it seems axiomatic that representative assemblies are essential institutions for democracy in large-scale societies. Theorizing about or analyzing democratic transitions without including parliaments in the story makes for theory that is grossly atomistic and analysis that is glaringly devoid of institutional grounding. This series of books is founded on the assumption that parliaments and legislatures are at the heart of democracy. The study of democratic politics must entail anatomizing the selection, structure, performance, and impact of parliamentary or legislative institutions.

In *Creating Parliamentary Government* Al Melone tells the fascinating story of the negotiations and struggles in the early 1990s that transformed the Bulgarian political regime from a Soviet-style puppet state to a freestanding democracy. In so doing, Melone proceeds in a theoretically sensitive fashion that informs his analysis of a concrete case of democratic transition and consolidation. He articulates sequences and events in the Bulgarian democratic transition by closely examining the actual processes of negotiating a change in regime and establishing democratic political institutions. By conducting in-depth interviews with leading actors in the Bulgarian transition, including members of Parliament, Melone is able to reconstruct the politics through which the process of shaping a new national constitution was hammered out, and parliamentary institutions were made to work.

The author first recounts the fascinating story of the Roundtable Talks among major Bulgarian politicians who met after the demise of the communist regime to put into motion the mechanism for forging a democratic constitution. Melone brings these politicians to life by letting them tell the story in their own words. As in other Eastern and Central European countries, the Bulgarian transition process embraced a remarkable array of individual leaders, independent groups, and organizations that ultimately formed a loose coalition. The personal accounts of the leading actors in this drama reveal both the political and the human features of the transition to democracy in Bulgaria. Then, the author describes the work of the constitutional convention agreed upon at the Roundtable Talks. Interestingly, former communists, running in the election under the Bulgarian Socialist Party label, won a majority of the seats in this Grand National Assembly (as the Constitutional Convention was named), the seventh such convocation in Bulgarian history.

Once the new constitution is in place, Melone examines the consolidation of the new democracy, focusing on parliament, parliamentary representation, and interinstitutional conflicts. Noting that "the legislative arena is the centerpiece of parliamentary democracy," the author presents a rich and vivid account of the parliamentary elections and the crucial institution-building events of the early and difficult days of democratic political life. Melone's sensitive analysis of the emergence of democratic parliamentary politics in Bulgaria sheds important light on the general nature of transitions to democracy, and underscores the possibilities for parliamentary government under fragile and even adverse circumstances. Moreover, this analysis allows us to understand the context of struggle and change in which the new Bulgarian parliament is emerging today.

Samuel C. Patterson

Acknowledgments

A PROPER ACKNOWLEDGMENT of those who helped me to prepare this book requires first a brief sketch detailing my involvement in things Bulgarian. Since my graduate school days in the late 1960s, I was aware of the in-principle importance of conducting comparative research. My primary research and teaching focus in the 1970s and 1980s was on judicial politics and related topics, including American legislative and interest group politics. Yet, I had long ago internalized the view that the comparative method is essential if as a discipline we are to develop a science of politics. No doubt a cross-cultural approach is preferable to the parochialism and ethnocentrism of American politics. But how does one move from an exclusive attention on the U.S. scene to other political cultures? As my case illustrates, it can happen when there is a combination of a university support system that encourages international exchanges, changing world events, and the good fortune of being in the right place at the right time.

The relationship between Southern Illinois University at Carbondale (SIUC) and the Republic of Bulgaria began in 1983. Dr. Emilia Kandeva-Spiridonova of Bulgaria's Academy of Science Institute for State and Law (since renamed the Institute for Legal Studies) received a Fulbright grant to study at SIUC during the 1983–84 academic year. During her stay in Carbondale, Emilia and I became friends. Since then she has been a source of information and encouragement. Her own work at SIUC culminated in a widely read and influential book in public administration published in Bulgaria about five years ago. Subsequently, Dr. Kandeva-Spiridonova became the director of Bulgaria's Center for Administration. Personnel of this organization hosted visits and provided support to SIUC scholars. In 1997, Kandeva-Spiridonova became the Bulgarian Lead Advisor to the Public Administration Reform Programme (Phare).

During her spring 1984 visit to the SIUC campus, Dr. Kandeva-

Spiridonova arranged for a campus visit by two representatives of the Bulgarian Embassy. The outgrowth of that visit was the formulation and signing of a Memorandum of Understanding between the Bulgarian Council of Higher Education and SIUC. The first visitor to SIUC under this linkage agreement was Professor Matey Mateev. He spent one month working with colleagues in the Department of Physics. Following the demise of the old regime in November 1989, Mateev became the first minister of public education in the new government.

As a result of several visits by SIUC administrators to Bulgaria, these officials submitted a proposal to the United States Information Agency (USIA) under the University Affiliations Program. This proposal was funded for the period 1987 to 1991, and it resulted in the exchange of nine SIUC faculty and nine Bulgarian researchers and faculty. Exchanges were conducted during that period in law, sociological research, radio-television, higher education administration, educational psychology, and art.

A major result of the grant was the first Annual Bulgarian-American Law Days. It was sponsored jointly by the Institute of State and Law of Sofia and SIUC. The theme of this May 1991 conference held at the Black Sea resort city of Varna, Bulgaria, was the impact of constitutional change on the Bulgarian legal and political system. Three political science professors, three law professors, and the SIUC executive assistant to the president for international and economic development, the late Charles Klasek, composed the official SIUC contingent. The official and unofficial Bulgarian participants far outnumbered the Americans. They included scholars of the Institute of State and Law, government officials, practicing attorneys, and law professors.

The timing of the Varna conference was particularly fortuitous. It was held after much of the work of the Grand National Assembly was completed. This part legislature and part constitutional convention was fashioning Bulgaria's new Constitution, and as a result of its work a new democratic document was promulgated in July 1991. Some Bulgarian participants at the Varna conference had an intimate knowledge of the politics of constitution-making by virtue of their personal involvement in drafting various provisions. By way of explanation, they sometimes argued with one another. In the process, they provided the American delegation with graphic descriptions and explanations for the likely changes in the Bulgarian political and constitutional system.

Some papers by the American participants at the Varna conference were explicitly cross-cultural while others focused exclusively on the U.S. experience. Actually, it mattered little what we spoke about. With their forty-five years of relative isolation from Americans, our Bulgarian hosts could find little wrong with anything American, including our papers. Needless to say, they carried this admiration to an unjustifiable extreme. However, the extent to which our Bulgarian hosts understood the constitutional issues within a comparative political context was particularly striking. We found their knowledge of alternative constitutional and political systems remarkable. A volume containing the conference papers was published in 1994 by the official press of Sofia University, St. Kliment Ohridski University Press. It is titled *Law in a Fast-Changing Society,* edited by Silvy Chernev.

There was a sequel to the first Bulgarian/American Law Days. This time Bulgarians journeyed to Carbondale for a conference in May and June 1992. Their stay in the United States included visits to Washington, D.C., and other cities. The USIA-funded 1992 Carbondale conference was jointly hosted by the SIUC Law School and the Department of Political Science. The conference theme was the U.S. judicial process and constitutional system. Fifteen visiting Bulgarian jurists attended the conference. They included judges and justices at each jurisdictional level, prosecuting attorneys, private lawyers, and law professors. The Bulgarian participants were selected because of their probable impact on the future of the Bulgarian judicial system and for their lack of ties to the old regime.

Unlike at the previous conference, only the American participants presented papers. These papers became part of a single volume published in 1993 by the St. Kliment Ohridski University Press. Maria Frankowska and I are the coeditors of this volume, titled *The Legal System and American Constitutional Democracy.* This dual-language book contains twelve chapters by SIUC political scientists and law professors.

The presence of the Bulgarian jurists on the SIUC campus offered a rare opportunity to gain insight into problems facing parliamentary institutions and judiciaries in a transitional society. We asked all the Bulgarians to respond to a closed-ended questionnaire and to participate in an additional in-depth personal interview. All but one participant agreed to fill out the closed-ended questionnaire and fourteen agreed to in-depth personal interviews. The closed-item schedule was written in English with a Bulgarian translation.

Composing the interview schedules required a careful look at the new Bulgarian Constitution promulgated in July 1991. To design these interview schedules, two graduate students, Marc George Pufong, now a faculty member in the Department of Political Science at Valdosta State University, and Carol E. Hays, and I worked closely with a Bulgarian legal scholar, Silvy Chernev, the same person who edited the Varna papers. He was in residence at the SIUC Law School during the spring term preceding the conference. Along the way, we gained an appreciation for the extraordinary political acumen and commitment to human rights and parliamentary government that went into writing the Constitution.

The knowledge gained through these interviews made it possible for me to better understand the principles and politics surrounding various constitutional provisions. I was also able to glimpse whether these jurists believed a new constitutional system could change existing attitudes. Indeed, a year later I came to understand the importance of the preliminary research in terms of the new institutionalism movement in political research. Can democratic institutions coax into existence a civil society? The results of the interviews produced a mixed interpretation. My own reading and research conducted since those initial interviews compel me to question the conventional wisdom. Albeit with some trepidation and much hope, I now respond in the affirmative: folkways can follow stateways.

In October 1992 I attended a "Conference on Legal Education and the New Democratic Societies—Transition Toward Democracy and the Rule of Law," held at South-West University "NEOPHIT RISLKI" Blagoevgrad, Bulgaria. The invitation came as the result of contacts developed at the Varna meeting, but it had nothing to do with the USIA program in Carbondale. At that meeting and my subsequent stay in Sofia, my interest in Bulgaria's fledgling civil society intensified. I began to entertain the counterconventional idea that just maybe Bulgaria could experience a successful transition from totalitarianism to democracy. This might happen although as a nation-state the so-called prerequisites for democracy are not present. While visiting with colleagues in Sofia after the Blagoevgrad conference, the president of one of Bulgaria's many new nongovernmental foundations asked me to pen an article about problems associated with the creation of civil society. At the time, I was fixated on the problem of the debilitating effects of the twin traps of mass society and the iron law of oligarchy on the creation of pluralism. However, within nine months after writing that piece my attention was redirected to the prior and the more fundamental issue. Namely, is it possible to coax a civil society into existence from the rudiments of a democratic constitution without those commonly supposed prerequisites such as a strong economy, a middle class, and experience with democratic institutions such as competitive political parties? This is perhaps the most interesting question in political science today.

My first serious crack at this particular issue came in a paper presented at the 1993 Interim Meeting of the International Political Science Association Research Committee on Comparative Judicial Studies held in Santa Fe, New Mexico. It is a detailed account of Bulgaria's National Roundtable Talks held in late 1989 and early 1990. My sabbatical leave of absence in the fall of 1993 was devoted to exploring this question further. Among other activities, I interviewed a good number of Bulgarian elites, including persons who participated in the National Roundtable Talks in 1990, persons elected to the Grand National Assembly that drafted the July 1991 Constitution, and members of Parliament. I also interviewed legal professionals including justices of the Bulgarian Constitutional Court. These interviews form the core of materials found in this volume. A brief stay at the Socio-Legal Centre at Wolfson College, Oxford University, in the fall of 1993 was useful as a way to test ideas. I am particularly grateful to Professor Mavis Maclean for her invitation to Oxford and her encouraging colleagueship. In the months and years to follow, I presented a series of professional papers at political science association meetings including presentations at the American Political Science Association, the Midwest Political Science Association, the Western Political Science Association, and the International Political Science Association. Reactions from professional colleagues were both helpful and positive.

I am grateful to the Center for the Study of Constitutionalism in Eastern Europe at the University of Chicago Law School. The staff provided me first with a list of bibliographical materials in their possession. Upon request, they sent me both published and unpublished materials pertinent to the Bulgarian constitutional experience.

The first draft of this book manuscript was completed in time for the beginning of the fall 1995 academic term. As part of my graduate seminar in Constitutional Changes in Eastern Europe, the students and I critiqued this draft. I am particularly indebted to Bradley Best, Angelis Vlahou, Jay Stokes, and Alexander Danilovich for their insights and criticisms. I also asked colleagues, friends, and relatives to offer suggestions for changes. My colleagues in the SIUC Department of Political Science were pressed with questions and for criticisms. William Turley plowed through most of the first draft and a draft of an early article. He provided cogent comments and suggestions. William Garner, Susan Collins, and Scott Tarry graciously provided helpful bibliographical references. I also asked Bulgarians living in the United States and Bulgaria to read the manuscript, including Emilia Kandeva-Spiridonova, Ivan Nikolov, a host of Bulgarian students studying at SIUC, and Luben Nikolov and Krasimira Nikolova of Sofia. It was reassuring to learn from all the Bulgarians who read the manuscript that I had the story right.

Several professional papers and other segments of the larger study found their way into print as professional articles. These include Albert P. Melone and Carol E. Hays, "The Judicial Role in Bulgaria's Struggle for Human Rights," *Judicature* 77 (1994): 248–53; Albert P. Melone, "Bulgaria's National Roundtable Talks and the Politics of Accommodation," *International Political Science Review* 15 (1994): 257–73; Albert P. Melone, "Serendipity and International Experience in Political Science: The Bulgaria/Southern Illinois University at Carbondale Connection," *PS: Political Science and Politics* 27 (March 1994): 149–51; Albert P. Melone, "The Struggle for Judicial Independence and the Transition Toward Democracy in Bulgaria," *Communist and Post-Communist Studies* 29 (1996): 231–43; Albert P. Melone, "Bulgaria," in George Kurian, ed., *World Encyclopedia of Parliaments and Legislatures* (Washington, D.C.: Congressional Quarterly Press, 1998); Albert P. Melone, "Judicial Independence and Constitutional Politics in Post-Communist Bulgaria," *Judicature* 80 (May–June 1997): 280–85;

Albert P. Melone and Bradley Best, "Creating the Institutions for a Law-Governed State: The Constitutional Politics of Bulgaria's Grand National Assembly," in Stuart Nagel, ed., *Research in Law and Policy Studies,* vol. 6 (Greenwich, Conn.: JAI, (forthcoming). I gratefully acknowledge each publisher for permission to reprint portions of those pieces in this book.

My much gifted daughter, Ann Melone of Seattle, Washington, read the second draft of the manuscript with a particular eye toward readability. I adopted many of her suggestions. I then submitted a proposal and later a third draft of the manuscript to Samuel C. "Pat" Patterson, the advisory editor of the Parliaments and Legislatures Series at the Ohio State University Press. His enthusiastic endorsement of the manuscript led Charlotte Dihoff, OSU Press editor-in-chief, to send my work out for formal review. I have incorporated the suggestions for changes made by the anonymous reviewers. Because of their careful analyses, the final product is an improvement over the original submission.

Useful materials were provided to me by the Reference Service of the Bulgarian News and Telegraph Agency (BTA). I am grateful for a chronology of the National Roundtable Talks and another for the Grand National Assembly. Also, most of the photographs found in this volume are through the courtesy of the BTA. One photograph is provided courtesy of the Constitutional Court of the Republic of Bulgaria.

The BTA cooperation was facilitated by my friend Luben Nikolov. He is a former BTA foreign correspondent stationed for five years in London. Without his help, it is doubtful I could have successfully completed the research project. Tenyu Boyadjiev and Ivona Spiridonova, graduate students at SIUC, and Ivan Nikolov, research project specialist of the SIUC Office of International Development, provided helpful assistance in translating some Bulgarian sources. Ivona Spiridonova and Ivan Nikolov also read and commented upon early drafts of the manuscript. Other Bulgarians aided me in a variety of tasks. They include, but are not limited to, Justice Alexander Arabadjiev of Bulgaria's Constitutional Court; Stefka Naoumova, a legal scholar and onetime member of Parliament; Tsvetanta Kamenova, director of the Bulgarian Academy of Sciences Institute for Legal Studies; Dr. Snezhana Botusharova, ambassador extraordinaire and plenipotentiary of the Republic of Bulgaria, and her former first secretary, Dobra Takova-Garner; Dr. Mariana T. Karagiozova-Finkova of the St. Kliment Ohridski University Law faculty; Dr. Emilia Drumeva, secretary to Parliament; Antonina P. Bakardjieva, formerly a staff member of the European Parliament who presently lives in Sweden; Diman Dimov, my undergraduate student at SIUC, a Sofia attorney, and now studying abroad.

For financial aid in the form of a sabbatical leave extension, I am grateful to the special SIU graduate school committee in charge of such matters. The SIUC Office of International and Economic Development provided both financial assistance and staff help for this project. In particular, the late Charles Klasek, Richard Kuehl, Ivan Nikolov, and Rhonda Vinson provided valuable assistance. During my most recent visit to Bulgaria in March 1997, David Hampson of US MEDS provided me a place to stay in Sofia and other services that made my visit both financially possible and productive. Robert Jensen, the College of Liberal Arts acting dean; John S. Jackson III, the vice chancellor for academic affairs and provost; and the SIUC Department of Political Science all contributed support for my various Bulgarian activities.

At different stages, graduate research assistants helped me with this project. Marc George Pufong and Carol Hays were the first to labor over my thoughts, followed by Kevin Walsh and Bradley Best, in that order. Walsh and Best were compelled to read many different drafts of various chapters.

A special debt of gratitude goes to a friend in the SIUC history department. Michael Batinski was a cheerleader for this project, offering his moral support and encouragement from the very beginning.

Several secretaries in the Southern Illinois University at Carbondale Department of Political Science eased the task of producing this manuscript in its various iterations. Rebecca Burns and Marilyn Farthing formatted and printed many drafts along the way. Rhonda Musgrave was the final secretary to see the manuscript through to completion. It helps to have a secretary who believes in one's projects, and Rhonda Musgrave was particularly diligent in all aspects of bringing the final draft into existence.

I am grateful to the staff at the Ohio State University Press for their professionalism. Charlotte Dihoff, editor-in-chief, and the press staff are a joy to work with.

My spouse, Peggy Melone, contributed in a variety ways to this project. Most important, as efficient manager of the homefront she made it possible for me to conduct my busy research, teaching, and service duties in relative tranquility.

Finally, I take full responsibility for any errors of fact or interpretation found in this book. None of the above mentioned persons or institutions bear any responsibility for what is wrong with this book. Each, however, is responsible for what is right with the effort.

1

Introduction

Explaining transitions from authoritarian and totalitarian states to democratic ones is difficult enough in such places as Spain, Portugal, Greece, Turkey, Argentina, Brazil, and Uruguay.[1] The even more spectacular events in the former Soviet Union and Eastern bloc countries compel us to reconsider much of what is known about the dynamics of political development.[2] No less a venerable scholar than Samuel P. Huntington asserted in 1984 that the "likelihood of democratic developments in Eastern Europe is virtually nil."[3] Obviously, Huntington and most other respected scholars and pundits were mistaken. As Adam Przeworski correctly observes, the fall of communism was a "dismal failure of political science."[4]

Existing paradigms are of little aid in either predicting or explaining the massive transformations that are taking place in Eastern Europe, particularly since 1989. This includes Bulgaria, long regarded as among the world's most repressive regimes. However, Giuseppe Di Palma's 1990 book, *To Craft Democracies: An Essay on Democratic Transitions,*[5] is a candidly optimistic approach to understanding the conditions necessary for transition to democracy. This important work is a useful antidote to the pessimism and inadequacy of the conventional wisdom represented, for example, in the seminal works of Huntington and Dahl.[6] When applied to the Bulgarian experience, Di Palma's theoretical analysis proves superior as an explanation for what most scholars have regarded as an unlikely transformation.

There is little disagreement about the meaning of the theoretical and empirical evidence. It substantiates the view that democracy develops best where there are strong economies, large middle classes, and supportive civic cultures.[7] Plural groups mediate conflict by insulating the masses and elites from direct relations, and in the process they educate citizens about the virtues of tolerance and accommodation. Strong competing political parties aid the transition from authoritarianism and totalitarianism, help to organize public discourse, and deliver the political goods once the debate is complete.[8] Within Bulgaria, however, few of the factors commonly associated with building democracy were prominent when, in late 1989 and early 1990, the process of political change began to occur.

By July 1991, Bulgaria had adopted a new Constitution exhibiting the main features of democracy. Between 1991 and early 1997 politicians went about the task of making government institutions work, and in the process they helped to consolidate one of the world's new democracies. Though the road to democracy is a bumpy one, it appears that Bulgarians are intent upon completing the journey. This book chronicles the points of interest of the initial miles traveled along that remarkable journey, one that is a testament to the role individuals can play in the process. By an exercise in human will and against the theoretical odds, individual political actors successfully traversed the difficult terrain to arrive at a point approximating the vicinity of destination democracy.

Because Di Palma's alternative approach focuses attention at the micro level of analysis, emphasis is placed on the importance of crafting agreements that create alliances and coalitions. He is particularly interested in the tactics entailed in forging agreements necessary to bring about transitions. Thus, when societies such as those in Eastern Europe approach democracy without the structural or cultural qualities deemed important by Huntington and Dahl, for example, the task of crafting agreements becomes more crucial and challenging.[9]

If there is a movement away from authoritarian or totalitarian rule, is it toward genuine democracy? Of course, the answer depends upon how one defines the word. Di Palma chooses to define democracy in a procedural sense, not in terms of policy outcomes, or in other words, in some substantive sense. In contrast to his optimistic view that political actors can will a democracy into existence, Di Palma's idea of what they may get in the end is decidedly more pessimistic. He maintains that it is probably wrong to assume that democracy will produce a better standard of living for the people. It might or it might not. What is important about democracy is that it is a set of procedures making it possible for a people to obtain some version of the good life. Therefore, consistent with the view of other modern theorists of considerable reputation, including Joseph Schumpeter and Samuel Huntington,[10] Di Palma defines democracy in terms of civil liberties, competitive political parties, choice of alternative candidates for political office, and the existence of institutions that regulate the exercise of governmental power.[11]

Bulgaria meets Di Palma's test for a successful transition. Yet, many Bulgarians would dispute the contention that Bulgaria has become truly democratic. The argument is mainly one about ends and means. Yes, Bulgaria has achieved from a procedural perspective democratic institutions; it has a government that operates in a fashion that is more or less democratic. However, the transition to democracy has not brought about material progress. To be sure, the transition to a market economy has been slow and uncertain. Unemployment, inflation, and crime are serious problems.[12] For many, unfortunately, the promise of democracy as a means to the good life seems a cruel hoax.[13] Nevertheless, progress on the procedural front is impressive. In this sense, Bulgaria is an example of a successful transition.

There are at least two dominant ways by which a transition from authoritarian or totalitarian regimes toward democracy may take place. Each approach exhibits, of course, circumstantial variations. One well-practiced way is through violent revolution, and the second is through a peaceful transition wherein the previous ruling class is afforded a role in the new order. The first method requires the liquidation of the existing ruling elite by firing squad or forced exit from the scene through exile or house arrest. In this manner, it is more than probable that the ruling elite will be effectively eliminated and that, in the process, their influence over the course of future events will be minimized. But such processes provide an opportunity for the victims of the previous repressive regime to become themselves executioners in the name of the new order. This type of political change teaches the dubious lesson that violence will cause a meaningful change in the existing ruling elite. From a democratic viewpoint, this lesson is deficient in important respects. The scenario of violence does not instill respect for democratic procedures and institutions. Some may admonish, "If the policy outcomes or political actors are unsatisfactory, then eliminate the regime incumbents." But this approach to change does not create the conditions for building a civil society. Bulgarians chose instead the difficult path; they created institutions in which elements of the previous regime take their chances with the vagaries of politics that necessarily accompany the creation of democratic institutions. Along the way, these institutions are shaping the manner and nature of political discourse and coaxing civil society into a stable and vigorous existence. Bulgarians have made great strides in both respects.

By agreeing upon fundamental changes through the mechanisms of National Roundtable Talks in 1990 and the convocation of a Grand National Assembly to create and then to adopt in 1991 a new national Constitution, political leaders cast aside Bulgaria's Stalinist past and the pattern of violence and vendetta that marks that nation's tragic history. In the process, leaders representing reform elements of the old regime and the newly formed opposition laid the foundation for democratic political institutions and a market economy. Because the old regime suffered from a period of delegitimacy, the initial condition necessary for fundamental change had already occurred. Yet, there was no assurance that a new democratic order would emerge. Leaders from a variety of backgrounds with differing ideological beliefs had to agree to create a new order and to go about the task of willing democratic institutions into place. This qualifies as a monumental accomplishment. Nonetheless, the creation of a democratic polity requires more than the promulgation of agreements and a constitutional document that articulates democratic principles. The creation and maintenance of a social and cultural infrastructure that exhibits group pluralism is a necessary condition to insure the permanence of a transition from totalitarianism to democracy.

Scholars including Di Palma agree that a sense of civic virtue is a necessary concomitant of pluralist democracy. There must be a public spirit in the polis directing attention away from a preoccupation with individual self-interest to that of community well-being. Hence, public decisions should be made in the interest of all the people and not just a small group of self-seekers. Of course, self-interest is part of the rational calculation in public choice. Yet, it must be only a part and not the exclusive actuator of political behavior. The alternative is the clash of self-interested groups without a moral claim to justice. A most interesting and important facet of the transition to democracy in Bulgaria is the awareness exhibited by political leaders of all stripes about the importance of learning and instilling the democratic rules of the game. Opponents of the Communist regime came directly from the streets to negotiating rooms and the Parliament building to forge agreements, create new laws, and write a new Constitution. They had little personal experience with such institutions. Nonetheless, they understood that the ability to admonish their countrymen at mass rallies did not in itself qualify them for the art of democratic governance. They understood that having justice on their side was not enough. They needed to learn the rules of the democratic game and to teach them to their successors if the new system of governance was to work. For those individuals coming from within the ranks of the reform elements of the atrophied communist ruling elite, the task was less difficult, but it did require some adjustment in thinking. In such circumstances, a crisis in a dictatorship makes coexistence with democratic forces an appealing prospect; it is better than the alternative.

Therefore, while Bulgaria did not enjoy the structural or cultural prerequisites for democracy, it was in the interest of those political actors intent upon survival to work out an accommodation with their democratic opponents. Such an accommodation does not require that all the parties are genuine democrats. It only requires a set of rules dictating the terms of coexistence. The parties involved in Bulgaria were able to accomplish this task at the National Roundtable Talks and the Grand National Assembly that drafted the new Constitution. Yet, there remains among many opponents of the old regime the view that reform Communists are untrustworthy; in other words, the actions of these latter-day democrats must be carefully scrutinized for signs of backsliding. For some democrats, the pact with former Communist Party functionaries represents a betrayal of fundamental principles; they believe justice requires that the Communists pay for their collective and individual past misdeeds.

Focusing on Di Palma's political actor approach, one discovers that although it ran counter to the theoretical odds, Bulgaria's transition to democracy was a matter of careful political craftsmanship. Leading reform elements of the former discredited regime joined with its fledgling opponents to create a democratic Constitution. They accomplished this feat through a painstaking process of accommodation, negotiation, and compromise at National Roundtable Talks. At these meetings, participants negotiated most of the principles and many provisions found in Bulgaria's new Constitution. The Roundtable Talks rendered the violent option unnecessary and made democratic transition possible. Later, elected members to a constitutional convention created the new basic document. Since then, parliamentarians, jurists, and political executives have endeavored to make the new democratic order work. Three parliamentary elections between 1990 and 1996 with instances of turnover in party control of the law-making institution, hotly contested elections for local officials, two elections for president of the Republic, and the creation of judicial institutions that have exercised independence in the face of formidable opposition all attest to the viability of the new democratic order. The negotiations that took place at National Roundtable Talks were a key factor in securing agreement among the competing political forces on the ground rules for creating national unity.

In this book I describe how major elements within Bulgarian society sought coexistence through what Di Palma dubs *garantismo.*[14] The 1991 Constitution that the Roundtable process ultimately produced stresses pluralism, political competition, and the rule of law. Di Palma argues that carefully crafted transitions from totalitarianism or authoritarianism to democracy can work. Individuals can create a quality finished product resulting from negotiations among competing alliances. A primary goal of the process of negotiation is the inclusion of the old as well as new political forces in the new governmental system. At a minimum, guaranteeing a place in the new order to reform elements of the old guard is a key to a peaceful transition to democracy.

Parliament and Democracy

Political elites, including Bulgaria's intelligentsia, view the Parliament as the symbol of the rejection of the discredited past Communist regime. With all its faults, the National Assembly is the quintessential institution of democracy. As the reader will come to see, post-Communist leaders display a consistent concern with creating a parliamentary government that reflects democratic values. The task is not an easy one. Individual leaders stepped forward—whether at the National Roundtable Talks, the Grand National Assembly, or later during the period of democratic consolidation—to place this matter squarely on the national agenda.

This is the case because they remember the former regime, under which Parliament had little power and deputies acted upon instructions from the Communist Party. But old habits, particularly bad ones, are hard to break. In the months following the November 10, 1989, peaceful coup, parliamentary subservience was evident in the way the National Assembly received instructions from the elite assembled at the National Roundtable Talks. Nonetheless, Roundtable participants forged the basic agreements necessary for the creation of a parliamentary democracy. Leaders of the Grand National Assembly elected in June 1990 were clearly aware of the importance of creating norms of conduct that would make parliamentary democracy an ongoing enterprise.

Yet, the inculcation of legislative norms regulating political competition does not take place automatically. Some members of the Grand National Assembly resisted attempts to abide by parliamentary rules. They remained wedded to the ways of street demonstrations, walkouts, and inflammatory rhetoric. Even with the establishment of the July 1991 Constitution and the creation of a new parliamentary system, leaders continue to grapple with the task of creating and implementing reasonable expectations of conduct.

Parliamentary leaders reveal an acute awareness that the fate of the democratic regime is tied to how well the National Assembly performs its tasks. Framers of the July 1991 Constitution and party leaders speak of the importance of learning and abiding by the democratic rules of the game. To be sure, substantive policy matters occupy much of their attention. But successfully coping with the legislative process questions is essential if Bulgarian politicians are to learn the ways of parliamentary government.

Some leaders understand better than others the importance of establishing a system of parliamentary democracy. They consciously work to institutionalize the norms necessary for the smooth functioning of parliamentary government. Yet, as will become clear, some party leaders possess little appreciation for the task. Though not insurmountable, the tendency toward bipolar party pluralism creates difficulties for the consolidation toward democracy.[15]

Then too, some scholars and politicians argue that legislatures are ill-suited to making public policy and that strong executive authority is necessary to make government work.[16] Given their life experience with the past regime, I doubt many east Europeans would or should accept such a prescription. Be that as it may, the story of the clash between and among branches of government is instructive about the challenges leaders face in newly created democratic regimes. As evidence of its central importance in a democratic regime, Parliament seems part of most conflicts. We also learn from these instances of interinstitutional conflict that democratic government has a holistic quality about it. In brief, when studying transitions to democracy it is helpful to employ an interinstitutional conflict approach and not to rely solely on a single-institution perspective.

As a correlative proposition, there is sufficient evidence to conclude that public and elite support for a democratic regime is more important than support for a specific legislative institution.[17] From the very beginning of Bulgaria's democratic transition, some leaders understood that the National Assembly is the symbolic embodiment of democratic values. But there is more to the legislative function than providing symbolic support for democratic systems. These institutions also provide forums for criticizing executive and bureaucratic activity and allow the expression of political dissent. Parliaments can represent the social, religious, and ethnic diversity in a culture. In short, legislatures contribute to the day-to-day stability of a political system and to regime legitimation.[18]

We also know that most people view government as a seamless piece of cloth.[19] Government institutions interact to create public policy. It matters little to the person on the street whether the legislature, executive, or judiciary is responsible for the policy. What is important is that government has created a rule that affected populations are expected to follow.

The experiences of the transition to democracy and consolidation periods in Bulgaria clearly show that constitutional systems tend to create ambiguities in the legitimate loci of political power. The ways these boundaries of authority are resolved reflect the balance of power within the political system and how individual leaders play their roles.

Demonstration Effects

The format for dismantling the Communist system was rehearsed in other Eastern European countries. The Polish and Hungarian roundtable talks took place in the previous year (February–April in Poland and March–September 1989 in Hungary).[20] Demonstration effects occurred throughout Eastern Europe, and no doubt Bulgarians of all political persuasions learned from what had happened there and elsewhere. Throughout the region, it became clear that the promise of communism as a way to achieve economic well-being and social and political equality was unfulfilled. Economic stagnation and privilege for a few had become the observable rule. The demise of the Brezhnev doctrine was also a key factor in the politics of change. Mikhail Gorbachev and his aides made it clear that military force would no longer be used to maintain Soviet-style communism in the satellite states. Further, Gorbachev popularized perestroika and glasnost as a way to encourage economic and political experimentation within his orbit of influence. The combination of these two factors made it plain that the totalitarian and authoritarian communist regimes would either disappear from the scene altogether, or there would have to be some accommodation with the new reality. Obviously, if the party leaders in power throughout Eastern Europe were to opt for the latter alternative, they would need to find ways to legitimize their rule.[21]

For the reform-minded Communists and their democratic opponents in Bulgaria, the Poles and Hungarians provided the most likely scenario for peaceful change. Their comrades to the north were the first of the Eastern bloc states to attempt a transition to democracy. Yet, in Bulgaria there was no organized opposition with the character and strength of the Solidarity labor movement, nor did the opposition enjoy the backing of independent institutions such as Poland's Catholic Church.[22] Nevertheless, in Bulgaria the reform-minded Communists negotiated with a set of opposition political leaders. This process served to legitimize a loose organization of dissidents that came to be called the Union of Democratic Forces (UDF). Negotiating at National Roundtable Talks was also important in legitimizing existing institutions and the individuals who had led the coup d'état against the Zhivkov regime. In Hungary, the national negotiation was a triangular affair: the Communist government, an umbrella opposition joined by Communist-sponsored organizations (including trade unions), and neutral observers (including churches).[23] In the end, however, the shape of the negotiating table mattered little. In both Poland and Hungary, successful elections were held later: in Poland on June 4 and 18, 1989, and in Hungary on March 25 and April 8, 1990.[24] In both cases, the anticommunists won impressive victories in the initial elections. The democratic opponents to the reform Communists in Bulgaria could take heart from these events. They might reasonably suppose that they too would also have an excellent chance to gain control of the government.

Though Bulgarians successfully employed the format of National Roundtable Talks to negotiate the governing principles and rules for democratic elections, for the anti-Communist forces the initial result was disappointing. Instead, the reform Communists—now called the Bulgarian Socialist Party (BSP)—won a majority of the seats in the Grand National Assembly (GNA). This body functioned simultaneously as a working Parliament and as a constitutional convention. Thus, although the strategy created by the Polish Communist leaders to keep themselves in power did not work in that country, the Bulgarian Communists were able to exploit it to its fullest.

Other Eastern bloc countries did not follow the same scenario as found in Poland, Hungary, and Bulgaria. Yet in each of the remaining states, political change took place. In Czechoslovakia, on November 17, 1989, just seven days after the coup d'état in Bulgaria, there was a "velvet revolution." One week after the police brutally put down a student demonstration, the entire Communist leadership resigned. On December 10, 1990, a new Government of National Understanding was sworn in, and only ten members of a twenty-one-seat government remained under the control of the Communist Party.[25] In Romania, the Communist Party disappeared after the December 1989 revolution. There were no national roundtable talks, no visible reform-minded members of the nomenklatura to lead the Party to a democratic future. There was, however, violence. In Albania, the Communist leaders decided to hold early elections to legitimize their rule. But as in the Bulgarian case, they won the first election only to lose in the next.[26]

Although Bulgarians were familiar with the Polish and Hungarian experiences, they had to find their own solution to end the pattern of violence and vendetta characteristic of political change in Bulgaria's history. The bloody overthrow in 1923 of the peasant government led by Alexander Stamboliiski, the pattern of reprisals, the wave of terror and subsequent violent events haunt the national psyche to this day. And the graphic media reports of the December 1989 summary arrest and execution of Romania's dictator, Nicolae Ceauşescu, and his wife were not lost on Bulgaria's political elite.

Research Approach

After two trips to Bulgaria in 1991 and 1992 and after conferring with and interviewing Bulgarians both in the United States and in Bulgaria, I was able to formulate the schedules for the interviews that serve as the centerpiece of this book. During my October 1993 site visit to Bulgaria, I formally interviewed twenty-four parliamentarians, political party leaders, interest group officials, and legal professionals. They included, among other notables, two former prime ministers, a former vice president of the Republic (who was also responsible for dismantling the secret police system of the old regime), and two members of the Constitutional Court. Between late 1989 and July 1991, most of my interlocutors were intimately involved in the National Roundtable Talks that facilitated a peaceful transition to democracy, or they were deputies to the Grand National Assembly that drafted the new Constitution. Some persons I interviewed are legal professionals with intimate knowledge of developments in the judiciary before and after November 10, 1989.

Before my 1993 overseas research trip, I wrote six interview schedules. I was able to administer five of the six schedules to the following elites: sixteen Bulgarian leaders who were personally involved in Bulgaria's National Roundtable Talks and the Grand National Assembly that fashioned the July 1991 Constitution, two members of Bulgaria's Supreme Court, two members of the district court in Sofia (courts of original jurisdiction), two Constitutional Court judges, a law professor, and a member of the private bar.

I identified all but a few of the sixteen Bulgarian leaders personally involved in the National Roundtable Talks and the Grand National Assembly by reading media accounts of events appearing in the Foreign Broadcast Information Service (FBIS). A few more names were added to the list of potential interviewees by my contacts in Bulgaria. In this way, they helped me to better identify the array of opinions among the political elites who negotiated Bulgaria's transition toward democracy. And, in the process, I was able to reduce the opportunity for bias, while improving the efficiency of my observations.

Most of the legal professionals I interviewed during my October 1993 visit were known to me beforehand. I had previously interviewed all but two of them when they were part of a delegation visiting the United States during the summer of 1992; one judge I had met twice before and came to know fairly well during 1991 and 1992 visits to Bulgaria, and the interview with the remaining legal professional was arranged by a jurist I had known for two years. Consequently, I had a preexisting rapport with all but one jurist, making for candid and productive in-depth interview sessions. Actually, the one judge I had not known beforehand was very frank; he exhibited no signs of inhibition during the interview.

Before my arrival in Bulgaria, each person I wished to contact received a letter of introduction and a request for an interview. My preestablished primary and secondary contacts in Bulgaria followed up the letters with phone calls, and only a few persons declined interviews. Each interview lasted from one to two hours, and during the course of our conversations I found that persons with similar experiences answered certain questions with a uniform response. At that point, I stopped asking the redundant questions and instead allowed the interviewees to tell their stories with less structure than I had originally thought necessary. This approach proved rewarding because it allowed for greater spontaneity than might otherwise have been the case, and I learned about people and events that would otherwise have escaped my attention.

Luben Nikolov, a former foreign correspondent for the Bulgarian Telegraph Agency stationed for five years in London, served as an intermediary, interpreter, and transcriber of the taped interviews. Without the aid of this BTA insider it is doubtful I would have been able to conduct these interviews in a time-effective manner or, in some cases, at all. I learned after completing my interviews that a high-ranking figure within the BTA, now deceased, personally interceded on my behalf to arrange some of the interviews. One learns quickly that in Bulgaria access to important persons depends upon whom you know and who your friends might be. It sometimes matters who your enemies are as well, or, as in my case, whether I was a friend of a friend or a friend of an enemy. Despite the fascination with things Western, Bulgarians continue to practice the fine art of Byzantine politics.

Because this case study focuses on analytical generalization and is not a survey study attempting statistical generalization, a representative sample of all participants at the National Roundtable Talks, elected members of the Grand National Assembly, members of Parliament, and all jurists is unnecessary and not attempted.[27] What is important is whether the persons interviewed have the personal experience to make their statements of fact and opinion noteworthy. All of my interlocutors have been engaged in the transition to democracy through concrete activities and interactions. Their participation has been personal and often decisive. As King, Keohane, and Verba point out, inference is a central goal of scientific research, and it matters little if the data that researchers use are a random sample of the universe of all events or a case study employing qualitative information.[28] What is important is to take a scientific approach to the subject, to check assumptions and evidence carefully. As part of this process, I analyzed news reports in order to place the interviews in historical perspective. This helped me in the first instance to frame questions for the interviews. Every attempt was made to arrange interviews with persons representing differing viewpoints, and for the most part this goal was met with success. When, during the interviews, I discerned contradictory statements made by different persons, I pressed them for clarification, and this helped to identify the range of viewpoints. Only one person I sought to interview refused to meet with me because of a busy schedule (president of the Republic, Zhelyu Zhelev), and a few did not honor their appointments. Many persons I interviewed remained politically active through 1993, and all of them possess keen insights about the creation of democracy in their homeland. Luben Nikolov's literal transcription is at times altered to make the materials more readable and consistent with English usage. I took care not to change the sense of what was said. Nikolov has read my revisions and certifies my faithfulness to its original literal content. Biographies of most persons I interviewed are contained in the endnotes to the chapter where they are first quoted extensively.

This multifaceted approach to information gathering was also useful in alerting me to the possible existence of alternative descriptions and explanations of events. During interview sessions, I could explore apparent inconsistencies between what different interviewees were telling me and what I understood from the news reports, and contradictory interpretations of events presented by the interviewees. Later, when analyzing the interviews, I was able to refer to both news reports and interview transcripts to clarify factual points. Furthermore, officials of the state-operated Bulgarian news agency, the BTA, provided me with written reports relating the key events surrounding both the National Roundtable Talks and the Grand National Assembly. The BTA also provided me with biographies of many persons I interviewed.

Employing Di Palma's alternative framework, I describe the politics of the institutions responsible for the creation of a new democratic order in Bulgaria. Part 1 of this book contains three chapters centering on the National Roundtable Talks. It is particularly interesting how Roundtable participants interpret key events. To place these interpretations in historical relief, I first describe in chapter 2 key incidents in the political history of modern Bulgaria and report the sequence of events involving the National Roundtable Talks. Chapter 2 contains a brief historical narrative designed to provide readers with a frame of reference for understanding the perspectives of those who sought a peaceful transition to democracy. I then introduce readers to the key events and political actors of the National Roundtable Talks. In chapters 3, 4, and 5, I explore, in detailed interview format, many Roundtable events with those who were present at the time. It is in these chapters that readers will find much of the analysis that forms the basis for understanding the politics of the transition.

Part 2 centers on the Grand National Assembly that crafted the July 1991 Constitution. I begin this part of the book with a narrative of the sequence of events. In chapter 6, I give a brief description of events surrounding the creation of the new Constitution and then outline the main features of the basic document crafted in 1991. Chapter 7 contains interviews that reveal the politics and motivations of key figures who crafted the 1991 Constitution.

The third part of the book is devoted to a description and analysis of important political events since the adoption of the new Constitution in July 1991 through the first weeks of 1997: what some scholars refer to as the process of democratic consolidation. Chapter 8 contains a discussion of parliamentary politics as it relates to the successful transition to democracy, and chapter 9 centers on the struggle for judicial independence and the problem of interinstitutional conflict. This chapter especially highlights what might go wrong in the search for a "law-governed state."

Chapter 10 contains the conclusions. Summarizing the findings of the previous chapters, I focus upon the lessons for understanding transitions to democracy and the creation of parliamentary government. I maintain that this study provides considerable additional empirical evidence in support of Di Palma's claim that transitions to democracy may take place without the so-called prerequisites to democracy. This is not to say that ideas, interests, and institutions are unimportant but that the experience in Bulgaria requires scholars to reconsider the central role individuals may play in bringing about political change. We need to focus at the micro level while not ignoring macro-level phenomena. Extrapolating from the findings, I conclude that it is a mistake to provide development aid to repressive regimes as a way to encourage the creation of substructures to support democratic superstructures. If anything, Western democracies should withhold aid as a tactic to encourage authoritarian or totalitarian governments to negotiate democratic transitions.

PART I

National Roundtable Talks

There is nothing more difficult to take in hand, more perilous to conduct, or more uncertain in its success, than to take the lead in the introduction of a new order of things.

—NICCOLO MACHIAVELLI
The Prince

2

The End of Vendetta

THE STRUGGLE FOR constitutional democracy is a central and recurring theme in modern Bulgarian history. Since its liberation from five centuries of Ottoman control (1396–1878) Bulgaria has usually been governed either by a royal-military oligarchy or by Communist dictatorship.[1] During the nineteenth century, Western-educated Bulgarian leaders attempted to rally their people to the cause of national unity and democratic values. In the 1920s, there was a democratic experiment ending in bloodshed.

At a constitutional convention held at the medieval capital of Turnovo in 1879, Bulgarians adopted what was, by European standards, an advanced basic document that included a unicameral legislature elected on the basis of universal male suffrage, a limited monarchy, and provisions for civil liberties and rights. Historian John D. Bell maintains this attempt at Western democracy failed because of a weak middle class and a low level of political support from the rural masses. Furthermore, Bulgaria's foreign-born monarchs opposed democratic institutions, preferring the familiar system of royal absolutism.[2] Despite the many obstacles to democracy, the intelligentsia and professional classes supported democracy organized around political parties. Also, the nation's civil servants and part of the working class supported the Constitution. The Social Democratic Party (Broad Socialists) and the Bulgarian Agrarian National Union (BANU) were active supporters of democratic values.[3]

Yet, military coups and murder are certain deterrents to the creation of democratic institutions. As a prominent reformer within the current Bulgarian Socialist Party (formerly the Bulgarian Communist Party) and twice prime minister since 1990 plainly put it in an interview: "Political vendetta is an unfortunate part of Bulgaria's political history."[4]

In the name of political change, the Bulgarian people have either been victimized by outside forces or practiced fratricide. Under Ottoman rule, Bulgarians complained that they lived under the "Turkish Yoke." They were not only cut off from commercial and social intercourse with the rest of Europe, but they also suffered inhuman cruelties at the hands of the Sultan. Occasionally, bands of insurgents took up arms against the Turks. It was the Russian military, however, which ultimately liberated Bulgaria. After a series of wars, including Russia's own humiliating Crimean defeat (1854–56), Bulgaria was finally liberated in April of 1878.

The Cycle of Violence

The cost of victory was high. Russia lost two hundred thousand soldiers, and thousands of Bulgarian peasants were murdered during the military campaigns. On March 3, 1878, Russia imposed upon the defeated Turks the Treaty of San Stefano. In part, this agreement provided for the political independence of Bulgaria, Serbia, Romania, and Montenegro. It also ceded all of Macedonia and Eastern Rumelia (Thrace) to Bulgaria.[5]

The Russian boost to Bulgarian pride was short-lived, however. England was prepared to go to war unless Russia agreed to rescind the San Stefano accord. Consequently, only months after the signing of the San Stefano Treaty, a new one, the Treaty of Berlin (1878), stripped Bulgaria of Macedonia and Eastern Rumelia. At that time, Bulgaria became a principality within the Ottoman Empire. This fateful agreement is a source for much tension and conflict that has plagued the Balkans ever since.[6] The forfeiture of Macedonia was a particularly egregious result because Bulgarians regard its inhabitants as Bulgarian in origin, language, and customs.[7] Then, a few months after consummation of the Berlin Treaty, there was an unsuccessful uprising in Macedonia against Turkish rule. Defeated, many Bulgarians left Macedonia for the safe haven of the new Bulgarian Principality located in the northwest.[8]

In 1893, Bulgarian Macedonians created a secret and violent society with the goal of obtaining either autonomy from the Ottoman empire or annexation by Bulgaria. The Internal Macedonian and Adrianople Revolutionary Organization, later simply known as IMRO, engaged in kidnapping: one infamous incident involved an American missionary. The IMRO also launched unsuccessful uprisings in Bulgarian areas of Turkey that ended in bloody suppression and flight to Bulgaria by thousands of refugees.[9] For decades, IMRO remained a violent force: it engaged in murder and assassination in the name of reuniting the Bulgarian people separated in Macedonia, Rumelia, and Bulgaria.

The Principality itself was a product of the 1878 Berlin Treaty. It confined Bulgaria's boundaries to the northwestern section of what was once a larger Bulgaria. Treaty provisions required Bulgaria to install a prince elected by the Bulgarians, but the European powers had to approve the particulars. The Sultan was granted semiautonomous political control over the Principality. Alexander Battenberg, a German and officer in the Russian Army, was crowned prince, and delegates to a Grand National Assembly devised a Constitution at Turnovo in 1879.[10]

As a consequence of military defeat at the hands of the Russians, Turkey had grown politically and militarily weak. Therefore, the Bulgarian Principality exerted considerable independence from Turkey. In 1908, the Bulgarian government proclaimed its independence from the Ottoman Empire.[11] Bulgaria then fought two Balkan wars. Both the 1912 and the 1913 wars were fought to reclaim Macedonia for the Bulgarians. The first Balkan War was a successful joint effort with Serbia, Greece, and Montenegro against Turkey. Unfortunately, the victors had serious disagreements over Macedonia. In the ensuing brief war, the Bulgarian army won a stunning victory over the Turks. But the Serbians and Greeks captured Macedonia. Then, without a declaration of war, the Bulgarians attacked Serbian and Greek positions. However, Romania invaded quickly from the north, and the Turks reopened hostilities from the south. This left the Bulgarian forces surrounded, and they were forced to sue for a humiliating peace. The resulting Treaty of Bucharest (August 1913) divided Macedonia between Serbia and Greece, and Bulgaria received only a small parcel of the much coveted ground. The two Balkan wars cost Bulgaria sixty-six thousand lives and left the struggling new nation without friends. Even Russia sided with Romania and Serbia against Bulgaria.[12]

The loss of Macedonia explains in large part why Bulgaria entered

World War I on the German side. There were other factors, of course, including the fact that the prince was a German and that Bulgaria's ruling party was pro-German. The Bulgarians expected that a German victory would result in the restoration of territories lost in the Second Balkan War. Instead, being on the wrong side of a war once again, Bulgaria lost additional territory. It was also forced to pay large reparations, and its trade relations were severely restricted.[13]

The cumulative effect of these military and foreign policy defeats was a severe diminution in public support for Bulgaria's monarchy and the military-dominated ruling elite. In fear of losing his life, on October 3, 1918, Prince Ferdinand abdicated his throne in favor of his son, Boris. Ferdinand left Bulgaria for Germany on a train guarded by German troops. Bulgarians then created an interim government of national unity; it served for several months until parliamentary elections were held in August 1919. The government was composed of leaders of radical parties, including the Agrarians and the Broad Socialists. The elections demonstrated deep public support for these radical parties. The Agrarians won 85 seats; the Communists, who called themselves Narrow Socialists, won 47 seats; and the Broad Socialists won 36 seats.[14] The strongest bourgeois party, the Democrats, gained only 28 seats in the 233-member National Assembly. Alexander Stamboliiski, the leader of the Bulgarian Agrarian National Union (BANU), then went about the delicate task of forming a coalition government, the balance of which was shaky at best.[15]

Stamboliiski's Agrarian party is the only European peasant party ever to exercise government power and to put at least part of their program into practice. An exception to the normal pattern of oligarchical tendencies within political parties, BANU was internally democratic. It relied heavily upon local participation when making party policy. The movement was founded in December 1899 by a group of intellectuals known as the Bulgarian Agrarian Union (BAU). Its initial goal was exclusively educational. Agrarian leaders sought to make peasants more efficient producers and through education to make them more efficacious citizens.[16]

Soon after the formation of BAU, the royal-military government instituted tax increases that produced mass peasant protests. In a May 1900 confrontation, police violently repressed demonstrators: ninety peasants were killed and more than four hundred were wounded. In the following year, BAU became overtly political. It changed its name to the Bulgarian Agrarian National Union (BANU) and gained sufficient popularity to lead the government for a period of three years, from October 6, 1919, to June 9, 1923.[17]

BANU sought to redistribute wealth and power. It did so by focusing upon the agricultural basis of Bulgarian society and instituting land reform policy. The program included the expropriation of all absentee landowners' holdings of a certain size. Housing reform took the form of reallocation of apartment space based on family size. The government monopolized trade in grain and tobacco, and most profits were rebated to the producers. World War I profiteers had their earnings confiscated by the government. Stamboliiski's government imposed a progressive personal and corporate income tax. It made educational reforms, including major curriculum changes aimed at providing children with practical education and work experience at all primary and secondary schools. It also introduced compulsory labor service of one year for all twenty-year-old males and sixteen-year-old females. In a move that would alienate many intellectuals, BANU sought to simplify the spelling rules of the Bulgarian language. Some feared that the government was intending to abolish the monarchy. It was known that Stamboliiski held monarchs in contempt, referring to them as "poisonous snakes." Further, many believed that he intended to socialize industrial enterprises.[18] Stamboliiski's government also earned the undying enmity of the terrorist organization associated with reuniting the Bulgarian people. He dispatched his foreign minister, Alexander Dimitrov, to Belgrade to assure the Serbians that Bulgaria was not behind the IMRO terrorist violence taking place in southern Serbia and that his government would take strong measures against the terrorist leaders in Bulgaria. As punishment for carrying the message, foreign minister Dimitrov received a death sentence, and by order of the IMRO leadership he was assassinated in October 1921.[19]

There existed in Bulgaria a culture of violence. It was a fertile medium for the virulence that greeted Stamboliiski's ideas and programs. Included among conspirators who plotted against him were the fanatical IMRO and the refugees from what were dubbed the "lost territories," the military, the royalists, the various manifestations of the urban class, and some intellectuals. All sought the end of the BANU government.[20] By the end of 1921, a pro-fascist group composed of business, military, and university leaders came together to plot a coup d'état. In an admiring attempt to imitate Mussolini's rise to power in Italy, the conspirators held a series of mass meetings in the fall of 1922. However, the Agrarians mobilized armed peasants to suppress these demonstrations, and Stamboliiski's government arrested the entire leadership of the Bourgeois Bloc Party.[21]

Stamboliiski's initial victory over the forces of reaction made him overly confident. At the same time, however, it caused the pro-fascist conspirators to try again. They executed a surprise military coup in the early morning of June 9, 1923. This time they succeeded, although Stamboliiski himself was able to get safely away by fleeing to the mountains. Within weeks, however, he was arrested, tortured, and decapitated. His head was never found, but it is believed that it was presented to King Boris at the palace.[22]

Although some local Bulgarian Communist Party (BCP) organizations fought on the losing BANU side during the successful coup, the national leadership was neutral. The Comintern in Moscow later rebuffed the leadership for its lack of action, causing a purge of the compliant BCP leaders. The Party was then directed by the Comintern to subvert the new government by instigating an uprising of workers and peasants. This action is celebrated in Bulgarian folklore as the first anti-fascist insurrection, despite the fact that in the wake of its failure, five thousand people were counted dead. The pro-monarchy government then enacted legislation criminalizing the BCP, where it languished in legal oblivion until 1944.[23]

A few years later, in April 1925, there was a left-wing attempt to assassinate King Boris by blowing up a church. This terrorist act led to massive retaliation with the official executions of hundreds of people. The actual number of persons who lost their lives is uncertain. Between 1923 and 1925, one report suggests that an estimated sixteen thousand BCP and BANU members were murdered. Another report indicates that in 1923 alone twenty thousand persons were killed. During this period, the IMRO carried out assassinations. Most of what was left of the surviving BCP leaders fled to Moscow, although a crippled underground party remained to triumph another day.[24]

Because the BANU and BCP leadership were all but liquidated between 1923 and 1925, the new government, imbued with strong fascist tendencies, allowed the presence in Parliament of a watered-down

Agrarian representation. These tolerable Agrarians became part of a parliamentary opposition called the People's Bloc, which in 1931 won the elections. Although a considerably more moderate party than the one led by Alexander Stamboliiski in the previous decade, the Agrarians did not take a leading role in the government, fearing another coup. Their fears proved warranted when a coup in May 1934, led by the same military group that ousted Stamboliiski a decade earlier, succeeded in ousting the timid Agrarians. A pro-fascist government ruled without political parties for about a year, after which King Boris established a personal dictatorship. This government lasted until elections were reestablished in 1938, when the king felt confident he could control the outcome.[25]

During World War II, Bulgaria was again a German ally. The alliance is not difficult to understand given the fascist sympathies of most government leaders since the overthrow of Stamboliiski's Agrarian government. Moreover, King Boris was part of a continuous line of German monarchs to occupy Bulgaria's royal palace. Further, beginning in the 1930s, Bulgaria's economy grew increasingly dependent upon Germany. Also, the Germans made promises: at the end of a successful war effort, Bulgaria's claims to territories to its west and south would be honored by a grateful Third Reich.[26]

Post–World War II Developments

Often war serves to unite the peoples of a nation against a common enemy. Entry into World War II on March 1, 1941, however, did not signal a new age of Bulgarian national unity. Instead, it foretold another round of fratricide. The underground forces of the Bulgarian Communist Party joined forces with Moscow to commit sabotage and assassination of government functionaries and police officials. The BCP did not attempt a general insurrection. Nonetheless, many of its members were killed during the war, either in small unit actions or at the hands of the police. Working at the direction of the Nazi Gestapo, Bulgaria's secret police penetrated the Communist Party underground and destroyed most of its members.[27]

In 1943, the Fatherland Front coalition was organized. It was an umbrella organization open to all anti-fascist groups and individuals. It included members of the Agrarian Party, but the BCP dominated it.

At the end of World War II, on November 18, 1945, the Fatherland Front won a series of elections: the combined Front total was 82 percent of the vote. Bulgarians repudiated the monarchy in a popular referendum; 85 percent of the voters endorsed a republic. Later, in elections held on October 27, 1946, Fatherland Front candidates won over 70 percent of the votes. The BCP received over 53 percent of the votes in the election for the Grand National Assembly; among the responsibilities of this body was to rewrite the nation's Constitution.[28]

Nikola Petkov, a leader of a wing of the Agrarian Party, was the primary resistance to the complete domination of the government by the Communist Party. Consistent with learned behavior, Petkov and twenty-three other delegates were expelled from the National Assembly. He was later tried, convicted, and executed. During this postwar period, Bulgaria was the first state to hold war crimes trials. It resulted in nearly three thousand executions.[29]

The Communists did not gain immediate control of the nation in 1944. Instead, their power came gradually and with great effort between September 1944 and December 1947. They eliminated political opposition, destroyed the social power of the middle class, and effectively isolated Bulgaria from Western foreign influences.[30] In 1947, the first communist-inspired constitution, the "Dimitrov Constitution," was ratified. In 1971, Communist Party control was made permanent when a declaration in the new basic document stated that the constitutional edifice was founded upon the 1944 socialist revolution and that since then Bulgaria had become not only a people's democracy but also a socialist state of the working people headed by the working class. The creation of this new Constitution was engineered by Todor Zhivkov, the successor to the Stalinist Vulko Chervenkov.[31]

November 10, 1989, Coup

Zhivkov's imitative Soviet-style rule spanned the period 1956–89 and ended with a bloodless coup d'état on November 10, 1989, the day after the Berlin Wall fell.[32] Although the leader and his close associates lost power, most party and government officials remained in position. This could have happened only if the Party itself had caused the coup. The drastic action was thought necessary because of widespread discontent with the economy, the environment, and human rights matters.

By 1987 the economy in Bulgaria seemed to be on a downward path despite the efforts of the Zhivkov regime to reverse the trend. Bulgaria's per capita consumption in 1985 was the lowest in Europe. The realization of the price paid for industrialization spawned the creation of an environmental movement. In terms of political rights and civil rights, Freedom House ranks Bulgaria toward the bottom for the 1980s.[33] Petar Mladenov, in charge of foreign affairs since 1971, became the new leader. He and other new leaders pledged to promote pluralism and respect for the rule of law. They halted persecution of the ethnic Turkish minority initiated in 1982 by Zhivkov, inviting those ethnic Turks who had fled the country to return, and they also allowed opposition groups to register as legal entities. They further promised to curtail the role of the secret police in the internal life of the nation.[34]

The widespread contempt for the Zhivkov regime cannot be fully understood without recounting at least a few of its many human rights transgressions. During the 1950s and 1960s, the government operated forced labor camps. The People's Courts of 1944–46 were viewed by many as a way to eliminate opposition under the guise of prosecuting Nazi wartime collaborators. These courts convicted 12,000 people, of whom 2,730 were executed. In the contemporary period, the Zhivkov government covered up the nuclear contamination that resulted from the Chernobyl disaster, in the process exposing Bulgarians to serious physical harm. The forced assimilation of the Turkish minority was probably the single most notorious denial of human rights of the Zhivkov administration. Besides these ideologically motivated crimes, there is evidence that approximately $10 billion in Western loans have disappeared, and forty-seven former officials are believed responsible. Todor Zhivkov was convicted of embezzlement in 1992 and sentenced to seven years in prison. These and many more acts—including the famous poison umbrella death of the Bulgarian dissident Georgi Markov in London in 1978—are the basis of repeated calls for lustration, that is, societal purification (purges) through ritual sacrifice (punishments). Yet, there have been very few successful prosecutions of Bulgarians who led the nation during the Communist era.[35] This omission is a constant source of irritation for those seeking revenge.

There were three main features of the November 10, 1989, coup d'état.[36] First, high-ranking members of the Communist Party carried out the coup; it was change imposed from the top and not the result of a popular mass movement. In this respect, it resembles the political reforms in the Soviet Union under the banner of perestroika.[37] Informants tell me that especially among the younger members of the nomenklatura there was considerable discussion about the need for reform. Indeed, the dictator's popular daughter was among the early proponents of change. Because the old guard slavishly followed Moscow's line for years, it would have been difficult for them to quash the new openness associated with perestroika and glasnost. Second, the coup was thought necessary because of widespread discontent traceable to worsening economic problems. Further, given the Soviet Union's preoccupation with its own political problems, Bulgaria was becoming increasingly isolated from the rest of the world. The regime's handling of ethnic Turks was an additional factor in the overthrow of the old leadership. In the mid-1980s, the Zhivkov regime forced Moslims to change their names and limited the use of other languages besides the official Bulgarian language in everyday communication. As many as 350,000 ethnic Turks left Bulgaria to escape the persecution after the Bulgarian authorities opened the border in May 1989. Furthermore, the obvious unwillingness of the Soviet leadership to maintain military and political hegemony in Eastern Europe contributed to system breakdown. And third, leaders within the Party, the military, and the militia preferred reform and self-preservation to confrontation and possible defeat and banishment from politics altogether.

Party spokespersons began to speak of "socialist renewal" and of a willingness to enter roundtable talks to solve Bulgaria's mainly economic problems. As early as December 19, 1989, the media were quoting the new Communist leadership as desiring to bring about needed changes without imposing them from the top. Dialogue, discussion, and national consensus became key terms in what was touted as the need for "successful restructuring."[38] Many believe that the Bulgarian Communist Party leadership feared the possible adverse effects of mass protests and violence. Rather than accept the blame for the pending collapse of the economy, some opposition leaders speculate that the BCP leadership wanted to share with a weak opposition the responsibility for the economic crisis that was sure to come.[39]

As a general proposition for all of Eastern Europe, Di Palma suggests that the Communist Party leaders were faced with two choices. They might pursue the Chinese solution of brutal repression of regime opponents by tightly controlling civil society while simultaneously pursuing economic market reforms. Or they might seek accommodation with the forces demanding change.[40] Choosing the latter, the BCP sought to guarantee a future that required coexistence in a democratic political system. This approach carried with it the danger of losing power to the opposition. But it was a calculated risk that gave the BCP a chance to survive, albeit in a different political milieu. Though not referring to the Bulgarian situation directly, since he wrote before events completely unfolded there, Di Palma aptly describes the dilemma: "By choosing the democratic method, and therefore transferring loyalties or bestowing legitimacy on democracy, political actors are also choosing a degree of calculated uncertainty."[41]

Knowing the cycle of revenge and vendetta contributes to understanding why reformers within the BCP and their democratic opponents were anxious to avoid repeating history. The BCP leadership chose coexistence with the newly developing forces for change. But they needed and insisted upon a set of rules that would guarantee the future of their organization within the new order. Crafting that agreement was crucial for both the BCP and the creation of democratic institutions.

The single most important development in bringing about the transition to democracy in Bulgaria was the series of agreements reached at the National Roundtable Talks. With the overthrow of Todor Zhivkov, many persons questioned the legitimacy of the extant National People's Assembly. On December 7, 1989, the Union of Democratic Forces was created, instantly becoming the most powerful opposition force in Bulgaria. There is some ambiguity about the precise source of the idea for a body that would replace the National People's Assembly as a de facto policymaking institution for the nation. Nevertheless, the Roundtable became the vehicle for change despite the National People's Assembly's de jure status. Though the existing Parliament behaved as a rubber stamp for Roundtable decisions, the fact that leaders thought it necessary to follow normal legislative procedures in making changes in government policies and practices speaks eloquently about the future of parliamentary government in Bulgaria. There was a sense that change should proceed in an orderly fashion. Indeed, if Bulgaria was to avoid the violent models in her own history and in the process reject the French (1789) and Russian (1917) approach to revolution in favor of the British conservative model and the contemporary Polish approach, then change should proceed consistent with the rules of parliamentary government.[42] This meant that the existing National People's Assembly had to be consulted, no matter how perfunctory the process might appear. Moreover, for the old guard, because Roundtable leaders asked members of Parliament to pass on their recommendations, legitimacy was afforded those specific decisions. In terms of creating diffuse support among all factions in society, parliamentary government became the accepted vehicle for regime change. Thus, the National Roundtable Talks are properly regarded as the precursor to the creation of democratic government in Bulgaria.

The remaining sections of this chapter contain a brief narrative designed to provide a timeline sketch of those talks. I provide this outline because few readers outside of Bulgaria will be familiar with the key names and events central to making the transition to democracy in Bulgaria a reality. Readers with little patience for names and dates may wish to skip the remaining pages of this chapter and proceed to the chapters that follow. For those who seek a fuller appreciation of events, however, the sequence found here will serve to satisfy the urge for orderly progression.

December/January Developments

On December 14, 1989, a mass rally of students, workers, and others organized around the Parliament building in Sofia. They protested that the government was not proceeding quickly enough in its transition to democracy. The rally organizers were attempting to force the National Assembly to abolish immediately Article 1 of the existing Constitution on the leading role of the Communist Party. By all accounts, the rally might have resulted in mob violence but for the intervention of the little known organizers who later become key figures for the democratic opposition. They persuaded the crowd not to storm the Parliament building and to peacefully disperse. This event was widely perceived as a signal of the growing impatience of the masses and evidence that positive steps toward change had to be taken if serious civil disturbances were to be avoided.

On January 3 and 4, 1990, delegations from various political groups and coalitions came together in Sofia for preliminary consultations

Dramatic rally around the National Assembly building, December 14, 1989

about the procedures for National Roundtable Talks. The delegates for the Bulgarian Communist Party included Andrey Lukanov, Alexander Lilov, Belcho Belchev, Georgi Pirinski, Todor Kjurkchiev, and Ivan Angelov. Representatives of the Bulgarian Agrarian National Union (BZNS) included Viktor Vulkov, Svetla Daskalova, and Svetoslav Shivarov. There were two nonparty (independent) members of Parliament, Blagovest Sendov and Luben Kulishev. The major opposition group, the Union of Democratic Forces, was represented by Zhelyu Zhelev, Petar Beron, Petar Dertliev, Milan Drenchev, Dimitur Batalov, Rumen Vodenicharov, Georgi Avramov, Konstantin Trenchev, Petko Simeonov, Lyubomir Sobadjiev, Emil Koshlukov, Elka Konstantinova, Georgi Spasov, and Petar Kanev (on behalf of Christofor Sabev).

At meetings held early in January, participants agreed upon a Roundtable agenda, membership of the delegations, decision-making rules, approaches to the release of information to the public, and other procedural matters. They agreed that the Roundtable would focus its attention upon ways to obtain national agreement and reconciliation, a new political system, and a law-respecting state with a judicial system to carry out this goal. It was agreed that the Roundtable would make

A leading dissident, Neshka Robeva, asking the crowd at the December 14, 1989, mass rally not to resort to violence

preparations for a new electoral law and that the participants would address socioeconomic problems. The communicants issued a joint declaration they called *A Realistic Approach Toward National Reconciliation.* It supported the December 29, 1989, joint decision of the State Council and the Council of Ministers of the People's Republic of Bulgaria. It was designed to deal with the denial of the rights of the Turkish and Muslim minorities that the Zhivkov regime had imposed beginning in 1984. They also agreed that the National Roundtable Talks would commence its work during the week of January 16–24, 1990. At the same time delegations of the BCP, the BZNS, and the independent MPs held consultations with twenty groups not present at these preliminary talks. These included representatives of the Fatherland Union, the Komsomol (DKMS), the Independent Trade Unions, and other public organizations.

In an attempt to guarantee public access to their ideas, the UDF delegation placed before those present at the two-day meeting a re-

President Petar Mladenov appeasing the crowd at the December 14, 1989, mass rally just minutes before allegedly stating "better the tanks come"

quest for a suitable public building to headquarter their activities. They wanted permission to publish their own daily newspaper and sought an allotment of time on the public airwaves to transmit their views to a national radio and television audience.

Formal Roundtable Talks commenced on January 16, 1990. But to avoid the potential release of misinformation to the public, the deliberations were closed to the media. During the first meetings, the UDF delegation raised again their request to have their own newspaper, public building to house their activities, and a guarantee of free access to radio and TV transmissions. The plenary decided to create a contact group representing the various Roundtable factions to treat the UDF requests.

In a public appeal, Rossen Karadimov, the first secretary of the Central Committee of DKMS, insisted upon fair treatment for the Komsomol. He demanded Komsomol participation on an equal footing with the other delegations. The Independent Trade Unions also asked to participate in the talks. Finally, the Roundtable accepted Blagovest Sendov's suggestion that the two negotiating sides should reduce their quotas to give other "invited" organizations an opportunity to participate.

At this early stage the UDF made their purpose clear. In an official declaration they said that the UDF treated the Roundtable Talks with the utmost sense of duty, because the process could initiate a peaceful transition from totalitarianism toward democratic developments in the country.

During sessions held on January 22 and 23, Roundtable participants made brief statements about the first section of the previously agreed-upon agenda on the political system. Each side set out its conception of the fundamental principles of democratic political life. This dialogue included why and how the totalitarian bureaucratic political system should be dismantled and abolished. They discussed requirements for the law on political parties, public organizations, and movements, including guaranties against monopoly control over state institutions by any political party or public organization, and possible limitations on the creation of anticonstitutional parties or coalitions. Each side presented views on the depoliticization of certain state structures—the army, the militia (police), the public prosecutor and courts, and the educational system. In this context, they also suggested legislative guarantees for equal access of the political parties and public organizations to national television and radio. Finally, each side presented their view of the concept of separation of powers, including how legislative, executive, and judicial institutions might function in the future.

During the first day of the talks, four members of the Komsomol, the Independent Trade Unions, the Fatherland Union, and the Movement of Bulgarian Women were represented within the BCP's quota of forty-five delegates. Similarly, representatives of the Democratic Party and of the Green Party shared the UDF's quota.

On the second day of discussions the BCP quota included representatives of the Union of the Fighters Against Fascism and Capitalism, the Union of the Anti-Fascist Forces in Bulgaria, the Independent Trade Unions, the Komsomol, the Committee for Human Rights, the All-Peoples Committee for Defense of National Interests, the Fatherland Union, the Union of Bulgarian Journalists, the Bulgarian Writers Union, the Union of Bulgarian Artists, the Union of Bulgarian Film

Makers, the Bar Union, the Federation of Scientific and Technical Societies, and the Independent Union of Bulgarian Women. Also present but without invitation, the Bulgarian Union for Physical Culture and Sports participated in the talks. The UDF quota included one representative of the Committee for National Reconciliation. Representatives of the Bulgarian Orthodox Church Patriarchy and of the Chief Moslim Council were invited to the talks as guests.

At the request of Krastio Petkov, the participants discussed the advisability of issuing an appeal to cease all strikes and other protest activities during the duration of the Roundtable Talks. At this juncture, Roundtable participants also discussed the establishment of a committee to compile a document that specified all points of agreement among the parties about the dismantling of the totalitarian system.

It should be noted that at an early but unknown point in the negotiations to hold Roundtable Talks it was agreed that decisions of any such body should be made on a consensus basis. The thinking that motivated this decision was that the nation should proceed in a united fashion, on the basis of what Roundtable participants could agree upon. Therefore, it came as no surprise that on January 29 Roundtable participants debated the proposal of Svetla Daskalova, the leader of the BZNS, calling for the creation of a widely based government of national consensus. This new government would include the participation of the opposition parties and movements, a complete dismantling of the totalitarian system, and the opening of Bulgaria to the international community.[43]

Meanwhile the reform leaders of the Communist Party busied themselves with plans for reform within the Party itself. On January 30, 1990, leaders convened an extraordinary Party Congress. The main goal of the meeting was to rid the BCP of Stalinist tendencies, to commit themselves to democratic socialism rather than Marxism-Leninism, to create a civil society based on the principles of a law-governed state, to emphasize the role of intellectuals in political life, and to encourage a market economy. Introducing radical changes in its internal government, the Party changed its name to the Bulgarian Socialist Party and eliminated the oligarchical institutions of the Central Committee and the Politburo. It also permitted the youth organization, the Komsomol (Communist Youth League), and other factions to sever their ties to the Party.[44] These changes made plain the intentions of the post-Communist leaders that they were prepared to reach an accommodation with the UDF. It also had the consequence of signaling to the nation that what might be left of hard-liners within the Party would not be a significant factor in future Roundtable negotiations.

Between January and April, BSP leaders moved swiftly to portray themselves as among the leading progressive forces for democracy. As a further gesture toward democratic procedures, Party leaders submitted the name change to a referendum of Party members, with 86 percent voting in favor of the change and 12 percent voting against. They also changed the name of the official Party newspaper from *Rabotnichesko Delo* (Workers' Cause) to *Duma* (Word). Today, *Duma* is regarded as among the most objective and professional newspapers in Bulgaria.[45] As if by an act of contrition, Easter Sunday was named an official state holiday, and members of the Communist government were seen attending services at the historic St. Alexander Nevski Cathedral in central Sofia.[46] Finally, about one year later, in March 1991, the BSP published a detailed apology to the Bulgarian people for its past crimes and misdeeds. It announced the expulsion from its ranks of former leaders who had been responsible for many of the outrages against the people.[47]

February Discussions

On February 6, 1990, the Roundtable formally discussed the disbandment of Communist Party cells in the workplace and the dates for prospective parliamentary elections.

Thorny issues packed the agenda for the February 12 meeting. Participants gathered information about the progress of the contact group; reviewed the progress of the editing group that was preparing a draft agreement on Bulgaria's future political system; discussed the nation's economic situation based on recently published statistics for 1989 and the January 1990 trends; and exchanged information on the progress of talks with the European Economic Community (EEC) for potential membership and economic aid. Svetla Daskalova raised the issue of creating a third side at the Roundtable. But the UDF's Milan Drenchev strongly argued against any such proposal. And, again, Roundtable participants discussed the matter of dismantling Party cells in the workplace.

At this February 12 meeting, Roundtable participants discussed and agreed upon a declaration prepared by the contact group headed by the UDF's Zhelyu Zhelev and the BCP's Georgi Pirinski. It said that in securing widespread representation the National Roundtable reflects the political will of the Bulgarian people; and it is this fact that guarantees the irreversibility of the democratic process. The Roundtable's historical mission, the declaration asserts, is to achieve concrete agreements that will create the foundation for settling the nation's most crucial problems. These solutions entail the ways, means, and timing to liquidate totalitarian structures and to democratize the society. The Roundtable will establish the basic ideas and principles to guide future laws and other legislative acts and decisions that will create conditions for quick and decisive steps toward achieving national goals. To achieve these central purposes, the declaration calls for an atmosphere of mutual trust, constructiveness, and responsibility.

Rumors abounded that the Roundtable was about to fail. To head off such fears Roundtable participants met again on March 5, 1990. They worked to prepare texts concerning the issues debated at the first round of discussion and came near to completing written statements. Working groups led discussions on bills for amending the Constitution, for the regulation of political parties, and for the ground rules governing general elections. It was envisaged that the proposals would be introduced at the next session of the National People's Assembly. Roundtable participants created an additional working group to prepare for plenary discussion an analysis of the nation's socioeconomic problems. This matter centered on proposals for cooperation with the European Economic Community that the Bulgarian government had presented as a memorandum on February 12, 1990, addressed to the deputy-chairman of the EEC Commission.

March Agreements

Subsequently at a March 8 meeting, the contact group sanctioned all final draft agreements to be submitted to the plenary on March 12. At their meeting, Roundtable participants gave their approval and signed the *Agreement on the Political System,* the *National Agreement on the Guarantees for the Peaceful Development of the Transition Toward a Democratic Political System,* and a *Declaration on the Role and Status of the National Roundtable.*

The *Agreement on the Political System* stipulated as its core purpose the attainment of constitutionally and legislatively sanctioned judicial and political guarantees and mechanisms. It affirmed the sovereignty of the people represented by a democratically elected Parliament and a government under its supervision. It stipulated that there shall be independent functioning bodies of local governments created by free elections. Further, this agreement stipulated that the government shall function consistent with the principle of separation of powers and that the government shall operate with a multiparty system. This agreement also affirmed the principle of political freedom and guarantees equal treatment for all forms of ownership. It contained a list of legislative priorities calling for a law to amend the present Constitution, a law governing the activities of political parties, and a new statute regulating national radio and television. The *National Agreement on the Guarantees for the Peaceful Development of the Transition toward a Democratic Political System* is an eight-point statement declaring that peaceful mechanisms will be used to achieve political change in Bulgaria. The *Declaration on the Role and Status of the National Roundtable* reasserted the function of the Roundtable as an instrument of national consensus and obliged participants to employ their resources to ensure the implementation of Roundtable agreements.

At their March 15 meeting, Roundtable participants discussed economic reform and the government's anticrisis program. Opinions differed whether "shock therapy" or a gradual approach to a market economy would be best for the nation. All agreed that there was no alternative to a market economy. They then decided to form a group of experts composed of economists and lawyers. The experts were given the mandate to prepare a Roundtable agreement and to involve themselves in the work of the existing parliamentary committee on socioeconomic problems.

By the end of March, Roundtable participants discussed proposals for creating a presidential institution with a provision for a five- or six-year term of office, bills for amending the existing Constitution, plans for the election of the National Assembly, and laws for political parties and for the electoral system. In a public declaration, the UDF said it could not bind itself to the particulars of the proposed *Memorandum of the Government;* this was a document to be sent to the EEC countries on the subject of the implementation of economic reforms in Bulgaria.

Then, on March 30, Roundtable participants signed three documents. The first was *The Agreement on the Principles and the Basic Terms of the Bill for the Election of the Grand National Assembly.* It states that the anticipated elections shall be based upon the principles of universal, equal, and direct franchise by secret ballot. They agreed that this would be accomplished within the framework of a mixed electoral system that combined majority and proportional representation principles. This document specifies the rules for compiling constituency lists, the electoral bodies at central and regional levels, the procedure to promote candidates, the right of candidates to equal media access, the financing of election campaigns, the coalitions and parties allowed to compete in the elections, and the total number of seats in the Grand National Assembly.

The *Agreement on the Basic Concepts and Principles of the Bill for Political Parties* is the second document formalized by Roundtable participants on March 30. Its main items include guaranties for the citizens' right to free association in political parties, that political parties shall be entered in a separate registration file of the Sofia City Court, that political parties shall perform their activities within the framework of the Constitution and the laws of the country and in accordance with their charters and programs, and that all parties shall have equal legal rights. At the same time, this document explicitly forbids political parties from engaging in certain activities. These included change of the constitutional order by force, creation of political parties based on ethnic and religious principles, interference in the work of government bodies, and creation of Party cells in the workplace. It prohibited parties that are paramilitary, subversive, or ones that have youth organizations. This agreement on political parties also deals with financing political party activities. It provides that parties shall not receive funds from foreign states. Another provision entails the disbandment of parties and the role of the judiciary in that process.

The third accord signed on March 30 was *The Agreement on the*

Basic Concepts and Principles of the Bill for Amendment and Supplement of the Constitution of the People's Republic of Bulgaria. It contains statements about the general principles of the political system and about the fundamental civil rights and freedoms of the people. It also treats the organizational forms of state power during the transition toward parliamentary democracy, and the status of the central and local governments.

Participants decided at this eventful March 30 Roundtable meeting to abolish the State Council system created by the Communist Party in the old regime. In its place they agreed to substitute a president who would be elected by the People's National Assembly. They argued, however, about whether the proper title for the new head of the state should be president or chairman. Furthermore, the Roundtable set June 10 and 17, 1990, as the dates for parliamentary elections. They agreed upon the creation of a working group to prepare an *Agreement on the Guarantees for Democratic and Free Elections.*

May Completion

After six weeks, the Roundtable plenary reconvened to wrap up its work. On May 14 and 15, 1990, participants signed several pacts. The first is the *Agreement on the Guarantees for Free Elections.* It created a Public Council with twenty-one representatives from various political and nonpolitical organizations to supervise the implementation of the election agreements concluded at the Roundtable. It provided that the Public Council shall have local branches in municipalities. This agreement contains methods for carrying out the election law. The Roundtable participants attached an appendix to the agreement that specified measures to prevent persons from voting repeatedly in the same election. They also agreed to a separate document called *Ethical Code for the Elections' Campaign.* It contains recommendations for the behavior of political parties and independent candidates. The Roundtable also promulgated an *Agreement on the Basic Principles of the Statute of the Bulgarian Television and Bulgarian Radio* and an *Agreement on the Elections' Campaign over the Radio and the Television.* Finally, it passed a *Declaration for Amnesty of all Political Emigrants.* This document says that such persons may freely return to Bulgaria without fear of prosecution and that they may take part as candidates in the elections for the Grand National Assembly. The National Roundtable Talks ended its work on May 15, 1990.

Though it is a useful way to bring initial intellectual order to events, understanding the Roundtable requires more than this recitation of dates and names. In the next three chapters, I explore through the medium of personal interviews the process of decision making, the insights of persons actually involved in the talks, and the interaction of ideas, interests, institutions, and individuals that made the talks a success and the transition to democracy possible.

3

At the Creation: Internal Politics and Intragroup Dynamics

WITH THE APPARENT disarray within the socialist world order and the correlative fall of Todor Zhivkov's regime in late 1989, both the Communist Party and opposition forces were seeking to find their way. But the contours of the path were yet to be charted. While the Bulgarian Communist Party was considering its future, opposition political groups were developing rapidly; about fifty such organizations existed.[1] A coalition of these groups combined under the umbrella organization known as the Union of Democratic Forces. This body was formally created on December 7, 1989, almost a month after the November 10, 1989, coup d'état bringing down Zhivkov's regime. Fourteen of these groups became part of a delegation representing opposition forces at a National Roundtable with official authorities, which included the Bulgarian Workers Social Democratic Party (United), the Nikola Petkov Bulgarian Agrarian People's Union, the Club of Victims of Post-1945 Repressions, the Independent Association for the Protection of Human Rights, the Ecoglasnost Independent Association, the Podkrepa Independent Labor Federation, the Glasnost and Democracy Club, the Civic Initiative Movement, the Committee for Defense of Religious Rights, Freedom of Conscience and Spiritual Values, the Independent Student Societies, and the Radical Democratic Party.[2]

In civic culture terms these opposition groups hardly qualify as interest groups or political parties within a pluralist society. During the forty years of Communist Party domination, dissenting groups were repressed. Intellectuals and other individual dissidents in the Soviet tradition had an impact, but that was very different from organized opposition. As an expression of apolitical motives, many opposition groups called themselves independent, such as the Independent Society for the Protection of Human Rights. Citizen attachment to these groups was not so much a matter of deep psychological commitment and allegiance to mutually shared values as an expression of frustration with and a rejection of government policy.

Ecological Beginnings

The ecological movement was an ideal way for previously unattached individuals to coalesce around a cause and vent their anger at the existing regime without directly challenging its legitimacy. Indeed, the first dissident activities to gain national attention were the mass demonstrations at Ruse, a northern industrial city on the Romanian border. A Romanian chemical plant was spewing pollutants into the air that fell directly on the Bulgarian city. Citizens had objected to Bulgarian government officials, but nothing was done. But on March 8, 1988, a small band of activists created the Committee for the Ecological Defense of Ruse. A year later, a group of intellectuals and students created the widely popular movement called Ecoglasnost. It was established as a legal entity on April 11 in the apartment of Alexander Karakachanov, who at the time was a city council member in Sofia and later the chairman of the Green Party and participant at the National Roundtable Talks. Ecoglasnost was responsible for awakening public opinion and organizing the first protests with which most Bulgarians could identify. Yet, it would be a mistake to conclude that the ecological movement brought down the regime. As Karakachanov indicated in an interview with me, "The events which took place in Bulgaria were in fact a repercussion of what had happened worldwide and in Russia. . . . Left on its own . . . the ecological movement or any other dissident movement would have been mercilessly smashed if the year had been 1985, for example," and not 1989.[3]

But opposition does not develop out of thin or even polluted air. There must be a social basis or ideological foundation that serves as the precursor for the establishment of an organized opposition. In Bulgaria, the creation of an ecological movement served to unite persons from different backgrounds and experiences for the purpose of combating serious degradations to the environment that the existing government seemed either unable or unwilling to combat. Petar Beron, an entomologist with an international academic reputation and early leader of the opposition, explained in an interview that the foundations for the UDF opposition were present before the November coup d'état. In the process he related the roles individuals may play in bringing about political change. Beron, with his warm personality and charismatic speaking abilities, was headed toward a promising political future—that is, until he was accused by fellow opposition leaders of being an informer during the days of the old regime. In a cluttered office, much like those occupied by academics worldwide, I asked Professor Beron:

> You were one of the very first . . . you, Zhelev, and others . . . to give the opposition a face?[4]
>
> **PB:** Yes. I have been in the opposition movement, but I cannot make a hero of myself, and I do not want to. Many other people, even members of the Communist Party, who have been in high positions before—now everybody claims to have been repressed and so on, which is really not very decent. I have always been in science, traveling in . . . various parts of the world and I can say I have always been against communism. I have never concealed this. All my life, I considered communism a common utopia in the best case, as a theory, something, which is fantastic, you know; and as a practice—it is a crime. I have never been a member of the Communist Party and I have never approved in any way what they were doing. But I was living in the mountains, in the caves; I explored the high mountains, I had long journeys. I attempted to have as little to do with the Communist authorities as possible.
>
> When the many changes were taking place in other parts of Eastern Europe it was clear that change was also coming to Bulgaria. . . . There were some gatherings of dissidents—they are not persons who are now in the highest places; they were people who have been in jail and so on. Some of them are marginal people, who are not fit for normal life, you know. . . . So, they were pushed away very soon. Yet, they were the original dissidents. But the Communist dissidents, the so-called perestroikists, who are now pretending they

are responsible for bringing about the changes—do not believe them. When you speak to the BSP people, they will say, "Well, we were some sort of . . . [dissidents]." Do not believe them. They are trying to change their appearance. . . . But it is true that most of the politically active people have been in the Communist Party, because . . . nobody could be active in any field of political life unless they were Party members. . . . So, when the changes did occur on the tenth of November, the Communists were the persons who profited; they very quickly had the upper hand everywhere. And so, . . . in 1988 we founded this committee—the Civic Committee for the Protection of Ruse.

AM: You are referring to the Ecological Committee? Was this committee led by Communists?

PB: Yes, the Ecological Committee . . . at this time it was easier to pretend to be an ecologist because outright political opposition would be crushed very soon if we had not. So, we pretended to be ecologists, but we were also claiming some openness, glasnost. . . . It was clear, though, most members of this committee had been former Communists or actual Communists, members of the Communist Party. I was not a member of the leadership of this committee, but I participated as a group member.

After the first demonstration the committee was suppressed. Most people who participated were expelled from the Party, they lost their jobs and so on. And then in the spring of 1989 . . . we formed the organization called Ecoglasnost. I was one of the founding members of Ecoglasnost in April, and I became its secretary. We then staged different actions against various state projects, we collected signatures and so on. Thus, Ecoglasnost was the focal point for opposition against the government. Several other newly formed organizations gathered around us. They attended our meetings.

AM: You mean committees on human rights?

PB: Yes, human rights committees, then Podkrepa [the Labor Syndicate], then the religious committee of Christofor Sabev, then a few others. All these were created before the tenth of November. And it was the same case for the glasnost and perestroika clubs. These organizations were composed mostly by intelligentsia from Sofia University. Most of these people were also former Communists. Most were highly positioned members of the Communist Party, but they pretended they were something else.

You know, there are different stories about how these organizations were created. Some people claim that all these organizations were created by the State Security, that they were just the tools of the Communists. As a member of one of them, I can say that there is some truth in this . . . but it is not the absolute truth. It is truthful in part because with all that was happening in this and other countries the State Security would not just watch what was happening from the sidelines. They would intervene because it was their duty to take precautions. And they certainly tried to introduce some people in these organizations. Certainly there were some. . . .

AM: You mean . . . State Security infiltrated your organizations?

PB: Yes . . . I cannot say to what extent this happened, but to some extent it was done—certainly. But it is not true, as some people may tell you, that all of them, all of the fathers of the UDF were police or Communist agents, and that the UDF was created by the Communist Party and by the State Security. That is not true. The UDF was created by the genuine need of all these organizations, including the newly formed or restored political parties, to fight together, to create a common umbrella organization. All of us were feeling this. . . . I had talks with Andrey Lukanov . . . and with Petar Mladenov on some occasions. They were very much opposed to the idea of having this opposition umbrella organization [Lukanov and Mladenov were leading members of the reform leadership of the Communist Party]. They were asking us not to form it. But we did form it.

Zhelyu Zhelev led the initiative in this direction. I was his deputy. We have very strong reasons to think that Zhelev himself was, if not an infiltrator, . . . acting in very close agreement with the Communists. It is now known that he and his group of several Communists around him were in touch with Lukanov and company before all of this and that they had negotiated the way of doing these things.

AM: But because you were Zhelev's deputy, you knew about this at the time!

PB: I did not know about this. I was always kept outside. This group around Zhelev—all of them were former Party secretaries like Ivailo Trifonov, or active Komsomol leaders—you know the Komsomol, youth Communist organization. . . .

AM: Yes, I do.

PB: . . . like [Dimitar] Ludjev or Stoyan Ganev, or *Petko Simeonov* [emphasis added]. In the past they were all active Communists.

AM: Yes, I see.

PB: They were trusted by Zhelev—I was not. And finally we now know about these talks, about these negotiations, about these deals, made by Zhelev with the Communist dignitaries in the past—that they made him promises and he made them promises.

AM: When were these promises made?

PB: At a very early stage.

AM: Before the Roundtable actually commenced? Or during the Roundtable itself?

PB: Before the tenth of November!

AM: Before the tenth of November coup d'état!

PB: . . . We cannot prove it, but we have very strong reasons to believe that it happened like the way I have described.

AM: What is the starting date of the UDF?

PB: The starting date of the UDF is the seventh of December 1989.

AM: Almost a month after the coup. But your organization was formed before . . .

PB: Well, there had been informal contacts. During the first days of December we had several meetings at the university, and we negotiated the whole thing on the seventh of December. The UDF was founded in a building one hundred meters from here, very near. When you go out in the garden, I will show you the building. . . . It is the Institute of Sociology. At that time, the institute director who is now the head of the Confederation of the Independent Syndicates in Bulgaria was Professor Krastio Petkov. So, we created the UDF; Zhelev was elected chairman and I was elected secretary.

AM: Let me be clear on this point: the communications between Zhelev and the Communist leaders—Andrey Lukanov and others—did that take place before or after the creation of the UDF?

PB: We think it was before.

AM: I see.

PB: Or even much before. They deny it, but we have strong reasons to think that it happened like this. . . . We learn more all the time. For example, I read yesterday in a newspaper that Ivailo Trifonov—Zhelev's close associate—was a candidate to go to Moscow as Bulgaria's ambassador. But the Russians declined. Moscow newspapers revealed that Ivailo Trifonov was connected with the KGB [the secret police of the Soviet Union]. . . . But you must understand the nature of the times. Mladenov was president, but the main features of the old regime were still in their place. Lukanov and Mladenov were considered, if not revolutionaries, certainly they were regarded as reformers against the old guard, which was even worse. We supported the reform wing of the Bulgarian Socialist Party. Now, however, it is very easy to say, "You were behaving as traitors, because you were talking with Lukanov . . . " But at the time the opposition movement was weak. The army, the police—everything—was in the hands of the Communist Party. Now things are quite different. . . . We had to support the new trend, the new wave, the so-called reformers against Todor Zhivkov and his associates. Step by step we needed to push them out of power. It was not possible to do otherwise. Now it is very easy to exclaim against us, but those who accuse us were hiding at the time! We were busy provoking the Communists. But our detractors just sat back waiting to see what would happen. Now everywhere they protest loudly.

So after first establishing the UDF we decided by the end of the year that is was now necessary to create conditions for new elections. We subsequently formed a contact group and created the National Roundtable Talks. Today's radicals regard the Roundtable itself as an act of treason. They rhetorically proclaim: "Why talk with the Communists!" But we had no choice. There was no other way to solve the problems. . . . They say, "Why didn't you enter the ministries and throw them out?" It is easy to make such statements today, but I ask why did they not do this themselves? The answer is at the time it was dangerous to do so: 90 percent of the army officers were Communists, the whole police, everything. . . . The Soviet Union was still in existence at this time. All the treaties were still valid . . . the Warsaw Treaty and so on. . . . They were still valid and nobody knew what might happen if violence erupted.

AM: So, you had no choice. . . .

PB: Of course! We had to create the Roundtable—it was a correct step.

* * *

We learn from Beron that the ecological movement provided a respectable cover for dissidents. These were persons with a variety of objections to the old regime. They took advantage of widespread environmental concerns to present a broader indictment against communism. As Beron observes, many of the people who were the original ecological activists were quickly marginalized, a phenomenon that has often been repeated in the history of political change; revolutionaries who initiate change are replaced by more moderate types who are less disposed toward ideological extremes and who tend to be more practical in their orientation.[5] As personality types, Beron observes that the ecological radicals who were active during the initial days of the movement were generally people outside the mainstream of Bulgarian life. As he put it, they are people "not fit for normal life," people "who have been in jail and so on."

Beron accepts the proposition that there may have been police or Communist Party agents within Ecoglasnost. What else would we expect from a police state? Even in so-called democratic states, such as in the United States, intelligence agencies are known to infiltrate allegedly subversive organizations. Commonly, paid informants or agents posing as followers, or fellow-travelers, report to state authorities on the organizational activities of the infiltrated group. Although it was probably infiltrated, Beron insisted that the UDF was not a creature of the Communist Party as critics sometimes suggest. Dr. Konstantin Trenchev, the leader of the Podkrepa syndicate, further elaborated upon the dynamics of the UDF's formation. He explained why disagreements emerged among the various groups under its umbrella. On a few important points, Trenchev disagreed with Beron's analysis.

Organizational Militancy and Political Compromise

By training, Konstantin Trenchev is a physician. In February 1989, at the age of thirty-four, he became the leader of the independent trade union for intellectuals and workers that he helped to found, Podkrepa. This trade union played an important role in creating the Roundtable and in exerting pressure upon the state authorities for change. I interviewed him at Podkrepa headquarters, which is centrally located in downtown Sofia. Of all the organizational headquarters I visited to conduct my interviews, Podkrepa's was the best equipped and staffed suite of offices. I was impressed by the efficiency of the office and the staff's knowledge of worldwide events. With his support staff in attendance during the interview, I first asked Trenchev how, at a very early stage in the Roundtable Talks, Podkrepa became involved. He said:[6]

> We had created earlier an Independent Association for the Protection of Human Rights. It was made up of former political prisoners, and I was among the few exclusions in the membership. I became a political prisoner after that. But I will tell you why the organizational structure took the form of a trade union. We had three basic arguments for this. The first one was that the socialist economy was facing tremendous problems and because of this the social potential for a trade union association was very high. The second argument was that there existed negative attitudes among the people toward the men in power, because as a rule they used this power for their own purposes, while at the same time a trade union could have great influence without being directly involved in government. And the third argument was that there were loopholes in the legislation, which were creating the opportunity for such an organization to

be formed without restrictions, because at that time the creation of political parties was totally banned. Having in mind these three presumptions we established the organization, which started developing very quickly, because people were ready for change. . . .

We were the fourth opposition organization founded in Bulgaria. The first one was the Independent Society for Human Rights. It was also outside the scenario [acceptable groups to the governing elite] and its members were either dismissed from work or repressed in some other way. The second organization that emerged was the so-called Association of the Clubs for Glasnost and Perestroika. It was an organization totally manipulated by ex-Communists and also by active members of the Communist Party.

The third organization was the League for Human Rights; it was wholly made up of ethnic Turks. This one was smashed by the authorities, and its members were forced to emigrate. And the fourth organization was Podkrepa. I would also mention the fifth one, the so-called Ecoglasnost, which was a totally directed formation too.

AM: Directed formation? I do not understand the meaning of this term.

KT: . . . they were manipulated by the Communists. The events I am talking about took place in 1989. Our trade union was founded in February 1989. In May of that same year six activists were detained or arrested. We were released in September 1989. After this, the organization started growing very quickly because people saw that it was not so dangerous to be in it. On the tenth of November we had a membership of two thousand members. And this was the biggest of all the opposition organizations. We had a number of activities—meetings, demonstrations, rallies. Everybody was expressing their hopes for change. And we, the leaders of different organizations, got to know each other. Before that time we were personally unacquainted, although we knew each other by name. On December the seventh the Union of Democratic Forces was created. Of course, there were preliminary meetings prior to that date. After the tenth of November some other organizations and parties were hurriedly created. But on the tenth of November we numbered only seven organizations and there was not a single political party among them. The UDF emerged spontaneously as an association from these different forces.

In this period Podkrepa was extremely active. We organized a series of meetings and rallies and on the fourteenth of December we formed a life chain around the Parliament building. We insisted on the abolishment of Article 1 of the Constitution. And this article was about the Communist Party.

AM: About the leadership role of the Communist Party in society?

KT: Yes. At the end of the year we in Podkrepa asked for a Roundtable and we went on a national strike.

AM: Excuse me, was your organization the first to make this request for National Roundtable Talks? Was the idea for a Roundtable your idea, the idea of a number of UDF leaders, or was it an idea of the former Communist Party? I want to identify where the idea originated.

KT: We went on a national strike, requesting the abolition of Party cell organizations in the workplace, the restoration of rights of the ethnic Turks, the right for free association of syndicates. I have to admit that we were restrained by our colleagues from the UDF, but nevertheless we started our protest action, which frightened the government and it then proposed a Roundtable. But this idea was circulating in the opposition for quite some time before the government initiative. By the end of the month [December 1989], in fact at the very end of the month, the demonstrations of the ethnic Turks for restoration of their names took place. And the government had to step back on this issue too. I think that those two things—the national strike of the Podkrepa Syndicate and the protests of ethnic Turks—frightened the government. And it decided to act in this way to release the pressure.

At the very beginning there was disagreement over the distribution of power at the Roundtable. Podkrepa insisted on a Roundtable between the UDF and the government, while the Communists wanted a Roundtable between . . . the Communist Party, the Agrarian Party, the Women's Movement, the Synod of the Orthodox Church, the Supreme Spiritual Council of Moslems in Bulgaria, the Fatherland Front, and many other formations. . . . Oh, the trade unions were also included. So we were facing a gang who wanted to impose its point of view, to have an upper hand by any means. And on our side of the table some UDF people did not want representatives of the ethnic Turks to participate. On the whole the Roundtable was an endless succession of dialogues, aiming, I think, to confuse the opposition, so it could not prepare itself for elections. In fact this was an attempt by the Communists to convince the opposition (or at least its leaders) of the need for a Bulgarian perestroika [reform rather than genuine change]. All during those talks our organization defended staunch anti-Communist positions, and we are proud of it. I think our failure at the first election [June 1990] was due to the hesitant and collaborative stand the UDF took at the Roundtable.

AM: You mean that the UDF was not militant enough? It was not sufficiently anti-Communist! . . .

KT: Yes, there were too many compromises and the UDF was not militant enough.

AM: I think I understand. Please understand I do not mean to put words in your mouth—I just want a clarification . . .

KT: I can give you an example to illustrate my point, a scandalous example. We had in our possession a video recording, where President Mladenov mentions something about tanks coming during a protest rally around the National Assembly. I insisted upon full publicity of this recording—just to show people how far the Communists are willing to go to impede peaceful protest. The then chairman of the UDF and current president of the Republic, Mr. Zhelyu Zhelev, and the head of the electoral campaign, Mr. Petko Simeonov, did everything to prevent the showing of the tape; they asked our people to show restraint. The content of this cassette finally became known to the public just after the elections.

And there is another example. They banned the circulation of an election poster showing all the concentration camps created by the Communists. I consider this an illustration of a wavering and passive policy. Of course, I am not that kind of militant anti-Communist who recommends that everybody should be shot or imprisoned. But this hesitant position of the UDF was the main reason for our failure in the elections. Of course, there was bad organization and so on which also played a negative role. After all, the Communists won. We were the only organization that refused to accept the election results. Podkrepa was the only opposition group having organizational structures nationwide. And we had enough information to know that in many regions the elections were not fair.

* * *

Trenchev aptly relates the motivations behind the Communist Party's willingness to accommodate change. It was, according to Trenchev, a matter of adaptation and a very successful one at that. He said:

> This adaptation concerned first of all their tactics, because the main goal was to preserve their influence. Thus, when we in the opposition were coming to the point of open conflict with them, they would retract their position. Their main goal was to save their members from the people's anger. They wanted to gain time to regroup. They positioned new faces at the forefront. These new faces were persons not so directly connected with the former regime. These new personalities presented a flexible line, and after waiting out the tumult, for the transition to pass, they would then proclaim themselves social democrats. In this way they would avoid responsibility or guilt for the past. So, I can say the Bulgarian Communists were very flexible, indeed. . . . The struggle in Bulgaria is not a struggle to restore Communist principles. Rather, the struggle centers around the issue of who will become the capitalists. And the Communists want to transform themselves into this social group.
>
> **AM:** To become part of the capitalist class!
>
> **KT:** Nobody wants to restore the Communist principles.
>
> **AM:** Is it possible to give the UDF behavior a charitable interpretation? . . . That is, in a forgiving way. . . .
>
> **KT:** Indeed, at the time no one had any experience. So, to a certain extent it is historically forgivable. And do not forget that the UDF

was massively infiltrated by former Communists and secret services men. So, certain militant attitudes were blocked from within. And I stand by that interpretation.

The second generation of UDF leaders consisted of vociferous anti-communists. But they have not produced any real decommunistization. I have, of course, my own explanation why the UDF has failed. First of all, the formula around which it was created was not carefully considered. True, we have the excuse that we were not experienced enough to create the UDF in a better way. But later it should have been improved to adapt more adequately to the times.

As a matter of fact, the UDF was a coalition. But in its true sense, coalition means association among real structures. The structures in the UDF did not continue to develop organizationally, and in some ways these organizations remained as little more than groups of dozens of people, while other groups reached memberships of a couple of thousand. But practically the most important thing was that this conglomerate—for it was a conglomerate indeed—was actually exploiting the anti-communist feelings within the nation. Ordinary people thought of them not as a coalition of many organizations but as of one single entity; still, organizationally, they were not one piece, but a bunch of activists. Those activists were unable to create a real formation, to take control of state institutions, and to promote their ideas. When the Bulgarian Socialists were in control of the government the UDF did not even have a shadow government standing in opposition. It was not in a position after victory at the polls to put into place the right people to carry out its policies. . . . A government of this kind is doomed. Because even the best ideas fail if there is no one to put them into practice.

Currently [October 1993], the UDF is in an even more tragic situation. The first thing the UDF did when it came to power [October 1991] was to smash its two main supporters—one was Podkrepa and the other was the Movement for Rights and Freedoms. They also attacked the institutions of the Orthodox Church; they created tension with the president, who was, by the way, their candidate in the presidential elections. Overall they fought battles on many fronts against all the real [oppositional] structures in society. They blame everyone but themselves for their own failures. They blame us for our eagerness to have reform programs. They also blamed us for our desire for dialogue; Podkrepa wanted a tripartite dialogue. And, of course, they lost the battle.

Nowadays [beginning December 1992] we have a government, born of utmost compromise. No one regards it as responsible for anything. But at the moment we can find no replacement. We could topple this [Berov] government easily. The politicians in the Parliament could also do it, but they are hopelessly deadlocked; no one is doing a thing to find a way out.

AM: What has to happen to break the deadlock?

KT: I wish I knew the answer. If I could tell the members of my syndicate whom they should vote for I would not suffer the current rulers even for a month.

* * *

Thus, besides Ecoglasnost there were several other organizations created before the November 10, 1989, coup d'état that brought down the Zhivkov regime. After that event Podkrepa played an especially active role in organizing meetings, mass rallies, and strikes. These staged events served to exert pressure upon the Communists who were still in control of the government. The goal of these activities was to produce meaningful change. Trenchev claims parentage for the National Roundtable Talks, but, as he admits, others also called for the talks, including the leaders of the Communist Party. In fact, Party leaders formally proposed the talks, although the idea had been floated in other quarters. Trenchev recognized that the Communists were attempting to employ the age-old divide-and-conquer tactic. The government sought talks with many independent groups instead of what all finally agreed upon: namely, two sides represented at the Roundtable, the government on one side and the opposition united under the banner of the UDF. Yet, loose federations suffer from a major disadvantage. It is difficult for them to behave quickly and decisively. To keep the coalition together, such umbrella organizations must compromise among themselves, and this spirit may translate into what Trenchev calls a hesitant and collaborative stand toward the opposition. He is critical of the UDF because it was not sufficiently militant. Trenchev blames the initial election defeat at the hands of the Bulgarian Socialist Party and the subsequent disarray within UDF ranks on its all-too-willing desire to reach an accord with the government in power. Yet, as Trenchev readily admits, the opposition had little experience in such matters. Moreover, there was good reason for all the parties at the Roundtable to fear failure.

A Social Movement from the Top

Political outsiders may bring to political discourse the twin qualities of new ideas and honesty—virtues sometimes lacking in well-worn politicians—but they often lack the instincts and skills that come with experience. But within UDF leadership ranks were some who had firsthand knowledge of their Communist Party opponents. Former Communist Party members and activists were involved in the formation of the UDF, the National Roundtable Talks, and the Grand National Assembly that fashioned a new Constitution. By all accounts, these ex-Communists played at the very least the important role of intermediary. In that role they made the process of negotiation and compromise smoother than it might otherwise have been.

Petko Simeonov is among the most interesting ex-Communists to become active in Bulgaria's transition to democracy. His father was sent to prison twice before 1944, because he was a Communist and anti-fascist. Some members of his family were killed by what Simeonov describes as the fascist regime. Thus, he began his conscious political life as a true believer in communism. Simeonov explained that this perspective continued until he entered the university. Sometime around 1964–65, he began to see things in less dogmatic ways. He was a Communist Party member twice. The first time he was thrown out of the Party, but on the second occasion he left on his own. Unlike Petar Beron and Konstantin Trenchev, Petko Simeonov was politically engaged in a variety of ways all his life. Although his background and initial involvement in the transition to democracy are different from those of Beron and Trenchev, the recitation of facts about how the opposition forces were created and the understandings created between those forces and the reform communist leaders are similar. However, Simeonov provides, from a lifetime of political activity, insights that Beron and Trenchev are incapable of relating.

I interviewed Petko Simeonov at the headquarters of the Bulgarian Liberal Party.[7] At the time, he was the leader of this party, which had no elected representatives in the parliament. As was the case for many of the original opposition members, Simeonov found himself in the political wilderness with too few followers. Nevertheless, he was bounteous with vivid memories of the role he played in the transition to democracy. I first asked Simeonov how he got involved in the Roundtable and the Grand National Assembly.

PS: I had some credit among Bulgarian dissidents, and I guess, a certain position among the Sofia intelligentsia before November 10, 1989. . . .

I was the scientific secretary of the Institute of Sociology and it was in my study there . . . where the foundation . . . the decision to create the Ruse (ecological) club . . . took place. . . . Among the participants at this meeting were Zhelyu Zhelev, Ivailo Trifonov (currently chief of the Cabinet Office of the President), and some five or six other people, who later played different roles in Bulgaria's political life. Subsequently, I was among the founding fathers of the Club in Support of Glasnost and Perestroika. The first of the above-mentioned events happened at the end of February 1988, and the second one—the formation of the Club in Support of Glasnost and Perestroika—took place on November 3, 1988.

AM: So a whole year before the coup [November 10, 1989], you are part of the dissident movement?

PS: Yes. I had two personal acts of dissidence during that period. The first took place sometime at the beginning of 1988, I cannot remember exactly when, but it was when I started to speak on Radio Free Europe. The other thing I did was on May 4, 1988. I remember this exactly: I wrote a comprehensive letter against communism to Milko Balev (the second in command in the Communist Party, secretary of the Central Committee and Politburo member). Balev was the most trusted person around Todor Zhivkov. . . . This letter of mine was widely disseminated by the *samizdat* press.

AM: You mean by *samizdat,* the illegal or underground press?

PS: Yes. By the tenth of November 1989 I had already attained a certain position and prominence. Before November 10 I was in the leadership of the Club in Support of Glasnost and Perestroika, and after that date I became its chairman. I was actively involved in the consultations around the creation of the UDF as early as the summer of 1989. The UDF was founded on December 7, 1989, a month or so after the coup. The signing of the founding declaration took place at the Institute of Sociology. At the time, I was no longer the institute's scientific secretary, because I had been sacked after the demonstrations at Ruse. But I was still influential at the institute, and as a result I was able to secure its premises, where the signing took place. We had all our meetings there. Later we got the building at 134 Rakovska Street [the current UDF headquarters]. The UDF used the institute premises, which were secured by me.

AM: Very interesting. So intellectuals were very much involved. . . .

PS: The persons involved were mainly intellectuals. . . . In the first call of the UDF Coordinating Committee . . . all the members were intellectuals. There was not a single worker or a peasant as a member of the Coordinating Committee.

AM: So one might say that it was a social movement from the top.

PS: Yes, indeed. I was a member of the Coordinating Committee in my capacity of chairman of the Club in Support of Glasnost and Perestroika. Then, I became chairman of the Central Election Club and I was appointed manager of the election campaign during the first elections [June 1990]; I was a deputy leader of the UDF. There were no other deputies—just a chairman (Zhelev) and his deputies. During the election I was the director of the *Democracy* newspaper.

I want to ask you a question myself. Are you interested in the peaceful transition as such or certain kinds of events?

AM: Well, I am interested in the events and the roles played by individuals in those events. . . .

PS: I see. . . . On December 14, 1989, the Communist National Assembly under pressure from the informal dissident groups started debates on the abolishment of Article 1 of the Constitution on the leading role of the Communist Party. The UDF was born just one week before. A mass rally was organized around the National Assembly, and people for the first time in their lives felt free. Well, this new feeling of freedom is very intense, and it could become dangerous. There were appeals from the crowd around the National Assembly building to enter by force and to throw the deputies out. Mr. Zhelev, myself, and some other persons circulated around with megaphones, trying to appease the people. We appealed to them not to storm the building. There were others who admonished the crowd to get inside, saying that the bloodshed is unavoidable. And let me tell you this—because you mentioned an interest in the role of the individuals—at that point Mr. Zhelev and the rest of us, Mr. Ivailo Trifonov and Konstantin Trenchev, took to the rostrum in front of the building of the Students' House of Culture, just opposite the Parliament. From there, Mr. Zhelev for the first time said to the people that we are for a peaceful transition to democracy; we stand for changing the system through elections, through free elections. Be patient, he said. We have to advance step by step. So we appealed to the people to disperse and to go home and they did.

AM: Let me see if I understand. UDF forces organized this rally to begin with, before it got out of hand.

PS: Now, because I was one of the organizers of the rally, let me explain. There were two [parallel] gatherings, two meetings of informal dissident groups. One of these was organized by students. The other represented a life chain [picket line], which we, a group from the Coordinating Committee, helped to organize around the National Assembly when it was having its debate about Article 1 of the Constitution. This was a life chain made up of people holding their hands together.

AM: But what came first? Did the Communist Party officials first initiate the discussion on changing Article 1, and then demonstrations followed?

PS: The pressure [by the informal dissident groups] preceded the debates on Article 1. We entered into a dialogue with the authorities, with totalitarian authorities, right after Todor Zhivkov was deposed, and that happened before the creation of the UDF. And they gave us their word they would abolish Article 1 of the Constitution.

AM: Did they force persons within the Communist Party who may not have wanted to go along with the abolishment of Article 1 to do so?

PS: No, there were ongoing changes within the Communist Party.

AM: But I am interested in understanding whether UDF activities were important in strengthening the hand of the reform faction within the Communist Party, that group within the Party who wanted to abolish Article 1.

PS: The situation in the country was very peculiar then. Let me summarize: Todor Zhivkov had changed forcefully the names of the ethnic Turks in Bulgaria. The emerging organized opposition stood in defense of the Turks. This later proved to be of great importance for the preservation of ethnic peace. The third event—the Turks have started their mass exodus, their mass "excursion" to Turkey. This created an outcry within the ranks of the Communist Party itself over the approach used by the Party leadership. That is why the deposing of Todor Zhivkov on November 10, 1989, dealt a blow to all conservative forces in the Communist Party. They were the guilty ones. And because of this they lost their voice within the Communist Party. Thus, it was within the ranks of the Communist Party itself that the call for abolishing Article 1 was the strongest. We put pressure on them to speed up this abolishment.

AM: This is very important to understand, because it is not clear abroad that there was a conscious effort on your part to keep the pressure on the Communist Party.

PS: Do not forget that I was a Party member until December 31, 1989, when I declared that I quit. There were members of the Communist Party in the first [UDF] Coordinating Committee. The protest rally on December 14, 1989, which I mentioned before, is significant not only for Mr. Zhelev's slogans for a peaceful transition. . . . Article 1 of the then existing Constitution could not be abolished by a simple debate in the National Assembly—which took place on December 14. According to the provisions of the then existing Constitution the people would have to wait an additional month before the abolishment of Article 1 could occur. Therefore, at the December 14 mass rally we were trying to appease the people. We argued that the constitutional procedure should be followed. And indeed, on January 16, 1990, Article 1 was abolished. On January 3, 1990, the preliminary talks on the formation of the Roundtable began.

* * *

It is especially interesting that intellectuals from the university community were actively involved in the dissident movement at least one year before the November 10, 1989, coup d'état that brought down the Zhivkov regime. Simeonov and others used their positions within the university to network with others by disseminating their views through the underground press and other avenues, including Radio Free Europe. Of course, these dissidents could go only so far before they were relieved of their positions within the university. Clearly, then, the opposition to the regime was led by intellectuals. It was not a peasant or workers' movement. These intellectuals-turned-activists were little known to the public before the December 14 demonstrations. The intellectuals insisted upon a peaceful transition to democracy. They admonished the thousands that had circled the Parliament building demanding a change in the Party's constitutional role as the leading force in society to use nonviolent means to achieve democracy. The dramatic events of December 14 are definitive because they placed the intellectuals at the head of the mass movement to change the character of Bulgarian society. And they established a peaceful rather than a violent strategy for how it might be achieved.

The Party Line: Glasnost and Perestroika

Why did the new leaders of the former Communist Party negotiate with an opposition that it otherwise might have crushed with a show of force? The answer is not as straightforward as one might suppose. There is considerable evidence suggesting that many of the younger members of the Bulgarian Communist Party believed reform was necessary. It is true that Zhivkov's ruling oligarchy failed to adapt sufficiently to the changing times and conditions, and there was widespread recognition that the system had failed. Yet, it is also true that Zhivkov wisely realized that political organizations need new talent to bring life to structures that would otherwise atrophy. Ironically, it was this cadre of relatively young Party apparatchiks created by Zhivkov that caused the November 10 coup d'état, bringing down his regime. Matters were made worse for Zhivkov because of his tendency and that of his predecessors in office to follow slavishly the policy cues of the Soviet Union. By all accounts, the doctrines and actions of the Soviet Union's Mikhail Gorbachev played a significant part in strengthening the hand of reform elements within Bulgaria's Communist Party.

Given this habitual pattern of conformity, it was possible for reformers within the Communist Party to embrace glasnost and perestroika without being accused of anti-communist activity. President Gorbachev of the Soviet Union encouraged public discussion and dissent; he reduced censorship and made it fashionable to challenge the authority of the Party apparat. None of this was lost on the people of Eastern Europe, including those in Bulgaria. Perestroika ("restructuring") and glasnost ("openness") played an important role within the then existing Bulgarian Communist Party to encourage reformers to create new political and economic structures to meet the challenges of the age. A new freedom to voice different views combated those entrenched forces that defended the status quo.

Georgi Bliznashki is a faculty member at Sofia University specializing in constitutional law. He was a Socialist member of one of the Roundtable's contact groups, and when I interviewed him in 1993 he was a member of Parliament.[8] He helps us to understand the internal political dynamics of the Bulgarian Communist Party and how it was possible for reformers to gain an upper hand over the old guard. Georgi Bliznashki said:

> Well, I believe the things that happened in Bulgaria were substantially influenced by events that already had taken place in other countries in 1989. This means that the basic opposition in the country against Todor Zhivkov and his regime was coming from inside, from the ranks of the Communist Party itself. And the main factor influencing the emerging trends was perestroika. It was not by chance that among the founding fathers of the first organized

dissident groups in Bulgaria were such prominent intellectuals as Professor Chavdar Kjuranov, Stefan Prodev, and many others who, subsequently, after the removal of Todor Zhivkov, occupied key positions in the Socialist Party leadership [the BCP changed its name to the Bulgarian Socialist Party]. There were, of course, differences of opinion because before the tenth of November 1989, most of the Central Committee members were personally selected by Todor Zhivkov. Because of this fact, different concepts within the Socialist Party about its political prospects were taking shape gradually. Mr. Petar Mladenov, in particular, the man who replaced Todor Zhivkov, was using the typical perestroika phraseology of the time. But I want to point out that his key thesis was that the Bulgarian people had made their socialist choice once and forever. If you remember, Mr. Gorbachev was talking the same way.

AM: Yes, reform for Gorbachev was a matter of reform within the general framework of the existing political order.

GB: Yes, within the framework of the totalitarian rule. And, well, there was another group within the Party and it was formed around Mr. Andrey Lukanov, who was then the leading reformer within the ranks of the Socialist Party [BSP]. This faction was united around the idea that the transition should go further than the totalitarian system—it should be about creating a new system. We were discussing the theme for the change of the political system; . . . well, you know, there was considerable discussion within the Party. It entailed the kind of regime we would have here in Bulgaria. I remember very well the aspirations of Mr. Lilov, who was elected as the new chairman of the Party after the BCP's Thirty-eighth Congress in January 1990. He was a reform-minded leader, but he was not going to stray too far away . . . from the status quo. I remember we discussed with him the topic of what is the main characteristic of the political regime here in Bulgaria; that is, whether it was authoritarian or totalitarian. And his thesis was that it was administrative . . . there is a Russian word for this view—I think Gavriil Popov used this term. He was the first to use the term several years ago—that in Bulgaria we should have an administrative-command system, a kind of authoritarian rule and not a totalitarian one.

Well, it was an important discussion, and at the first stage of the National Roundtable it was one of the points that the Socialist Party was fighting for. We would not accept the proposition that Bulgarian socialism was equivalent to totalitarian rule, because such a rule is characteristic of repressive regimes. And, you know, I was using then another political category which seemed rather strange to most foreign observers. Well, I was using a term, it was well known, but it was not accepted within the leadership and especially by those foreigners not well informed on the subject. But I was trying to use the term *autarchy* as a totalitarian democracy. It seems strange at first. . . .

AM: You mean a contradiction in terms . . . ?

GB: Yes, because Mr. Zhivkov and the old regime were not isolated. They have had for a long period of years grassroots support within the society. Because Bulgaria was a very poor country—one of the poorest in Europe—and during his rule there was a trend toward modernization, especially economic modernization. And, well, there are some specifics here in Bulgaria about our own history. The regime was not as repressive as was the case for Poland, Czechoslovakia, or Hungary. This is so because the Russians were considered . . . old friends of Bulgaria. The Russians liberated Bulgaria from the Turkish yoke and, especially you know, after the First World War there was a very deep crisis in Bulgaria . . . The ruling class just . . . *prosto se sruti* [just collapsed]. And you know, there was conflict within the left between the Communists and the Agrarians. After the killing of Stamboliiski in 1923 the strongest party on the left was the Communist Party, and on the right the strongest parties and movements were of a fascist kind. You know, Bulgarian society was very much divided for more than fifty or sixty years. After the catastrophes in the Balkan wars and the First World War we lost our sense of national unity. There is a very complex history of what happened later in Bulgaria. It is important to know that the Communist Party was not an invention of the Russians. You know what happened in Hungary: the Russians came and they created a Communist Party, which later took the power and so on. Well, it was not . . .

AM: An indigenous party . . . ?

GB: Yes. The Social Democrats here were very weak because they fought against Stamboliiski in the coup d'état, so they paid the price—there are very deep divisions in our history. And well, the socialist regime contributed to the well-being of the mass of the population. It was a totalitarian rule. But, well, in the everyday life you are not interested in freedom—you are looking for your work, for having a job, and for having something to eat and so on. You know, all those absolute values—they come later on.

AM: Right. I understand you to mean that eating comes first and then comes liberty.

GB: Yes . . .

AM: So, you say it was by consent—totalitarianism by consent?

GB: Yes. For many years there was no official opposition. We did not have events here in Bulgaria like those in Germany or Poland during the 1960s; nothing occurred in Bulgaria like the events in Czechoslovakia during the 1970s, nor in our own days, events like those that transpired in Poland. Nothing happened here. . . . Mr. Zhivkov was at the highest place for many years. There was a group at the top, his circle of followers and very close friends for many years at the top; it was a kind of septuagenarism. They were not stepping down—they were staying. You know, there was opposition from within the Socialist Party. . . . In the beginning there was considerable discussion within the Party about the future of the country.

And perhaps the key figure during this period was Mr. Lukanov . . . he may have played the same role here in Bulgaria as Adolfo Suarez did in Spain. He is from an old family: his father, his grandfather were active in politics. His grandfather was leader of the Party in the twenties—he was second in command of the Party here in the twenties.[9] Well, Andrey Lukanov was the man who could make the social contract with the opposition coming from within the Party. He was the same figure as Adolfo Suarez, who came from the ranks of the Phalanges and forged reform in Spain changing the political system.

AM: How long was this reform thinking going on in Bulgaria? Did this type of thinking take place long before November the tenth?

GB: Yes of course.

AM: I mean, would you say several years? That is, when did people start talking seriously about reform? Was it simply a matter of thinking and talking, but it was all very quiet until the events surrounding the collapse of . . . ?

GB: Perestroika was the big catalyst for the events . . . of developing opposition. . . .

AM: Okay. And you are suggesting that perestroika seemed to free people to start talking openly about reform. Is that what happened?

GB: Yes . . . there was great interest in the events in Russia. And people went to the post offices wanting subscriptions to *Ogoniok* [the largest circulating Russian weekly magazine] and all the Russian papers. In fact, because of the great demand it became very difficult to obtain these publications.

Well, Mr. Zhivkov was trying to maneuver amidst all the talk about reform. He made expressions in support of the concept of change, but it was just talk and nothing happened. And people knew that he was just talking. His expression was a very famous one: that we should keep quiet, that we should just lay down while the storm is raging and later we will see what will happen, in the wake of the storm. That is, we will react after the storm passes . . . to lay low.

* * *

Andrey Lukanov was unmistakably a principal actor in the reform movement within the Bulgarian Communist Party. He served as a member of the Politburo and was responsible for the economic reforms under Zhivkov from 1984 to November 10, 1989. He helped to organize the coup that toppled Todor Zhivkov. He later became the first prime minister under the new July 1991 Constitution. Lukanov sought a peaceful transition based on the premise that change was necessary.

In an interview with me that took place in a lounge of the Parliament building Lukanov phrased the problem in historic terms:[10]

> The idea we had from the very beginning was to move the . . . notion of peaceful transition into the center of the political debate, being aware not only of the dangers of the transition as such, but the additional dangers, that have been rooted in the Bulgarian civil war, as I call it—in the fact that the Left and the Right sectors, the Bulgarian leftist and rightist sectors of the Bulgarian society, have been in conditions of a civil war, hot and cold—for seventy years, starting from the end of the First World War and the well-known September 1923 uprising against the coup d'état, carried out in June 1923.
>
> Since then, vendetta was—I would say—the principle of Bulgarian politics. One side persecutes the other, oppressing it in different forms, starting with very violent forms—killings, summary executions, and both the Left and the Right are responsible for these acts . . . these persecutions severely limit one's opportunities and civil rights because of belonging to the losing side at a given period of time.
>
> So, this was a fact of life we were very clearly aware of, because, many of us, especially Mladenov and myself, had been on that side. His father has been killed; my grandfather has been killed.
>
> So, although I happened to spend a great part of my life as a representative of the winning side, I was deeply aware of the injustice, dangers, and constant confrontations.[11] And some of the other active participants in the reform process at the beginning were themselves participants in this civil war—the armed struggle during the resistance. Mr. Djourov, the minister of defense; the minister of the interior, who was previously chief of staff [of the Bulgarian Army], Mr. Semerjiev, were themselves guerrillas.
>
> I am trying to emphasize the idea that the reformers within the Bulgarian Communist Party were not only politically and intellectually but also morally committed to stop the civil war: to avoid the dangers of physical confrontation inherent both in Bulgaria's history and in the difficulties inherent in the process of transition.

AM: You said something that is especially interesting to me. You speak of vendetta. This vendetta is deeply ingrained in Bulgarian life, isn't it? It penetrates beyond politics . . . ?

AL: To some extent it is in the national character. Which is the nasty side of our altogether interesting national character.

So this was one of the sides. On the other side at that time the leading positions in the opposition itself were taken by dissidents, who were fighting the totalitarian society. Of course, dissidence in Bulgaria was much weaker than in other ex-socialist countries, but still they were fighting totalitarianism under the slogans of civil society, democratic rights, and other personal rights.

And we were altogether sincere believers in democracy. The right-wing part of the UDF at that time was not known; it was present, but it was playing third- and fourth-rate roles behind the scene. . . . Many of the frontline dissidents and creators of the new opposition in Bulgaria were themselves ex-Communists. Some of them were Communists even at the time they were forming the opposition against us. They left the Party two or three months after the tenth of November. So, in a way they also understood—because of their background—that democracy could not be achieved through repetition of vendetta, through revenge in the form of repression against the other side . . .

AM: But as the leader of the reform movement you certainly encountered opposition from within your Party? How did you deal with that opposition?

AL: Yes. To some extent, but at the time it was not too difficult to overcome it, because, first of all, there was a general recognition in the society that totalitarian socialism has failed. So, at that time people who liked to defend it uncritically were rather subdued; they felt that it was not the right kind of statement to make. And our authority was unchallenged absolutely. The five of us [the Politburo members who rebelled against the Zhivkov regime] were enjoying high opinion rankings from . . . all sectors of the society—even those who hate me today gave me . . .

AM: Excuse me, are you referring to public opinion polls?

AL: Yes, they gave, for example, Mladenov 80 percent confidence rating, which was . . .

AM: Fantastic, yes.

AL: So, both within the Party and the general public our support was so great that we could impose our own way of thinking . . . without using any other means than conviction and our own . . . I should say . . . our own statement as to how things should be done if we want to achieve democracy.

So, from that point of view we had such strong support—public support and internal support within the Party—that it was not a problem. Really! Opposition and discussion came later, when things started to normalize, and after we insisted on transforming the Party itself into a democratic institution, doing away with democratic centralism and Marxist-Leninist dogma. Three or four months later we faced opposition from conservatives within the Party. But at the beginning there was no resistance to change—everybody understood that change was inevitable.

AM: But nonetheless you needed an opposition not within the Party, but outside the Party in order to use it against potential opponents from within the Party. You know, I am surmising this.

AL: Not from that point of view. Actually we . . . argued rather schematically, starting from the principle that a democratic society should be based on pluralism.

AM: Yes.

AL: And that is why I think everybody recognized that we were very constructive in helping the opposition to establish itself. That is to say, dissidence was very weak in Bulgaria—there was no opposition force at the moment of the great change.

AM: But from time to time you did challenge the legitimacy of the opposition . . . ?

AL: No. In formal terms—never. We challenged them sometimes on . . . their line of confrontation. Because the way the Bulgarian opposition was formed they were opposing everything. This is one of the ways to set up an opposition. But to establish themselves they had to divide the nation; they had to say that others are bad and we are good. They drew the dividing line in a way that made Bulgarian political life more confrontational than is healthy for such a period.

AM: I have noticed in a number of press reports from those days that you talked about avoiding witch-hunts against—you used the words—honest Communists.

AL: Not only that. We invited the opposition to form a coalition government as early as December 1989. Before the Roundtable!

AM: Oh, I did not know that.

AL: Two or three weeks before the Roundtable we said that we are ready to share power, not because we have similar views but because we think the nation is facing a very difficult transition period with many crises to come. And in these conditions we should try to concentrate on finding a national consensus on basic, fundamental issues. That is why . . . I was insisting all along that we form a coalition government and that we should keep places in the government for the opposition.

* * *

Bulgarian leaders had long imitated the Soviet Union. With the announcement of new directions and programs of each successive Soviet leader, beginning with Stalin, Bulgaria's leaders had sought to please their patrons. At one time, following the Soviet lead, Bulgaria embarked upon a program of massive industrialization at the expense of agriculture. At one point, Bulgaria had a foreign policy hostile toward China and the West. Devotion to the Soviet Union was so complete that Todor Zhivkov had offered to Khrushchev and Brezhnev that Bulgaria become the Soviet Union's sixteenth republic![12] It is ironic that this habit of ideological subservience might in the end encourage the development of democracy in Bulgaria. The Soviet ideas of glasnost and perestroika were quickly adopted by Bulgarians in part because they had always followed the latest fashions in Soviet doctrine. Todor Zhivkov could hardly renounce the new doctrines since he had in the past so devoutly followed the Soviet line. This provided the opportunity for the younger generation of Party officials and leaders to ask questions and to propose changes. As Lukanov said, everyone knew "totalitarian socialism has failed." Thus, what remained of the Leninist/Stalinist opposition within the Party was easily circumvented, and the instinct for survival took hold for those who had nowhere else to go in what surely had become a world dominated by capitalism and democratic ideas.

Not only the political logic inherent in the situation but also the history of Bulgaria served to motivate thoughtful people to consider seriously a peaceful transition rather than the alternative. The history of violence, lost wars, and the practice of vendetta in Bulgarian life reminded all of the principal actors that there ought to be a better way to achieve change. And indeed, they did find a way. However, the path was encumbered with distrust, misunderstanding, and fear. Agreements at the National Roundtable Talks would need careful crafting.

4

Start of the Roundtable: Initial Posturing, Gamesmanship, and the Secret Police

On December 27, 1989, a spokesperson for the Central Committee of the Communist Party announced that it had agreed with the UDF to hold Roundtable consultations.[1] The first meeting between representatives of the government and the UDF was held on January 3 and 4 at the National Assembly building in Sofia, the nation's capital. Before the meeting between the two sides, there was consultation among representatives of the Bulgarian Communist Party, the Bulgarian National Agrarian Union (BZNS), public organizations, and the creative workers' unions.[2] Some groups, including trade unions and communist youth organizations, insisted upon representation at the talks. However, the UDF refused to sit at the Roundtable with the Fatherland Front, Bulgarian trade unions, the youth association, and other "formal" organizations, claiming these organizations were linked to the Communist Party. The UDF characterized them as a "third wheel on a two-wheel carriage," with the UDF on one side and the BCP, the National Agrarian Union, and the government on the other.[3] The major players negotiated an agreement to provide forty-three participants for each side. The UDF and the BCP could choose representatives of any organization to be part of their delegations.[4]

Though the opposition made assumptions about widespread popular support, the BCP nonetheless had the greatest single membership in Bulgarian society: BCP members made up one-eighth of the population and were in one-fourth of all Bulgarian households. Consequently, individual opposition organizations could not command widespread loyalty, which left leaders of those organizations without a firm foundation of citizen support. It made political sense to combine individual protest groups under the loosely knit alliance called the Union of Democratic Forces.

The apparent fragility of the opposition prompted the BCP to challenge its legitimacy, so the UDF demonstrated its authenticity by organizing mass protest rallies. It did so after leaving the Roundtable Talks because government forces seemed to be dragging their feet, and negotiations stalled. Also adding to the UDF's legitimacy was the apparent preference for it by Western observers and diplomats. With other Eastern European countries undergoing radical change, additional legitimacy was bestowed upon opposition forces.[5]

To Include the Turkish Ethnic Minority?

On several occasions participants raised the matter of Turkish ethnic minority representation at the Roundtable Talks, but they did not discuss it publicly. Although representatives of the Movement for Rights and Freedoms (MRF) were invited to attend, this Turkish minority group never became part of either the UDF or BCP delegations. Both sides feared reprisals from anti-Turkish nationalist forces within Bulgarian society. In fact, the Turkish question was never given a full public airing. However, it was the subject of private discussions in the closed contact groups established by the two sides to prepare the agenda and work out the details for agreements at the plenary meetings.[6] Stefan Gaitanjiev is an academic sociologist with the Institute for State and Law, and in October 1993 he was the secretary of the Bulgarian Democratic Center Party. In 1990 he was an active participant in the National Roundtable Talks. His interpretation of why the MRF was not seated at the Roundtable is substantiated by others I have spoken with about this matter. Gaitanjiev said:[7]

> most of the participants were in favor of the idea that the UDF should represent the interests of the national minorities, . . . to take the role of their only defender and to rightfully count on their votes in future elections. But the Movement for Rights and Freedoms of Ahmed Dogan declared that it did not want to enter the UDF; instead, it wanted a share of the UDF quota at the Roundtable. This

[MRF] proposal was most strongly rejected by Rumen Vodenicharov from the Independent Society for the Defense of Human Rights, who at that time had the support of most Bulgarian Moslems. And I think this reflected to a great extent a struggle for influence over those people. Nationalistic convictions were at the time more pronounced in people like Petko Simeonov and Zhelyu Zhelev. Another conflict was . . .

AM: Before you discuss other conflicts please finish discussing the conflict concerning the representatives of the Movement for Rights and Freedoms at the Roundtable. Press reports indicate that the Movement for Rights and Freedoms was invited to participate, but ultimately it did not. If I understand your response, they did not participate because within the UDF there were elements that did not agree to give them standing within the UDF quota. Is that correct?

SG: The basic principle of the Roundtable was that there were two sides only. On the one side stood the UDF—and on the other the BCP. From its initial quota of thirty-seven representatives, the BCP agreed to give spots to the Agrarian Union, the Fatherland Front, and some other organizations. On the UDF side, apart from the member organizations, the only additional quota allocated was for the Committee for National Reconciliation. Mihail Ivanov was one of its representatives. . . . Other representatives of that organization included Ibrahim Tatarla, who currently is in the Movement for Rights and Freedoms, and Manush Romanov—the present leader of the [Gypsy] Democratic Union, Roma.

AM: So, this was one source of conflict within the UDF at the Roundtable?

SG: Yes. . . . The problem, I repeat, is this: the Movement for Rights and Freedoms requested participation from the UDF quota. They were not invited. And the bulk of the members of the [UDF] Coordinating Committee as well the participants in the Roundtable Talks were not sure that the MRF would stick to the goals of the UDF. The Movement for Rights and Freedoms was not considered a big organization—at the time it was a newly created organization. The disagreement was over a matter of principle . . . never mind that

> at the time I supported as a matter of principle the inclusion of the Movement for Rights and Freedoms. In retrospect, it was a correct decision not to seat the Movement. As it has turned out, the fact that they were not seated has not been an obstacle for the peaceful transition. The reason for this conclusion is that a fundamental problem for Bulgaria is to avoid ethnic conflicts.

* * *

Stefan Gaitanjiev's justification for not including the RFM may seem at first disingenuous. After all, if representatives of significant populations are not included in decisions about the future of the country in which they reside why should these minorities obey? Surely, one might conclude, the decision not to include the RFM is a problem of legitimacy. Yet, there is another important aspect of this issue. Given the history of ethnic unrest in the entire Balkan region it may be wise to treat ethnic and religious differences as outside the bounds of acceptable political discourse. Indeed, playing the so-called "nationalistic card" is a charge that the various factions within Bulgaria's political community level at each other from time to time. This issue does not go away, as subsequent events attest. The Constitution adopted in July 1991 treats ethnic and religious minorities in a special way, thereby creating serious constitutional issues; and beginning with the June 1990 elections, the Movement for Rights and Freedoms has played an important role in parliamentary politics.

Initial Roundtable Meetings

The initial January 3, 1990, meeting between the two sides of the Roundtable lasted for three hours. A major discussion item was the creation of contact groups to make reform proposals. The UDF wanted to concentrate on reforming the political system. It sought elimination of the Communist Party's monopoly with a call for a multiparty system, disbandment of Party organizations in the workplace, and depoliticization of the army, the militia, the courts, and the procuracy.[8] The Bulgarian Communist Party sought to discuss reform of the economy, ecology, the legal system, and politics.[9] Collectively, Roundtable participants decided to focus on national agreement and reconciliation, the political system, the legal system, drafting a new election law, and socioeconomic problems.[10] The UDF also placed on the agenda questions relating to their ability to communicate views to the general public. They asked for an adequate building to house their operations and also sought unrestricted media access, first by requesting the right to publish their own daily newspaper and then by demanding access to radio and television. Government representatives agreed to put this matter to the appropriate officials for resolution before the first formal Roundtable meeting. The UDF clearly sought to place the BCP in the glare of the public spotlight. In this way, the UDF might garner public concessions for the immediate task at hand and make UDF leaders familiar household names. This tactic might also enhance their ability to win general elections later.

The major resolution of the January 4 meeting was an expression of support for the joint resolution of the State Council and the Council of Ministers of Bulgaria adopted on December 29, 1989. This measure repudiated the actions of the former Zhivkov regime in repressing the Turkish ethnic minority. The statement of the UDF, the BCP, and twenty-three political and public organizations called for national reconciliation, denounced the old regime's program to change Moslem names, and upheld people's right to use other languages besides Bulgarian in informal communication and to observe traditional customs. The declaration appealed to universal principles of human rights and respect for law with equal protection for all groups in society.[11]

The Roundtable resumed deliberations on January 16, 1990. However, a January 14, 1990, mass rally, estimated at 150,000 persons, was organized by the UDF to keep political pressure on the government. UDF representatives reiterated their demands for political reform, which included, among other things, that elections be held later rather than earlier (November 1990 was suggested), a government building to house the UDF, and access to the press.[12] A few days later, a UDF spokesperson said that an agreement had been achieved in principle with government forces led by the BCP. This agreement provided that Roundtable proceedings would be broadcast live on Bulgarian radio and that Bulgarian television would air substantial parts of them.[13]

Still, UDF forces threatened to walk out of the Roundtable Talks immediately after the first session. They reiterated demands for the publication of a UDF newspaper, a building to house its activities, and access to radio and television. The government stated that the issue of the building had been resolved in principle. The Sofia City People's Council was to provide the premises by the end of the week, and the authorities were to resolve the matter of opposition access to radio and television.[14] In the end, UDF officials agreed to compromise and go on with the talks; "for yet another time we will show good will despite the foot dragging on the decision."[15] The next day, however, the UDF demanded postponement of Roundtable deliberations until its demands were met. Furthermore, it objected to the editing procedures for television reports, which were contrary to the original agreement. The UDF thought it unfair for proceedings to be edited without the presence of representatives of the two sides. Both sides reached a compromise on January 22, 1990, agreeing not to participate in the selection of television material in exchange for the promise that the television crew would work closely with members of each delegation in preparing broadcasts.[16] Radio broadcasts were aired live during the day, and edited versions of the proceedings were televised in the evening.

Meanwhile, Zhelyu Zhelev, leader of the UDF delegation, kept pressure on the BCP. He charged that the Party leadership was afraid to undertake serious negotiations with the opposition before the BCP Extraordinary Congress at the end of January. According to Zhelev, BCP leaders feared internal attacks by Stalinists and Zhivkovists.[17] He apparently understood, as the BCP leadership had earlier, that the exposure and exploitation of group disunity were old and useful tactics to reduce an opponent's legitimacy.

For its part, the Bulgarian Communist Party leadership attempted to portray itself as a force for reason and democracy. It publicly objected to the rally organized by the UDF in Sofia on January 14, 1990. Anti-Communism and new forms of totalitarian thought threatened the transition to democracy and a law-governed state, so went the refrain. Andrey Lukanov, member of the Politburo and secretary of the Central Committee of the BCP, said that the Party fully assumed responsibility for the damage inflicted by the totalitarian system and for the crisis facing the country. However, Lukanov emphasized that "we categorically protest against the attempts to identify the totalitarian system with the entire Party and its 984,000 members."[18] This statement emphasizing reconciliation pleaded that opponents should not

The National Roundtable Sessions, the site of long and substantive debates between opposing forces

blame the entire membership for the transgressions of a few. The Party, it suggested, is responsible for making the transition from totalitarianism to democracy possible. Permit it to remain a viable force in society and it will accede to the reasonable demands of the opposition forces.

Substantive Posturing and Gamesmanship

On January 23, 1990, Roundtable participants got down to substantive discussions. Zhelyu Zhelev, the philosophy professor turned UDF leader and later president of the Republic, argued that the transition should be rapid and modeled on what had happened in the German Democratic Republic and Czechoslovakia as well as in Poland and Hungary. He pointed to the dangers of civil war and military dictatorship, dangers the Soviet Union also faced, if Bulgaria should move slowly toward democracy. Zhelev argued that if Bulgaria moved fast it would help the Soviet Union make reform there irreversible, which would result in the complete collapse of the center of European totalitarianism.[19]

The BCP leader agreed with Zhelev. Andrey Lukanov said that he too sought quick revolutionary changes in the Eastern European countries and that he understood the linkage between the future of the

The National Roundtable. The Communists and their allies display confidence and flexibility. Andrey Lukanov is seated third from right.

The opposition side at the National Roundtable. The three persons seated in the center are Zhelyu Zhelev (hand on mouth), to his left Petar Beron and Petko Simeonov.

Soviet Union and that of Bulgaria. Lukanov's main point, however, was that socialism should not be regarded as dead. Rather, Bulgaria should renounce the Stalinist model of socialism. The BCP declared its support for a democratic and humane form of socialism as the only way to guarantee social justice, economic progress, and spiritual development. Professing the Party's willingness to enter discussions with all forces seeking change, the leader of the BCP delegation stressed that the Party had a program for democratization and de-Stalinization. The first step in the process was to repeal paragraphs 2 and 3 of Article 1 of the existing Constitution. This provision proclaims that Bulgaria is a socialist state headed by the working class. Repealing this constitutional provision would effectively end the BCP monopoly of political power. Lukanov also urged Parliament to enact laws immediately that would make it possible for free elections to take place. The Party agreed that the state and economy should be dissociated from political parties. Further, the power of political parties was to be limited in the exercise of legislative, executive, and judicial authority. Lukanov went on public record to support the establishment of a constitutional court as a guarantee against a return to monopoly power. He also endorsed depoliticization of the law courts, the chief prosecutor's office, and the office of minister of the interior. However, given its special place in national security, he urged a go-slow approach to depoliticization of the armed forces. Finally, he denounced, as he had done earlier, "the nationwide witch-hunt" against "honest Communists."[20]

Various other participants spoke of the importance of restoring religious freedoms; effecting meaningful emancipation of women; and shifting emphasis from heavy industry to agriculture, light industry, and tourism.[21] Svetla Daskalova, minister of justice and secretary of the Standing Committee of the Bulgarian Agrarian Party (BZNS), the nation's other ruling party, called for early elections because postponement would "destabilize the situation in the country."[22] She agreed with most of what BCP representative Lukanov said. But placing distance between the BZNS and the BCP, and thereby enhancing the legitimacy of her own organization, she disagreed that the Constitution should proclaim Bulgaria a socialist state. She said this would taint the legal status of non-Marxist parties and handicap development of a multiparty system. She also expressed the view that the future president should have limited political functions and stated her preference for this person being elected by the National Assembly for a five-year term only. Daskalova also argued for the election of members of Parliament by a system of proportional representation as opposed to the then current winner-take-all majority election system. She agreed with other speakers that in the future there should be a ban on political parties in the workplace.[23]

Milan Drenchev, leader of the opposition Nikola Petkov Bulgarian Agrarian Party, spoke about Bulgaria's unpreparedness for a multiparty system and argued therefore that parliamentary elections should take place in the autumn—meaning better later than earlier. As Zhivko Zhivkov, chairman of the National Council of the Fatherland Front, aptly pointed out, this is the one major issue that divided representatives of the official government and the opposition. "On about four-fifths of the problems under discussion, however, it is possible to reach a consensus."[24] Although this statement oversimplifies what finally happened, there is no doubt that jockeying for political advantage in the forthcoming elections was on the minds of everyone. In power for more than forty years, the Communists had the political apparatus in place to wage election battles successfully. While confident that their message would ultimately carry the nation, the opposition forces needed time to organize for victory at the polls.

The BCP strategy for early elections proved to be the winning one. Parliamentary elections were held June 10–17, 1990. They combined proportional representation with a majority system, and the former Communist Party, by then renamed the Bulgarian Socialist Party, won a majority (211) of the 400 seats with 47.15 percent of all votes. The Union of Democratic Forces won 144 seats with 36.2 percent of the votes, the Bulgarian Agrarian Union won 8.03 percent of the votes and 16 seats, and the Rights and Freedoms Movement, the Turkish ethnic minority party, won 23 seats and 6.03 percent of the vote. Assorted other parties won 2.59 percent of the total votes and 6 seats.[25] The voter turnout was 91 percent of the eligible citizens.[26] Thus, the original BCP strategy prevailed, at least in the short term. The UDF went along with early elections, professing that the people sought rapid resolution of the national problems.[27] But by so doing, the Reds, as the forces of the former BCP were called (the UDF forces were called Blues), could capitalize on their considerable organizational ability to deliver the vote. They not only guaranteed their place in a new Bulgarian political system but also were able to maintain Communist Party dominance, however fragile or uncertain it may have been.[28]

The successful gamesmanship entailed in *garantismo* requires considerable attention to detail and delicate negotiation. The willingness of the Communist Party to end its formal dominance in the government, army, and workplace made credible the Party's claim that it too sought basic reform of the political system. What made its claim particularly convincing was that, through its control of the existing government, it instituted fundamental changes. However, when it organized professional party clubs as a substitute for the Communist Party in the workplace, Party leaders made it plain through their actions that they did not intend to give up their influence altogether.[29]

A particularly useful negotiating tool was the early creation of small contact groups that kept talking when the two sides were publicly at an impasse. When negotiations first started in January 1990, the Roundtable leadership created six of these groups dealing with separate issues: legislation, national security, economic changes, religious freedoms, mass media, and Communist Party property. Therefore, it was possible to avoid public discussion on issues that both sides preferred to skirt. The contact groups also saved time by identifying matters where there were no significant disagreements.[30]

Party Monopoly Ends

Did BCP officials consciously invent specific proposals for ending the Party monopoly, or did they respond to suggestions from other quarters? Although there is good reason to believe that reform leaders of the Communist Party anticipated needed changes, there is evidence that the BCP also responded to events. Less than a month after the November 10, 1989, coup d'état, lawyers working in Sofia's legal offices took part in a December 4, 1989, mass meeting. Decrying the weakness of legislative and judicial institutions, they shouted democratic slogans such as "Enough legal nihilism!" The lawyers fashioned a resolution calling for the repeal of Article 1 (referring to the Party's leading role in society); the separation of legislative, executive, and judicial power; the establishment of a constitutional court to protect human rights; and other measures that eventually became part of the Constitution adopted in July 1991.[31]

One week after the lawyers' rally, the BCP Central Committee at its December 11–13 plenum agreed to repeal paragraphs 2 and 3 of Article 1. It instructed its parliamentary members to introduce the appropriate proposal at the National Assembly.[32] Parliamentarians submitted a draft law on December 14. After the obligatory one-month waiting period, the National Assembly took up the proposal on January 15, 1990. It amended paragraphs 2 and 3 of Article 1 by eliminating any constitutional reference to the Party playing a leadership role in the affairs of state. However, some members of the National Assembly objected to retaining paragraph 1 of Article 1, which proclaimed Bulgaria a socialist state,[33] and referred the matter to an Assembly commission. After debate among commission members, they eliminated from Article 1 any reference to the word *socialism* and approved the simple statement that "The People's Republic of Bulgaria is a democratic and law-governed state."[34] The Constitution as finally adopted in July 1991 does not contain "the *People's*" reference, a code term for socialist government. Article 1(1) reads: "Bulgaria shall be a republic with a parliamentary form of government."

By seizing the moment, the BCP leadership could argue that they were solidly behind the movement for eliminating the Party's political monopoly. In a speech delivered to the National Assembly, Andrey Lukanov made a point he was to later emphasize at the Roundtable Talks:

> This plenum decision and the consequent actions of the parliamentary group are a clear confirmation of the BCP willingness to be a factor in the real democratization of the Bulgarian society and in the renewal of socialism in our motherland, to relinquish its monopoly over political power that has been established by the law, view political pluralism as the natural environment of its political activity, and conduct an honest and open dialogue without privileges and discrimination with all sociopolitical forces in our country.[35]

The Politburo of the Central Committee and the State Council by a decree dated January 24, 1990, disbanded the Party's propaganda agency within the armed forces. By doing so, it demonstrated that the BCP could be trusted to carry out political reform, control the military, and deflate anxieties about a military coup. For forty years the army had imposed political education upon its personnel as a way to insure

Party discipline and control. This action was cited as further proof of the Party's commitment to end its monopoly, consistent with the repeal of paragraphs 2 and 3 of Article 1 of the Constitution. Lieutenant General Radnyu Minchev, spokesperson of the Ministry of National Defense, said: "With the multiparty system already being created in the country, it is impermissible for any party to build its own organizations and conduct political propaganda in the Army. This would negatively impact the troops' combat readiness and discipline. . . . The BPA [Bulgarian People's Army] will continue in the future to be governed solely by the Constitution of the country, the orders of the supreme state and military leadership, and the national military doctrine."[36]

Opposition forces led by Zhelyu Zhelev, chairman of the Union of Democratic Forces, well understood the motives of the Bulgarian Communist Party. If there was to be a coalition government that would legitimize the Communists having an ongoing role in the nation's political life, then the BCP must be prepared to yield more of its power and information about its internal operations. If this weakened its voter appeal, so be it, and so much the better. Probably responding to widespread rumors that BCP leaders were using the organization's financial resources for their personal benefit, Zhelev asked the BCP to provide the Roundtable with information related to its structures, financial and property situation, and income sources. UDF participation in a coalition government and its possible refusal to take part in general elections, projected at the time to be held in May 1990, turned on the BCP's willingness to accede to these UDF demands.[37] There is no evidence, however, that Roundtable participants seriously discussed in public the matter of BCP property and income or subjected the matter to a negotiated settlement.

Disbanding the State Security System

Zhelev welcomed the changes that had been taking place, but he wanted more and insisted on discussing in greater detail the depoliticization of not only the army but also the militia forces, the courts of justice, and the prosecution. He called for disbanding the State Security Department and depoliticizing the Ministry of Internal Affairs.[38] This demand was answered in a speech by General Attanas Semerjiev, head of the Ministry of Internal Affairs and later vice president of the

Republic. Semerjiev admitted to past transgressions of civil liberties, but he said that the traditional structures of the State Security Service had been disbanded. In its place, he mentioned the establishment of a National Intelligence Service and a Protection Service. Semerjiev promised that they would be law-abiding. He also pledged that those who had abused their power and broken the law in the past would have no role in the new regime. He assured Roundtable participants that they would not be subject to electronic surveillance, as some had alleged, and stated categorically that he would not release the names of informers in the previous regime. To do so, he said, would be a violation of law.[39]

By all accounts, General Semerjiev exhibited extraordinary leadership. He assured Roundtable participants of his good intentions, and he substantially transformed the Interior Ministry from a heretofore fearsome secret police agency into an intelligence operation that exercises greater respect for civil liberties. At least temporarily, Semerjiev was able to silence opposition leaders with evidence that the bad old days of police state abuses were over. Additionally, when dealing with public protests, Semerjiev exhibited restraint. His personal commitment to a peaceful transition to democracy and the organizational acumen he exhibited may have been key factors in breaking the cycle of political violence so prevalent in Bulgaria's history.

I interviewed Semerjiev at his tastefully decorated Sofia apartment.[40] Our meeting took place several years after his retirement. At the time, he was working on a memoir, and I found this urbane man in a reflective mood. I first asked him: "How is it that you got involved in the Roundtable deliberations?"

> **AS:** My participation at the Roundtable was mainly due to the fact that I was the minister of the interior. In the first place, it was quite natural that the security and public order forces were greatly scrutinized by the society and the then existing opposition. One of their main tasks was the disbandment of these structures. Because of the role the security and public order structures had played in the society and because of their past repressive functions, they were considered as one of the pillars of the totalitarian regime. Naturally their restructuring, their democratic transformation, was one of the key factors in the transition towards democracy, a market economy, and a civil society. The Roundtable could not avoid tackling these problems.

General Attanas Semerjiev, interior minister and first vice president of the Republic

I have to say that the former Communist Party leadership totally realized the legitimacy of the interest and the insistence of the newborn opposition in knowing what was going on in the security services. And it responded to this request by agreeing that the interior minister ought to take part in the work of the Roundtable, that its representative should make a thorough statement at the Roundtable and participate in a wide-ranging discussion. So it happened.

AM: Pardon me. Did you participate at the request of the opposition forces?

AS: This happened . . . by mutual consent. In the course of the preliminary talks between the ruling party . . . and the just created coordinating structures of the opposition.

Yet I will speak parenthetically and inform you, dear Professor Melone, that preceding the Roundtable Talks there was a dialogue between the leadership of the Interior Ministry, the leaders of the newly created UDF, and critical elements of Bulgaria's intelligentsia. This dialogue started on my initiative. I was appointed minister of the interior the night before the twenty-eighth of December. On the twenty-ninth of December, the State Council, the government, and the Plenum of the Central Committee of the ruling Communist Party made a decision to abolish the discriminatory acts aimed at the population with a Turkish ethnic identity and the Bulgarian Moslems [the so-called Pomacks]. The country was stormed by waves of public meetings, rallies, demonstrations, and strikes.

To better understand the complexity of the situation just contemplate that in the Kirdjaly region [borders Turkey] and in many other places there were parallel public rallies going on: on one side there were ten to fifteen thousand people, and on the other side twelve to fifteen thousand massed in demonstrations and counterdemonstrations; on one side people were expressing nationalistic, pro-Bulgarian slogans: they sought to nullify the decision taken by the top state and party institutions, or at least to have a moratorium placed on it. On the other side, we had the Bulgarian Turks and Moslems. They supported the decision, but at the same time they were using some unrealistic, I dare say, provocative slogans aimed at the Bulgarian population. In general, this was the situation everywhere. . . .

On the second of January, less than a week after we started the changes at the Interior Ministry, the Ministry leadership took the initiative. I want to stress this once more: we initiated the effort to meet with the most respected and most active members of the former dissident organizations and of the emerging opposition. We made great efforts to get in touch with them on the first and second of January—official holiday dates—to invite them to the Interior Ministry for talks.

I will mention just some of the names because they speak about the level of representation at this meeting: Mr. Petar Beron; Mr. Stefan Prodev, who was among the most active and staunch dissidents [currently he is editor-in-chief of the Socialist Party *Duma* newspaper]; the poet Marco Ganchev (maybe you had a chance to listen to his essays broadcasted on Radio Free Europe before the changes started on the tenth of November 1989); the writer Georgi Mishev; the academician Nikola Popov, the rector of the Sofia University; Mr. Hristo Ganev, cinematographer; and Mr. Anjel Vagenstein, the playwright and one of the most prominent film directors. Vagenstein is also well-known in the West: he was a very straightforward and principled dissident indeed. At this meeting, I announced our ideas about far-reaching reforms within the Interior Ministry. We aimed to transform the Ministry from a pillar of the totalitarian system into a modern institution, expressing the interests of the society as a whole and safeguarding the national interests: the interests of the citizens and the preservation of public order.

I add to this description of events the acknowledgment that the idea for these reforms should not be considered General Semerjiev's personal credit. They were borne out of the course taken by the new leadership of the Party and the country—a course towards straightforward democratization of the national life, towards a market economy, towards the establishment and development of a pluralistic society and parliamentarianism, towards the creation of a law-respecting state based upon the principles of parliamentarianism. . . .

I have to state that despite the hangovers from the totalitarian past, the officers in the Ministry were ripe for these changes. The conceptualization of these reforms was a process that came to fruition and was effected inside the Ministry by the officers of that same Ministry. . . . We clearly understood that those institutions should be set totally free from the tutelage of the ruling party. By the way, the new party leadership also advocated the dissociation of the Party from the state. . . .

This was one of the key points of the new policy. Adopting a course towards liberation of the structures of the security and public order from the patronage of the former Communist Party, we began the deideologization and depoliticization of these structures. I do not want to sound immodest. But I was one of the people who generated these initiatives, relying upon the support of the president, Mr. Petar Mladenov. . . . And if memory serves me correctly, on the seventh of January, only ten days after I took office, the State Council issued a decree to disband the Party and the Komsomol committee structures. . . . I will not conceal the fact that almost 90 to 95 percent of the people in the security services were Party members. It was not easy for them to abandon the Party and the Komsomol, or, to be more precise, to quit these organizations. But their strong allegiance to the institution [the Interior Ministry] and the realization of their duty as citizens prevailed.

AM: This is a very interesting story because, as you know, it is typically very difficult to ask bureaucrats to change their perspective, to change their point of view. It seems to me that you are describing a situation where these people were ready for this change. What was it about their experience or perhaps even their education that made them ready?

AS: I will tell you. People who worked at the Interior Ministry and its branches were bright and well-educated. Long ago the cadres were of a far lower quality. But at the right moment a new generation of well-educated, experienced, self-motivated, and responsible people formed the staff of the security services. It was not difficult for them to come to terms with the new realities emerging in Bulgaria and Europe; they were able to realize that the new situation requires a redefinition of Ministry functions. It was also understood that it was necessary to identify a new role for the security services. That is why they wanted the changes and helped to promote them. It is in this context that they not only accepted the changes as a fact of life but they also became supportive of depoliticization. A similar situation existed at the Ministry of Defense.

I will take the liberty to quote for you some of the data from a sociological poll of the armed forces; it was conducted in April–May 1990. The results show that approximately 80 percent of the officers of lower military ranks, up to the rank of captain, between 50 and 60 percent of the senior officers, from major upward, and over 60 percent of the sergeants and soldiers categorically supported the law for depoliticization of these structures.

I will speak parenthetically and give you some more details, taking into consideration your scientific interests, because an academic study needs greater depth and preciseness. The State Council's decree for the abolition of the structures of the former ruling Party and the Komsomol did not forbid the staff of the security service from being members of a political party. These structures [the Party and Komsomol cells at the workplace] were disbanded, and political parties were forbidden to promote any kind of political activity in the units of the Interior Ministry and the army. At the same time, however, there were no limitations whatsoever on the right of servicemen to be members of political parties outside the workplace. This is why it became necessary at a later stage to pass the law on depoliticization. It regulates such things not only in the armed forces and in the security structures but also in the judiciary: namely, in courts, prosecution offices and also in the diplomatic service. In other words, all of the so-called law-enforcing institutions have been depoliticized. The law makes it illegal for these civil servants to be political party members even outside their institutions.

AM: Just a brief point of clarification. In many different spheres parties in the workplace were prohibited, but political clubs were created in their place. Did that happen in the Interior?

AS: No, it did not happen—neither in the armed forces, nor in the Interior Ministry. . . . We strongly believed that depoliticization and deideologization were necessities, that it was necessary for these structures to stay neutral, to keep them away from any involvement in the emerging political confrontation. Otherwise, it could be suicidal for their own existence. By the way, I was among the most active figures who insisted and argued before parliamentary committees that it was necessary to enact as quickly as possible the law for depoliticization. In my capacity as vice president, I energetically argued for this position at the Parliament, at a special meeting of all standing parliamentary committees. . . . Let me add that the bill that was passed by the Grand National Assembly was introduced there by President Zhelev. I was a strong proponent of this law, but it was he who introduced it in the National Assembly.

Let me go back and follow the logic of my narration. As I have already said, on the seventh of January [1990] a decree for disbandment of the Party structures at the institutions in the defense and security sphere was published.

AM: Was it published in the *State Gazette*?

AS: Yes. That is an official document. On the fifteenth and sixteenth of January I proclaimed a program for reforms in the security forces of the Interior Ministry. This program was duly discussed and approved. If I rightly remember, on the seventeenth of January, at the request of the writers-dissidents whom I had already met on the second of January, I went to a meeting with the Governing Council of the Bulgarian Writers Union. This was the most respected public organization of Bulgarian intellectuals. Over a hundred of the most active members of the union were in attendance at that meeting. I informed them how the restructuring and the democratic reforms in the Interior Ministry were intended to go. I must say I was extremely pleased by their response. Tons of questions were asked, and we gave them straightforward and fair answers. And believe me, deep and far-going structural reforms took place virtually in a month's time after that meeting.

AM: Within a month after this meeting?

AS: Well, the changes took place almost in parallel with the above-mentioned events. At the end of January and the beginning of February the bureaucracy of the Ministry had already changed shape. Along with these structural changes our substantive activity also changed; namely, the functions of the security services. There were far-reaching and very radical . . . personnel changes. . . . Almost all the top people in the Ministry, with very few exceptions, were released from office and were replaced by professional people from the new generation. There were also significant reductions in staff numbers.

AM: Well, I am a little confused. I thought you said earlier that there was an agreement within Interior about the necessity for these changes, but now you are saying that you found it necessary to fire or to release a number of officials.

AS: Indeed, they wanted changes, but you understand that the new times, the new policy, the new concept for security quite naturally needed new people to implement them.

AM: Despite the fact that the old people were ready for change themselves?

AS: I am talking about changes at the top, for the top officials.

AM: At the top—at the very top! Okay, I understand. So the substructure of the bureaucracy was ready for change?

AS: Well, see, I have to tell you that even the deputy ministers themselves and the directors of the national security services were ready for changes. . . . So when on the third, fourth, or fifth day after I took office we decided to start the changes. But we had to face the fact that it would be difficult to accomplish. Because all these changes strongly influenced the lives of many people. We had to sack them because of the overall restructuring in the organization, and this was very painful. Then I consulted my colleagues from the Interior Ministry leadership and asked them: "Are we all ready to submit immediately our collective resignation and by this act to make others understand the necessity for change?" All the people I asked declared they were ready to do this.

I want to make clear the extent to which things were well considered and the democratic nature of decision-making procedures. We convened about four thousand people gathered in four halls; these halls were connected with hi-fi speakers. The whole Ministry leadership stood in front of six hundred people in the main hall to explain and debate the problems facing us. My opening words began with the following statement: "As the changes will be inevitably detrimental to employee and social status [for many people in the Ministry], we declare our intention to resign from office the day after the reform is implemented."

AM: Did all of you write letters of resignation—all the top people? Or was it simply a declaration?

AS: Most of my colleagues submitted immediately their formal letters of resignation. Subsequently, however, some of them began to have second thoughts, but I reminded them of our "gentlemen's agreement," and they had to stand by their word. In one way or another the personnel changes were implemented. Additionally—as I have said already, but want to repeat again, because it is my impression that the fact has not received enough notice—the total number of Ministry personnel was cut. Some structures were totally disbanded.

AM: Did the budget remain the same or did it shrink?

AS: The budget shrunk as well. I want to explain right away that the notorious Sixth Directorate, which was, from a legal point of view, a political police, was disbanded. Sorry, I have to correct myself—its [main] task was to scrutinize the so-called dissidents, but its functions also included the fight against terrorism and the preservation of art treasures [from theft and so forth] . . .

The former Directorate for Security and Protection—the

proverbial UBO [the corresponding Bulgarian initials of the directorate] . . . was trimmed by 70 to 75 percent; it was reorganized into the National Protection Services. Yet, I am afraid that currently, under the conditions of democracy, this service is back again to its former being.

AM: Oh, it is back to what it was doing formerly—secret KGB-style activities?

AS: No, this structure always had purely protective and auxiliary functions, serving the top leadership [of the state].

AM: Bodyguards?

AS: Yes, bodyguards. Such services exist everywhere. In the United States it is a state within the state. But we had to cut its size, because formerly it performed functions not typical for organizations of this kind. It is not right for the Interior Ministry to be burdened with [household functions].[41] However, we successfully reorganized and trimmed this service and then had it transferred to and placed under the auspice of the presidency. So, currently, it is under the presidency.

The same thing happened to the famous First Main Directorate [PGU], this was the Bulgarian Intelligence Service. It was reorganized into the National Intelligence Services [NRS], removed from the jurisdiction of the Interior Ministry, and placed under the authority of the presidency. It has kept this status to this day. Yet the issue of who shall supervise it has become a cause for political conflict during the last two years; it is mainly a dispute between the UDF and the president.

In the second place, the military counterintelligence [VKR] was withdrawn from the state security system and from the Interior Ministry. It was placed under the command of the General Staff of the Army. It has retained this position ever since.

AM: So, what is left to the Interior Ministry?

AS: I will explain. There was a department within the Ministry that supervised prisons. On my own initiative it was transferred to the Ministry of Justice. I was deeply convinced that the supervision of the penal regime and its behavioral function, more specifically the execution of a prisoner's sentence, should not be part of the Interior Ministry's prerogatives. That is properly a responsibility of the Ministry of Justice. Well, what then was left to the Interior Ministry? Those . . . structures assigned the responsibility for safeguarding public order, the police in particular, remained as part of the Interior Ministry. By "police" I mean the wide range of its functions, including the fight against terrorism, drug trafficking, trade with people, corruption, and so on.

Another large concern left for the Interior Ministry is counterintelligence. In your country its functions are performed by the FBI. Indeed, I am not well aware of its exact functions, but it seems to me they are similar. I also need to mention the internal forces; these are the forces that guard the borders of the country. Another part of the organization concerns auxiliary services that provide logistic and technical support.

In short, the organizational reforms and the democratic transformation within the Interior Ministry were in-depth operations. They were not mere changes in the facade. . . . This was not gimmickry. There was great disrespect for this institution, and just after the tenth of November [1989] the Interior Ministry was the focus of public criticism. It was subjected to a number of severe social and political actions. Yet after the reforms in March and April [1990] it began to quickly gain respectability.

There was another factor that played an instrumental role in these changes. As minister of the interior I decided to avoid and abandon totally the use of force. This happened at a time when the streets and squares were full with tens of thousands of people. There were many meetings, marches, vigils, hunger strikes, occupation strikes. And as might be expected . . . there appeared all kinds of marginal people: degenerates, anarchists, recidivists, criminals. The forces of public order had to face many provocations. It was our duty to keep public order at huge mass rallies, where over two hundred or three hundred thousand people gathered. All during this period the security forces did not harm a single citizen.

AM: No incidents?

AS: There were no incidents. We based our activity upon dialogue. In my capacity as minister of the interior, on just my second day in office, I created a special department for liaison with the political forces and all other civil organizations. My cabinet office was turned into a meeting place, where every political leader, activist, or government functionary was most welcome any time of the day. On my initiative we proclaimed the guiding principles in the activity of the Ministry; namely, the supremacy of the law and the Constitution, respect for all civil and democratic human rights, the nonuse of force including the ways and means for suppression, and the full openness and transparency of Ministry activities (of course, without penetrating some special spheres that required secrecy). All these measures played positive roles. And we showed great self-restraint. I believed—and my colleagues shared this belief—that the arguments for force, of machine-guns and tanks, should be totally discarded. We succeeded in safeguarding public order during the first free democratic elections in June 1990. If memory serves me correctly, there were over 1,100 foreign observers, including a big group from the United States, headed by a congressman. They stated unanimously, although with some minor reservations, that the general elections had been absolutely democratic and fair and that the elections represent a big step forward for democracy in Bulgaria. I do not want to exaggerate the role of the Interior Ministry and the role played by its structures. All the political forces, the government, and the president contributed to this success. But I cannot deny the significant role of the council for nonviolence that was created on my initiative. I came up with this idea, and I made an appeal to the BSP, the UDF, the Agrarian Union, the Fatherland Union, and all other political forces to create this public body. They sent their representatives, and an independent civil council was created with the aim to safeguard civil peace by promoting the nonuse of force.

The council met a couple of times every week. Its meetings were public, and television and radio sent their representatives to cover them. It became routine for one of the deputy ministers to analyze the situation in the country: the minister would point to certain infringements of public order and other dangerous events that could threaten civil peace. Open debate would follow about whether we were following the proper course and then we would issue appeals.

AM: General, when exactly was this council created?

AS: It was created in April, on the eve of the general elections, when the tension, the polarization in the society, increased and the social temperature rose substantially, reaching dangerous levels.

AM: Was it officially created pursuant to the Roundtable political agreement on the peaceful transition? There was a Roundtable agreement in March—was your action taken pursuant to that agreement?

AS: No, this was an independent initiative of ours. We spared no effort to invent forms and mechanisms that could secure a peaceful, bloodless transition to democracy. We sought a well-balanced transition, guaranteed not by the use of force but through dialogue, through reasonable compromise between the political forces—a civilized transition. And despite the fact that we were pressed to the wall all too often, we did not step back from this approach.

Now, allow me to explain one more thing. The former Bulgarian Communist Party, renamed . . . the Bulgarian Socialist Party, is not a party conceived and operated in the fashion of the Soviet Union. . . . In fact it [the BSP] initiated the changes in the country. In Bulgaria there was no opposition against the former regime of the sort that existed in Poland, Hungary, Czechoslovakia. The Bulgarian dissidents were few, and they came mainly from the circles of the old Communist Party. That is why the changes had to begin and were started by reformers (the perestroika supporters) and top people from the Party leadership. The new leaders of the Party established contacts right after the tenth of November [1989] not because of outside pressure but because they themselves believed they should do this. The Party leadership declared null and void dozens of articles in the then existing criminal code that had limited civil liberties; in other words, it restored all civil rights of the people. . . . These actions were due to the new party leaders like Petar Mladenov, Andrey Lukanov, Georgi Atanasov. As the minister of the interior, I provided, so to speak, the opposition with telephones and cars. I helped them in every possible way because we understood that without proper material conditions they would be unable to carry out real political activity. By government decision, the UDF was given two public buildings, one of them on 134 Rakovsky Street and the other on 39 Dondukov Boulevard, I think. These are nice, spacious buildings.

The Party based its policy on the dialogue that was taking place. At its initiative the Roundtable worked out a national agreement on a peaceful, nonviolent transition. At its XIV Extraordinary Congress on the thirty-first of January, and the first and second of February 1990, the Party rejected all the theory and practice belonging to the past. It accepted a new system of political values and a new political platform, based, so to speak, on a European system of values. It abandoned democratic centralism,[42] which unfortunately reigns currently in the UDF and many other opposition parties. I beg your pardon for this straightforward opinion—you may find it offensive, for I really do not know what you believe in—but that is the truth.

AM: To say organization is to say oligarchy.

AS: Indeed. Despite the fact that at the elections for the Grand National Assembly the Bulgarian Socialist Party won an absolute majority of 52 or 53 percent, it insisted that a coalition government should be formed. By the way, it had approached the opposition with the proposal to participate in the government of the country as early as February and March; that is, before the election. After the election victory in 1990, which by the way was a landslide victory, the party [BSP] alone decided not to assume the presidency. Instead, it brought about the election [in Parliament] of Dr. Zhelev for this post. This was done in the name of national understanding and agreement. Party leaders were deeply convinced that Bulgaria's way out of its national crisis can be found only if the full potential of the nation is mobilized.

Now let me add a few more words along this line and get back to the Roundtable Talks. When, during the Roundtable Talks, some time around the beginning of February 1990, I informed the participants about the range of the changes in the Interior Ministry, Mr. Petko Simeonov and some other leaders of the opposition said: "Well, it seems that you had been successful in dismantling the system."

I don't think "dismantling" is the proper word. It was in fact a democratic transformation of the system. The Bulgarian understanding of this word "dismantling" carries the connotation of liquidation followed by re-creation of certain structures. Bulgaria could not afford this: we did not have a West Germany to shelter us, and we were not in the position of Poland and Hungary. There continues to be a turbulent situation along our borders. We cannot turn our country into a fenceless yard. That is why we needed to implement these democratic reforms, to transform the system from an instrument of totalitarianism into an institution that serves the democratic process. We need to create democratic order in the country and yet at the same time we must safeguard the national interest.

The U.S. secretary of state could not understand the substance of these reforms, but I think it was your ambassador Mr. Sol Polansky who should take the blame. The State Department sent a letter or two to the foreign minister of Bulgaria and expressed its satisfaction with the ongoing changes. But at the same time, the State Department claimed that the security forces' organizations remained intact, that they were not yet disbanded. I think this was a totally unfounded and unfair accusation. I believe I share the opinion of Mr. Alvin Toffler,[43] a politologist [political scientist] and colleague of yours in the USA, who said to survive in the new realities we need to change. Indeed, the Interior Ministry survived because it changed. The change, as painful and difficult as it was to accomplish, was necessary to preserve the institutions that guarantee the security of Bulgaria.

The State Department became enchanted by a thesis of Dr. Rolf Darendorf. He argued that one of the main prerequisites of democratic change is the disbandment of or the change of the nomenklatura.

But I ask you: who was not in Bulgaria's nomenklatura? The whole elite—in political life, management, science, or in the economy—they were all on the nomenklatura lists. And . . . most of the intelligentsia were keen to enter the nomenklatura. To waste this national potential . . . bodes ill for the country. Mind you that over a half or even two-thirds of the UDF MPs are former members of this party [BCP] and were in the nomenklatura. In the GDR, the eastern provinces of Germany, they did not proceed like this. And, therefore, we were unwilling to proceed foolishly with the cadres of the Ministry. Okay, we might have said, we will sack them—a couple of thousand people—but how would we find replacements? For this reason I definitely disagree with Mr. Darendorf's thesis. That is why I was shocked by the State Department's statement that they saw nothing changed in Bulgaria. Not to mention the fact that such statements represent an interference in the internal affairs of a sovereign state. I will stop at this point.

So, let me repeat, when I made my speech at the Roundtable—and they were very inquisitive; they asked me questions for four hours and twenty minutes—finally they were all satisfied by what they had heard.

AM: I know, I read some of their statements.

AS: And now let us express a personal point of view. You are aware there was a great fire in August 1990. The party building, the Supreme Council's building of the Bulgarian Socialist Party was set on fire. Do you know this?

AM: I heard about this, yes.[44]

AS: This was a very dramatic night. The people who organized this plot obviously wanted to cause bloodshed. Dr. Zhelev happened to be in Varna at that time, the Prime Minister Andrey Lukanov was abroad. So I immediately went to the spot where I spent the whole night. There was a hurricane, . . . a terrible eruption of extremism, mob aggression beyond description. Yet, I did not permit the violence to escalate or for a single drop of blood to be shed. I knew that after the first blood the square would be soaked with it all over. Nowadays there are some people who blame me for my patience and restraint. There are old party veterans, dogmatics. They call me a traitor.

AM: Because you did not put down mob violence?

AS: Because this [mob violence] represented a gross infringement of public order and there is a reasonable expectation that security forces should put it down. Indeed, a building was set on fire and the security forces did their best to stop it. But I forbade them to use force, because those people [the provocateurs] were just waiting for this to happen. They were armed with pipes and iron bars; they were bloodthirsty. That is why people blame me: faced with such a brutal infringement of the public order, with an outrage, the police should have performed its duties. But they ignore the fact that this was not purely criminal activity. It had a broad political background and was part of a political plot to cause bloodshed.

AM: Did you arrest anyone at the time or afterwards?

AS: There were some arrests, and we had an investigation. It lasted for over a year—a year and a half—but yet to this very day the court has not proceeded with the prosecution's case.

AM: But as a tactic of crowd control did you make any arrests or did you refrain from arresting anyone? At the time, did you just try to protect public buildings? Did you arrest people during that night or afterwards?

AS: Oh, yes, some people were arrested on the spot. However, the next morning Mr. Petar Dertliev—I greatly respect him, he is a friend of mine but I disapprove of his behavior in the circumstances—and some other people like Ludjev intervened, and we had to set free those we had arrested. . . .

AM: Let me ask one more question. We are taking a tremendous amount of your time. As a former chief of staff, are you convinced that the army will not be a factor in the future?

AS: I am totally convinced . . . the army will not interfere in politics.

AM: What is the reason? Is it because of the new army leadership?

AS: The Bulgarian Army has never been in a position to intervene in the internal affairs of the state. . . .

I am not a historian, neither a politologist [political scientist] or philosopher, but I dare express some considerations, which might be useful for you in contemplating this matter.

According to Marxist-Leninist teaching on army and warfare, an army performs two functions. They are external and internal: namely, defense against the foreign enemy and inside the country—neutralization, so to speak, of forces that attempt to change the social order . . . to safeguard the existing political system. After the war [World War II] there was no reason for the Bulgarian People's

> Army . . . to perform any internal functions. This was due to two factors: first there were Soviet troops stationed here until 1947. And secondly, the new regime of the people's democracy was widely accepted by a great many people. This is not a distortion of the truth but a fact of life. As far as the existence of an opposition here, it was not strong and it was suppressed. Its suppression was conducted by the forces of law and order like the Interior Ministry, the courts, and the public prosecutor. It was not necessary for the army to play the role of an instrument for the suppression of an internal opposition. . . . We in the Ministry of Defense were convinced that because of the postwar pattern of behavior and the new sociopolitical situation that the internal functions of the Bulgarian Army were defunct; the army had no internal functions any more. It is in this spirit that the current officers have been reared; they were taught that we have just one task—to guarantee the sovereignty, the independence, and the territorial integrity of Bulgaria. So there were only the external functions left. The officer's corps does not belong to any particular class and along with this the whole teaching of Marxism-Leninism proclaims respect for the people and for their democratic traditions.

* * *

This interview is especially enlightening because General Semerjiev makes clear the role of police state functionaries in bringing about the peaceful transition to democracy. His statements illustrate that, in addition to the forces of the Communist Party on one hand and the opposition UDF forces on the other, the Interior Ministry played a vital role in making accommodation possible. Semerjiev's testimonial underlines Di Palma's point that individuals can make a huge difference in the transition to democracy. Most people I encountered in Bulgarian political circles expressed great respect and even admiration whenever the name of Attanas Semerjiev came up. The main reason he was named by Parliament as Bulgaria's first vice president was the respect and stature he had attained with the reorganization of the Interior Ministry and his exercise of restraint when faced with provocation.

Semerjiev understood that a peaceful transition was possible only if all sides worked closely together. In fact, Semerjiev actively sought to bring all the sides together, assuring them that he was sincere in reorganizing the services of the Interior Ministry. He made the opposition aware of his intentions, and he kept it informed about progress made on this front.

Perhaps an even more delicate matter concerned his own bureaucracy. Semerjiev makes a strong case that Ministry personnel were predisposed to change. Nevertheless, bureaucrats everywhere are loath to give up their domains, routines, and authority. Semerjiev had to seize the window of opportunity available to him at the beginning of his tenure to obtain promises from Ministry functionaries to give up their power. Yes, it was for them a matter of rational calculation. They concluded that serious mistakes were made in the past and that under the circumstances change was inevitable. Moreover, given the fact that the Party was now in control of reformers and that the Ministry head was an advocate of change, they had little choice but to transform their bureaucracy. Nonetheless, the tactic used by Semerjiev to obtain written resignations from the Ministry's top leadership was a brilliant stroke to compel compliance in the event that some of the bureaucrats might at some later date change their minds.

Results of Initial Steps

The preliminary steps taken during the first month or six weeks of the National Roundtable Talks laid the foundation for more substantive agreements that would follow. But there was a final bone of contention that was raised early during the Roundtable and has been repeated many times since: the matter of the property of the Bulgarian Communist Party. In February 1990, Zhelyu Zhelev asked the BCP to provide the Roundtable with information relating to its structures, financial and property situation, and income sources. It was widely charged that BCP leaders were using the organization's financial resources for their personal benefit. Zhelev insisted that participation by the UDF in a coalition government and its possible refusal to take part in general elections to be held in May 1990 turned on the BCP's willingness to accede to these UDF demands.[45] However, there is no evidence that Roundtable participants seriously discussed the matter of BCP property and income or subjected the matter to a negotiated settlement. Still, many years after the Roundtable Talks, the charge of personal gain by Party leaders is widely circulated and believed. No doubt this charge has weakened the credibility of the Bulgarian Socialist Party.

In summary, the early Roundtable actions required adjustments on the part of all participants, and there remained considerable distrust particularly toward the representatives of the government in power. Nevertheless, the accomplishments of ending the constitutional monopoly of the Communist Party, restricting BCP control in the workplace, providing the UDF with facilities to conduct its affairs, and reorganizing the Interior Ministry were important initial steps toward negotiating a pact for a peaceful transition to democracy. Despite their genuine differences, both sides proved by their actions that it was possible to work with the other to achieve meaningful political change.

5

Roundtable Agreements and the Election for the Grand National Assembly

For a month the Roundtable made no visible progress.[1] Amid charges of a lack of cooperation, there were rumors of walkouts, personal illness, and the creation of an alternative roundtable composed of organizations not included in the official talks. However, during the hiatus a contact group met to iron out details of an agreement. It was cochaired by UDF leader Zhelyu Zhelev and BCP representative Georgi Pirinski.[2]

On March 12, 1990, the leadership of the BCP, UDF, and twenty-six other Roundtable participants signed three significant agreements: (1) Declaration on the Role and Status of the National Roundtable, (2) National Agreement on Guaranteeing the Peaceful Development of the Transition Toward a Democratic Political System, and (3) Agreement on the Political System.[3]

Rules Establishing Political Civility

The Declaration on the Role and Status of the National Roundtable was necessary because there were public suggestions that the Roundtable had no right to interfere with the activities of the government and the National Assembly.[4] This declaration obligated Roundtable participants to "utilize their representation in the legislative and executive organs and their public influence in order to ensure the implementation of the agreements that have been adopted by consensus, and to initiate action related to the most important issues."[5] The acting

National Assembly was to accept the determinations of the Roundtable and to faithfully make constitutional changes and legislative initiatives. This declaration served that purpose, although there were moments when the result was in doubt.

The National Agreement on Guaranteeing the Peaceful Development of the Transition Toward a Democratic Political System is a model statement about nonviolent political mechanisms for achieving peaceful transition. It contains in eight points the following set of principles and rules:

1. To refrain from using violent methods and means, as well as from preaching violence and threatening with violence, and to prevent the emergence of disorder and chaos in the country in any form.
2. To view political confrontation as a competition between ideas, platforms, and programs; to demonstrate tolerance for the convictions and views of opponents that is characteristic of every democratic and civilized society; and to strive to reach agreement through constructive dialogue.
3. To guarantee mutual noninterference in their political activity, to refrain from illegally interrupting or hindering any political manifestations including peaceful meetings and rallies, and to exclude any attempts against the propaganda methods of other sides.
4. To refrain from using printed matter and the mass media for political provocation and instigation to violence.
5. To prevent and intercept all acts of violence and to be politically and morally responsible for all illegal activities of parties' members or adherents.
6. To make maximum efforts to create the necessary conditions for the normal and peaceful preparation and conduct of elections in conditions of total democracy and equal participation for all.
7. To prevent state organs from abusing power in favor of any single party.
8. To demand an increase in the responsibility of law and order institutions in anything related to maintaining safety and public order, by making their activity fully conform to the democratic changes taking place in the country's Constitution and legislation; decisively preventing and intercepting all attempts to use physical, moral, and psychological pressure and terror against

> both political leaders and individual citizens; demanding the assumption of responsibility, including legal responsibility, by all those who had engaged in such actions in favor of any political party, including the employees of them, seizing illegal weapons; and ensuring equal protection of premises, buildings, and other property of legally registered political and public forces.[6]

This declaration represents an article of peace among the leading political forces and is consistent with Di Palma's conceptualization.[7] It demonstrates the fallacy of reducing probability statements about the composition of aggregate phenomena to individual cases. Though Bulgaria did not have the structural and cultural prerequisites commonly thought necessary for democracy, this agreement represents a modus vivendi, making it possible for the Communist leadership and governing functionaries to transfer loyalty and bestow legitimacy peacefully in order to institute political change. For their part, opposition forces promised to recognize the BCP's right to exist and to compete in the political system. The uncertainties of rejecting this approach made peaceful coexistence the reasonable choice.

The Political System Agreement laid the foundation for the new constitution that was completed sixteen months later. Roundtable participants agreed that the political system should guarantee all the international rights and freedoms of man, social justice, and creation of a civil society. Government institutions were to include (a) a parliament elected by free and competitive elections, (b) separation of powers, and (c) a multiparty system. The Constitution would guarantee all forms of ownership. It called for a national election to be held halfway through the year (1990) with equal participation by all political parties. To insure fairness, authorities were to invite observers from around the world to monitor the elections. Moreover, draft laws facilitating fair elections were to be introduced at the forthcoming National Assembly session.[8] On May 14, 1990, the Roundtable produced a detailed Code of Ethics for the Election Campaign.[9]

The Economy Issue

The Roundtable dealt separately with the economy. Both the BCP and the UDF accepted the need for serious economic restructuring and for infusing more private enterprise into the economy. However, government forces wanted the economic transition to take place in stages, while the opposition forces favored "shock therapy."[10] Government participants at the Roundtable offered to cooperate with opposition forces in devising measures to reform the economy, including creating alternative forms of property, integrating the Bulgarian economy with that of Europe, and lifting price controls on 40 percent of the nation's goods and services. Opposition forces identified the need to provide constitutional protection of private ownership. They argued for radical agrarian reform and limiting government's exercise of economic power, a new taxation policy, and creation of legal rules for the conduct of economic activity. Zhelyu Zhelev accused the government of failing to acknowledge the failure of the state-controlled economic system and alleged that the Communist Party was attempting to evade its responsibility for the economic debacle. However, he declared that the significant economic problems could not be resolved without resolving political ones first.[11] He clearly recognized that economic policies flow from the allocation of political authority. Creating a political system in which democratic forces could defeat the old regime would create the necessary conditions for meaningful economic reform.

Di Palma reminds us that democracy was once thought to be the key to material progress.[12] The notion is that by liberating individuals to do what comes naturally to them, namely, the pursuit of self-interest, societies progress almost continuously. Yet, capitalism does not always have the promised results because the free market does not always operate as its proponents proclaim. Either private power subverts the market system or government intervention needlessly obstructs its operation. A stronger claim for democracy is that it protects human rights. However, many Bulgarians, like other former Eastern bloc inhabitants, embraced the view that a return to a system of private property would rescue their bankrupt state-controlled economy.

The Constitution as finally adopted in July 1991 provides for both private and public property. It declares that private property shall be *inviolable,* but it also allows for a regulatory role by the government.[13] Within the context of inflation and high unemployment, Bulgarians have debated, along with the rest of Eastern Europe, the relative value of gradualism versus shock therapy.

Reaching Final Agreements

By the end of March 1990, Roundtable participants were close to a final agreement. But several thorny political questions remained. First was the matter of the election of a new parliament. This body would function as both an ordinary legislature and a constitutional convention. The second issue was the future constitutional role of a president of the Republic. Again, compromise solutions were necessary.

The BCP first proposed a mixed system of representation: 175 majority and 75 proportional mandates with national party lists. The employment of a majority system whereby the election of legislators is on a winner-take-all basis in single-member districts makes it possible for one party to gain a majority of seats. Because the BCP was clearly the best organized party, such a system, even if only used in part, would clearly be to its benefit. The BCP could form a strong single-party government rendering coalition-making unnecessary. Predictably, opposition forces proposed a system of proportional representation. Composition of the proposed Grand National Assembly would be based upon the proportion of votes received by each party. This system would favor opposition parties because it would assure parliamentary representation consistent with the parties' share of the electoral vote. Interestingly, the Roundtable compromised on a mixed system resembling the BCP proposal. It provided for the election of two hundred members in one-mandate election districts based on the majority principle of more than half the votes. An additional two hundred seats would be filled by proportional representation. Each voter had the right to two votes: one for a single-member election district and the other for multimember districts under a party list. Political parties or other groups with a membership of at least five hundred people had the right to nominate candidates.[14] The Roundtable agreed to the BCP proposal for the Grand Constituent National Assembly elections. They were firmly set for June 10 and 17, 1990,[15] although the same UDF forces that once argued for elections no earlier than November now urged that there be elections in September that same year.[16]

Roundtable participants agreed that the duly elected Grand National Assembly would prepare and adopt a new constitution within a year and a half and would hold a national referendum. The Grand National Assembly would also assume all the tasks of a working parliament associated with a functioning government. Further releasing this new body from Roundtable control, participants agreed that the Grand National Assembly could introduce amendments to the existing Constitution except for regulations relating to the head of state.[17]

Few Roundtable participants disagreed that Bulgaria should have a presidential institution, or that the existing State Council was unnecessary. Government and opposition forces agreed in principle that future presidents of the Republic should be elected directly by the people. The BCP wanted the election of a president to take place simultaneously with parliamentary elections.[18] If this happened it would guarantee a four- or five-year period of control over the presidency. This could have happened because it was widely understood that Petar Mladenov, a prominent figure in the 1989 coup that removed Todor Zhivkov from power, would in all likelihood win a popular election. The UDF, however, thought that election details and presidential rights and duties should be left to the future Grand National Assembly to decide. BANU representatives supported the UDF proposal and threatened that if it was not accepted they would insist on retaining the State Council, an institutional hangover from totalitarian days.[19]

The BCP proposed a compromise that was ultimately accepted by the Roundtable participants: the president was to be elected by the existing Parliament, and this person would have the mandate for the next National Assembly as well.[20] A day later, Petar Mladenov, president of the State Council, was made head of state, and the Roundtable participants agreed to leave it to the Grand National Assembly to determine his functions and mandate.[21] Later, Mladenov was forced to resign for an indiscreet remark captured on videotape, extolling the desirability of using force against street protestors.[22] The Grand National Assembly then elected Zhelyu Zhelev after several ballots.[23] Article 93(1) of the Constitution, adopted by the Grand National Assembly in July 1991, provides that the president shall be elected for a term of five years. Zhelev won the first presidential election.

The Roundtable concluded its most important work on March 30, 1990. The Agreement on the Basic Ideas and Principles of the Draft Law on Amendments and Addenda to the Constitution of the People's Republic of Bulgaria is a six-part document representing national consensus on common principles with respect to the political system; the economic system; basic rights and freedoms of citizens; the organization of state power under the transition of parliamentary democracy; a strong, competent, and responsible government; and a call for elections.[24]

Although Roundtable participants signed an agreement hailed as important evidence of national consensus, the memory of four decades of totalitarian rule remained. On April 4, 1990, the UDF protested that the government was violating agreements reached at the Roundtable. It indicated that Parliament had wrongly decided that the head of state had the right to declare martial law or a state of emergency and even to annul acts approved by the government.[25] It is also true that although the proceedings of the Grand National Assembly resulted in the adoption of a new Constitution, the proceedings were not without moments of high drama and tension. Nevertheless, the Roundtable proved a valuable consensus-building tool for forging coexistence among powerful and potentially destructive forces.

Election for Grand National Assembly

The National Roundtable Talks represent an effective step in the de-Stalinization of Bulgarian society, laying the foundation for creating a democratic constitution instrumental in nurturing a civil society. Yet, the Roundtable has been criticized because it failed to eliminate completely the power and influence of the Communist Party, which changed its name to the Bulgarian Socialist Party.

The election for the four hundred–member body Grand National Assembly was held on June 10 and 17, 1990. Many Bulgarians regard this election as the first free and democratic expression of the people since 1931, when voters were last given a genuine opportunity to choose from among competing political parties. Four hundred deputies were chosen under a mixed system of representation. Officially sanctioned by the existing National Assembly, the Roundtable agreement on elections provided for a combination of proportional representation and majority systems. In accordance with the election law, two hundred seats were apportioned consistent with the boundaries of the extant administrative units. An additional two hundred seats were apportioned by single-mandate constituencies. A Central Electoral Commission as well as regional and local electoral commissions were created to oversee the electoral process. Forty political parties, including three coalitions, registered with the Central Electoral Commission.

Coming as a surprise to many observers, the renamed Communist Party, the Bulgarian Socialist Party, won the Grand National Assembly elections. It won 57 percent, or 211 of the seats (114 seats in the single-mandate constituencies and 96 seats in the multimandate constituencies), with the opposition forces dividing among a variety of loosely defined parties. The main opposition came from members of the umbrella organization, the Union of Democratic Forces. They earned 144 seats (69 seats in the single-mandate constituencies and 76 seats in the multimandate constituencies), or 36 percent of the total number of seats. The Bulgarian Agrarian National Union won 16 seats, the Rights and Freedoms Movement won 23 seats (11 seats in the single-mandate constituencies and 12 seats in the multimandate constituencies), or 5.75 percent of the total seats. Assorted other individuals won six seats. More than half the deputies were between forty and sixty years old at the time of election, and the average age was forty-nine years. Men outnumbered women by a 12 to 1 ratio.[26]

How did it come to pass that the thinly disguised former Communist Party won the election? Changing its name to the Bulgarian Socialist Party may have fooled some voters, but it is unlikely that its pedigree was unknown to most. If the voters had wanted to punish the Communists for forty-five years of repression, the election was a convenient device indeed. Several explanations for their failure to do so seem plausible.

First, the Bulgarian Socialist Party was well organized. This was particularly true in the rural areas of the country. Although Article 1 of the old Constitution making the Communist Party the leading force in society had been repealed, many Party functionaries and organizations remained intact. They possessed the political skills and experience necessary to get voters to the polls. Their opponents did not. Second, the inexperienced opposition was overconfident. They were guilty of believing their own propaganda. Trusting that the former Communist Party was widely despised and therefore could not hope to win the election, the opposition failed to make the effort required to win. As history attests, moral correctness does not necessarily translate into victory at the polls. Finally, UDF leaders were ill-advised when they acceded to the request to hold the election for the Grand

National Assembly at an earlier date than they had originally thought prudent. In this respect, pressure, including that coming from the United States, may have impaired their better judgment. Leaders on both sides were queried for an explanation of events. In my interview with him, Andrey Lukanov of the BSP said:[27]

> Oh, to some extent it was inertia, of course. But on the other hand—there was a recognition that we were changing fast; that we were not the old totalitarian Party. We got quite a lot of trust—from that point of view. . . .
>
> Our platform was in some respects unrealistic. There were too many promises in it. And there were some differences, not fundamental ones, but . . . nonetheless nuances of differences, between what the government . . . said and what the party [promised]. This type of thing also happens in Western countries. You know that very well. . . .
>
> Extremism worked to the disadvantage of the UDF. . . . This was the first time that labels and all kinds of false accusations were used on a massive scale in Bulgarian politics. And we [BSP] did not do it. We were subdued; we were being reasonable. We said to the people: "Let us agree at least on some minimal national goals. We should not quarrel; forget about the civil war; unite to work together for Bulgaria." And this was the winning line, of course, and—I still think—the right path.
>
> **AM:** Yes, I see.
>
> **AL:** We did not take a demagogic line. And I remain a very ardent proponent of national consensus as a must for the transition period. I do not think that fighting one another helps to overcome the crisis and to solve the problems.
>
> **AM:** Several people told me they are quite convinced that within the UDF there were informers. . . .
>
> **AL:** . . . And then the party had a very good prime minister . . . ! [laughter]
>
> **AM:** Yes, that is right! . . . Some people have said to me that . . . within the UDF there were informers who told their opponents

what they were thinking. Without naming names, is there anything to that proposition? Or is that claim just a fabrication?

AL: No, I don't think so. . . .

AM: There is something to it?

AL: No, I would not say so. There were different people, but on the whole public life was cleaner than it is now. . . .

I think we had a fantastically successful election from that point of view. Of course, there were some who attempted to nullify the election results. These were people with extreme views or they were monarchists . . . they understood that if they cannot change the situation, they would instead challenge the legitimacy of the Grand National Assembly.

AM: Your party had great influence in rural areas, in the countryside; that is, the UDF is strongest in the big cities. Is that true?

AL: It is partly true. We are also strong in big cities. Sofia is a very special case. Sofia, by the way, has the greatest amount of restitution, so people are materially interested, socially interested in driving the social balance. This is legitimate and understandable.[28]

AM: Yes.

AL: And Sofia is very lumpenized.[29] . . . the negative social effects . . . of alienation and rapid industrialization are mostly felt in Sofia and in the big cities. Therefore, there is a very strange element of voting power within the UDF and . . . this consists partly of people who are interested in getting back their positions. But they could not form a majority; they represent only about 15 to 20 percent of the population, not more than this. . . . This population has started to melt rapidly in the last two years. That is why the overall political strength of the UDF is coming down—because the lumpenized part of their electorate is not socially interested in their program, or even economically interested in their program. And they suffer from the shock-therapy and the monetarist approaches and mistakes in government more than the others. City dwellers bear the greatest burden of change. And that is why their [UDF] electorate is . . . internally contradictory. They have two large sectors; they basically can hardly live in the same bed or be in the same boat for a very long time. There are differences from the point of view of their social status and interests. . . .

So, we [BSP] still have a rather strong position in Sofia—about 35 percent which is a strong position, but less than the UDF. And also in the other big cities, when the UDF was stronger. . . . But on the whole, I think we still have strength in these cities and much more in rural areas, where our predominance was quite impressive and it still is.

AM: . . . I have been asking people about the social structure. And one of the things I am discovering is that apparently there is considerable property ownership. Many Bulgarians own their own flats or homes, or whatever . . .

AL: This is one of the Bulgarian specifics. Actually, I think 70 to 80 percent of Bulgarians own a flat. And many—I mean hundreds of thousands of families—have more than one flat. Even before restitution! A villa, a house in the village from which they came, and the flat they bought.

AM: I wonder: Is this a characteristic of a middle class?

AL: In a way, yes. Mr. Kjuranov, my colleague, who is heading the Social Democratic wing of the Socialist Party, says that a Bulgarian middle class exists. It is a very strange middle class because it is not the means of production that matters. What matters is the means of consumption—a car, a villa, a flat or two. And from that point of view, he says, it is not true that a middle class does not exist in Bulgaria. In a way it does . . .

And in general in Bulgaria—in the good sense—the petty bourgeois has been preserved. Our socialism was a petty bourgeois socialism—very similar to the Hungarian one. The ownership feeling is there, the entrepreneurial feeling, the love of land, the link with . . . land is still there. That is why especially small trade is flourishing in Bulgaria. It is not only because change was quick and radical, thereby providing small business opportunities, but also because of the preserved nature of the Bulgarian people. The Russians do not have it, coming as they do from a feudal to a socialist society—a

Bolshevik society. They do not have this spirit, or they have it to a lesser degree.

AM: So privatization is not such a radical idea?

AL: No, no, no. The young people are prepared mentally, intellectually, and professionally. . . .

* * *

Though Andrey Lukanov may be guilty of exaggerating the people's affinity for the BSP, there is little doubt that during the initial years of the transition to democracy the most competent political professionals were in the former Communist Party. Opposition forces were just learning the art and science of democratic politics. Stefan Gaitanjiev and others I interviewed believe that early elections were a tactical mistake. They blame to some degree the United States for the mistaken decision to go along with the BSP request for early elections. I asked Gaitanjiev:[30]

Why did the UDF agree to early elections? At first, UDF leaders said they wanted elections to be held a little later and the Communist Party wanted them earlier and eventually the UDF compromised. Why?

SG: It was by the explicit insistence of the U.S. state secretary, Mr. James Baker.

AM: Do you know this from firsthand knowledge?

SG: There was a meeting at the Sheraton Hotel,[31] where we expressed our thought that the elections should be held at a later date, because the opposition was not at the time sufficiently consolidated.

AM: Right.

SG: The State Department, however, was obviously misled by the election results in Poland. It might be that it had a plan to hold all elections in Eastern Europe at the same time.

AM: How many UDF leaders were at that meeting with Mr. Baker?

SG: Konstantin Trenchev, Georgi Avramov, Petko Simeonov, Zhelyu Zhelev, Milan Drenchev, perhaps a couple more people. Georgi Avramov participated. If he comes [to the office] we could ask him who exactly was there. [Later in the interview Avramov appears. His illuminating comments appear below.]

AM: Did you argue with Mr. Baker about this or did you simply agree?

SG: . . . Mr. Milan Drenchev as well as the Social Democrats took the position that we were still unprepared, that this takes time. Actually there was a long internal debate within the UDF on the elections date. The issue was intensely discussed in December, January, and February.

The basic argument in favor of holding elections later was our unpreparedness. As a matter of fact, we in the opposition were most prominent and relatively influential in Sofia and some other big cities. I also supported this view because as chief of the UDF's all-union services, I knew the situation pretty well. I had regular communications with the countryside. I was aware that our local organizations were very weak and unable to run a serious election campaign. The proponents of the idea for early elections were mainly those leaders who gathered their information of the general situation by virtue of standing before rostrums at big rallies.

AM: I am interested in the influence of outside forces, not only American, but others, such as Greek. What type of support did these outside forces gave to the UDF?

SG: Foreign dignitaries, ambassadors, and foreign ministers established contacts with the UDF. They expressed their appreciation and support for our democratic goals. Who specifically gave us support of real importance? The Greeks were helping us mainly through the New Democracy Party. They sent us campaign promotion materials—in fact all such materials were printed there [in Greece]. They provided blue paint and even workers to install hi-fi stereo systems. The Americans and French sent advisers and consultants. They explained the different ways to run election campaigns. My personal opinion is that these instructions were not that informative or they were not applicable to the situation in Bulgaria. Anyway, as far as advisory work was concerned, I think that the most substantial help came from the Polish, Solidarity. Their advice was most practical; it concerned the tactics we needed to follow at the Roundtable and at the elections. I am aware that a great deal of promotional materials were donated by different foundations; we also received some office equipment—mainly computers and copying machines. But I should not underestimate the material support given to us by the [Bulgarian] state. Actually, I would say this aid was the most instrumental of all.[32]

A couple of million leva were allocated for the UDF. We received about fifty brand-new automobiles. The Communist government of Lukanov was doing this very reluctantly . . . but nevertheless it stood by its obligations. We got offices to house our clubs all around the country. . . .

And Robert Maxwell [the British publisher and business tycoon] supplied us with printing paper. It arrived a bit late, but better late than never. On balance, the Greeks or the Polish people provided the most helpful aid. Jacue Seigella delivered a couple of spectacular lectures, but they were not very practical.

AM: . . . do you still have the automobiles? Or did they make you return them?

SG: No, we did not return them. Most of them are still at the UDF's disposal, but the condition of these cars is extremely bad. Some of them have had tires stolen, others are immovable. We received substantial help from Bulgarian emigrants, too—mainly from Germany. Actually their donations came first—in January 1990, when it was most needed.

AM: How about the Bulgarian emigrants in the United States? Did they help?

SG: Well, as far as I am aware, they did not aid the UDF directly, but they did help the Agrarian Union, Nikola Petkov. There were individual donations—mainly money.

AM: Was the outside influence well known in Bulgaria? Did you demonstrate it? Did you try to show you had Western support?

SG: On the contrary, we were trying not to evidence the material support we were getting. Because the Socialists were criticizing us for selling out the national interests, our common understanding was to avoid making too much fuss about this aid. For propaganda purposes we preferred to use the statements of Western political leaders made during their visits here. . . .

AM: Did you want to be seen publicly with some of them?

SG: Yes, indeed.

AM: But you did not want it known that you were receiving financial support from abroad?

SG: There were legal restrictions. The agreement on political parties approved by the Roundtable and then enacted into law by Parliament strictly limits the amounts of foreign aid that may be received. But, in fact, as a rule, the value of these donations exceeded the imposed limitations. . . . We were able to circumvent these restrictions, and actually nobody cared much about this.

AM: Do you mean that authorities were not watching carefully? . . .

SG: I think that in most cases they knew because everything came under customs' control. But as far as I know they were "advised" that if they behave too negatively with respect to this aid they would accordingly receive bad treatment from the West. Simply a suggestion was made to them to turn a blind eye. . . .

[Georgi Avramov enters the room. He is warmly greeted and introduced.]

SG: Now that Mr. Avramov is here I would like to use the opportunity to verify my story about Secretary of State Baker. This gentleman was among the participants.

AM: Ah, I see, you were at the meeting held at the Sheraton Hotel!

Georgi Avramov then said:[33]

I had a confidential meeting the day before with one of his [Baker's] advisers. He wanted firsthand information about the situation in the country. On the next day there was that official meeting with Mr. Baker at the Sheraton Hotel.

AM: Can you give us a date?

GA: It was sometime at the beginning of February. He was on a visit to Moscow and from there he arrived in Sofia on the fifth or sixth of February [1990]. Here he met first with the Bulgarian Communist Party leadership, Lukanov and Mladenov; and, in fact, he came late from that meeting to meet the opposition. In attendance were all the UDF representatives, all leaders: Mr. Zhelyu Zhelev, Mr. Rumen Vodenicharov, Milan Drenchev, Petar Dertliev, Konstantin Trenchev, Petar Beron, Mr. Petko Simeonov. Apart from these UDF people, Petar Gogov was also present. [At this utterance the room breaks into laughter.]

AM: Why is that funny?

SG: Because he is a very peculiar exemplar. [At that point others in the room explain that Petar Gogov is a "very special person"; "marginal, you know: in fact he is ultra-right, a neo-Fascist leader."]

GA: This was still the nursery age of the UDF. So all the opposition representatives got the chance to talk. And they discussed in detail such things as the lack of print paper or that the circulation of the newspaper (*Democracy*) is far from enough, and that the UDF did not have access to national television or that access was very limited. It was Mr. Zhelev who described the general situation in the country. He said the opposition is not ready for elections. As a matter of fact, the UDF had organizations only in Sofia and other big cities. Therefore, we were realistic enough to know that we were not ready to hold elections.

It was then that Mr. Baker spoke. He said that in the whole of Eastern Europe the democratic process is progressing. There have been elections in Poland and Hungary and elections are nearing in Romania and Czechoslovakia. Consequently, we should not drag our feet behind this process and we should not postpone the elections for the fall. What matters now is to have fair and democratic elections.

At this point only Milan Drenchev showed his mature political instinct. He said if we have elections in the spring, we will surely lose and the Communists will win.

Then Mr. Baker repeated his thesis that what matters is to have fair and democratic elections. With this statement the meeting ended, and it influenced the decision to have elections in June.

SG: The Communists had wanted them in May, at the latest.

AM: When was the decision made to hold the elections? Was it made at this meeting with Baker or was it made sometime after that meeting?

SG: Oh, no, after that meeting, at a Coordinating Committee meeting.

AM: But was it clear to everyone involved that Mr. Baker's influence was decisive? His view became the accepted view?

SG: Well, see, we were people with no experience in government; we had been dissidents.

GA: This was our first meeting with such a high-ranking foreign dignitary; he was representing, by the way, a great power. So I believe his opinion played a decisive role in our decision about the dates set for the elections.

AM: Mr. Avramov, do you think it would have made any difference in the outcome of the June elections if they had been held six weeks later?

GA: No, the option we were considering were elections in the fall. Our idea was to have them in October or November. And I knew the position of the U.S. Embassy at the time. It was the same as ours, namely, the UDF had no chance in spring elections. They were convinced that we are unable to . . .

AM: Sorry, I am confused: the Americans were convinced that you were able to win the elections?

GA: No, that we were unable to win them. This was the stated position of the Embassy.

AM: Okay.

* * *

Some other participants at the Sheraton Hotel meeting corroborate the claim that Baker suggested to the assembled UDF leaders that they should agree to early elections. However, other persons I interviewed either discount the U.S. influence or deny it outright. Dr. Konstantin Trenchev, leader of the Podkrepa syndicate, is in the latter category. He said:[34]

Mr. Baker wanted to acquaint himself with our opinion of the situation and with our forecasts for its further development and evolution. I think Mr. Baker did not defend any thesis of any kind. He was just listening to us. And I think . . . the more talkative person was Mrs. Margaret Tutwiler, not him. It was she who asked most of the questions. So, it would be incorrect in this case to speak about any suggestions. A similar position was taken by Mr. Genscher, whom we met in a seaside resort. Well, as far as I know—and I consider myself a front-line participant—as far as election dates or strategy is concerned—there was no direct influence by the West. . . .

AM: Well, what I have heard is that Secretary Baker indicated because the rest of Eastern Europe was going to have early elections, Bulgaria ought to be part of the process.

KT: I did not get the impression that he insisted upon having early elections. I think his attitude on the elections was clear enough and he did not say anything about setting dates for elections. And if my memory serves me correctly, he came here in April. At that time the

Stefan Gaitanjiev, a founder of the Ecoglasnost Political Club, deputy of the Grand National Assembly, and leading member of the parliamentary group of the Democratic Left

elections were already pending; there was a decision to have them. The date was fixed. . . . Or maybe it was at the end of March. But still I do not think he influenced us on the date.

* * *

Whether or not Trenchev is correct in his recollections,[35] there exists in the minds of some UDF leaders present at the Sheraton Hotel meeting the notion that the West wanted early elections. The election results are hardly shocking, given the euphoria of the day, the UDF's lack of political experience, and the former Communist Party's organizational capability. These combined factors resulted in a Socialist Party victory and with it the domination of the Grand National Assembly by the former Communist Party operatives and some of its allies. This fact is a major reason that some people cannot accept the deliberations of

Konstantin Trenchev, influential leader of the Podkrepa Labor Federation

the Grand National Assembly as anything but a Communist plot to retain its hegemony. Then, too, if the opposition forces had won the election, they would have been charged with responsibility for whatever events might have gone wrong.

It is tempting to assign at least partial blame for the defeat of the UDF at the hands of the BSP to Secretary of State Baker's suggestion that UDF leaders go along with early elections. It might be said that Baker's interference in the internal affairs of Bulgaria is yet another example of Western imperialism or simply another example of State Department incompetence. Yet, one may place a more charitable construction on events. As Di Palma teaches, time is a tactical resource in the transition to democracy. In order to deter breakdown games by those who may possess vested interests in promoting an antidemocratic regime, pact members must give clear signals that the negotiated agreement is holding and the momentum for change is irreversible. Therefore, it is an advisable tactic to specify a speedy timetable for political reforms. Holding elections is among the clearest signals that democracy is a done deal.[36]

Thus, whether planned or accidental, Baker's admonishment, be it real or a misreading of events, contains considerable wisdom as a tactical tool in the hands of those who favored a successful transition to democracy. Though the decision to hold elections earlier rather than later may have been a contributing factor in the Socialist Party's victory over the UDF, this short-term result is outbalanced by the interest of all those seeking to secure democratic procedures for a nation-state that for forty-five years did not practice the fine art of political competition and parliamentary government.

PART II

The Grand National Assembly

This particular Parliament does not matter much. The important matter is the principle of parliamentarianism. The fact that the Grand National Assembly exists is important by itself. Otherwise, we could get into the bad habit of disbanding parliamentary institutions by illegal means any time it suits us.

—Ginio Ganev

6

Adopting a New Constitution

A GRAND NATIONAL ASSEMBLY differs from an ordinary parliament in that it is both a constitutional convention and a regular parliament. Its mandate is to meet contemporary problems by enacting ordinary legislation and to write a constitution to serve for years to come. Between 1879 and 1947 Bulgaria had six such assemblies; in each case the voters elected the deputies on a nationwide ballot. After they were liberated from what the Bulgarians routinely term "five hundred years of the Turkish yoke," the Turnovo Constitution was promulgated on April 16, 1879. This was done with the inspiration and under the guidance of their Russian liberators. By definition Grand National Assemblies have limited tasks, and they are relatively short-lived; for example, the Sixth Grand National Assembly that commenced in 1946 lasted three years. Roundtable participants agreed that the Seventh Grand National Assembly would complete its task of preparing a new constitution within a year and a half. Upon completion of that task, there was to be a vote of the people by referendum. Instead, however, the new Constitution was ratified by a vote of the Grand National Assembly.[1]

Convening Activity

After the June 1990 elections for the Grand National Assembly the four hundred–member body dominated by the Bulgarian Socialist Party was ready to convene. The election result was important because by virtue of their victory the BSP was in a position to control the outcome of most ordinary legislation, and it was in a strong, though not commanding, position to guide the creation of the new

Constitution. Thirteen months later on July 12, 1991, 309 members of the Grand National Assembly, with some rancor, ratified the new Constitution by more than the required two-thirds majority.[2]

By presidential decree Petar Mladenov called to order the newly elected Grand National Assembly on July 10, 1990, at Velico Turnovo, the site of the first constitutional convention held in 1879. The eldest deputy, Josif Petrov, a veteran of the Nikola Petkov Agrarian Union, opened the constituent session. With the preliminary protocols complete, the working parliamentary session commenced just a week later at the Parliament building located in Sofia, the nation's capital. On July 17, by a majority of 217 votes, the Grand National Assembly elected its chairperson, the academician and Bulgarian Socialist Party member Nikolay Todorov. The following day the GNA elected his deputies—Nikodim Popov and Ginio Ganev. On August 1, parliamentarians elected the nation's leaders. They elected the chairman of the UDF Coordinating Committee, Zhelyu Zhelev, for president. For vice president, the GNA elected Attanas Semerjiev, the BSP candidate and a widely respected army general put in charge of dismantling the dreaded secret police of the previous regime. The election of Zhelev and Semerjiev was necessary because Petar Mladenov, a leader of the BSP, tendered his resignation as the nation's president following revelations of the unguarded remark he had made on video.

On August 8, 1990, the Grand National Assembly enacted on its second reading its very first statute, the Law for Amendment of the Law for the Universal Military Service. On August 30, a leader of the reform faction within the old Communist Party and a chief architect of accommodation with UDF forces, Andrey Lukanov, was appointed chairman of the Council of Ministers. The GNA approved his cabinet choices on September 20, but Lukanov's one-party government collapsed after only two months in power. A new cabinet was created on December 19 and 20, 1990. The government was headed by Dimitar Popov, a lawyer and former secretary of the Central Electoral Commission at the June 1990 elections, and a person without a party affiliation. Popov named as deputy prime ministers a UDF politician, a BZNS member, and a BSP member.

Drafting the Constitution

On April 4, 1991, ten months after the June 1990 elections, the Grand National Assembly resolved that it would debate the matter of a new constitution by the beginning of May. It was stipulated further that the GNA would thereafter disband itself to conduct local elections and then a general one. The preliminary debates on basic constitutional principles began on April 12, 1991.

Reflecting discontent with the likely course of events, on April 26, 1991, the UDF parliamentary group issued a declaration insisting on the disbandment of the Grand National Assembly by May 15. They also wanted the GNA to set July 14 as the date for new general elections. Revealing a serious fracture within UDF ranks, the cochairman of its parliamentary group, Petar Dertliev (later dubbed the father of the Constitution) made a counterdeclaration. He proclaimed that the supporters of the first declaration were siding with surviving elements of the former Communist Party within the BSP and in the process endangering the nation's still fragile democracy. Then, on May 14, thirty-nine members of the UDF parliamentary group issued another declaration, making clear their fears. The signatories stated that the Communist majority was getting an upper hand in Parliament. They complained that arm-twisting was being employed as a tactic by the leadership and that the goal of economic reform toward a market system was hopelessly deadlocked. In a dramatic move, the disaffected thirty-nine from the Radical-Democratic Party, the Democratic Party, and the United Democratic Center, boycotted the assembly's plenary sessions. On May 29 the Group of Thirty-Nine formed a new parliamentary faction called the National Movement UDF. The remaining elements of the UDF coalition were steadfast in their support of GNA deliberations. But within the UDF parliamentary group, the split became permanent; it signaled the danger that the GNA might be unable to fulfill its mission to create a new constitution.

Meanwhile, the initial debates on the draft constitution took place on May 16, followed by a first reading of the proposed constitution on May 29. The second and third readings of the new document took place on June 28 and July 9. A May 28 vote set the timetable for debating and voting on the draft constitution, including the signing of the document on July 17 at Velico Turnovo. The deputies agreed that before the signing there should be a referendum on Article 1 concerning Bulgaria's form of government: a republic or monarchy. Later, however, the GNA reversed itself on the need for a vote of the people. On July 10, twenty-three of the disaffected thirty-nine members of the National Movement UDF began a dramatic hunger strike that would last until the GNA's self-disbandment and would end only after compromise was reached on a few key contentious issues.

Ratification

On July 12, 1991, five days before the set date, the Constitution of the Republic of Bulgaria was enacted by an affirmative vote of 309 of the 400 GNA members. The deputies also voted to disband the Grand National Assembly, with the proviso that it would continue to work as an ordinary National Assembly until a new parliament was elected. They envisaged the last session to assemble on September 13 and the election campaign to start right after it.

Though the Constitution was passed by a wide margin, there was considerable argument about the advisability of ratification. The UDF leadership voted to expel parties from its ranks if its GNA members signed the new Constitution. They disagreed fundamentally over whether the electoral system should be a proportional or a majority system of representation. The Bulgarian Socialist Party did not express a preference. The Agrarian Party favored a system of proportional representation. At the same time, the Union of Democratic Forces began its call for a referendum on the new Constitution.[3] Further, the GNA voted to require all members to take an oath to support the newly adopted Constitution: this new declaration in addition to the one they had already taken upon their election to the body. But this action precipitated, to a significant extent, the hunger strike of twenty-three members protesting the "new Constitution which is consolidating the Communists' rule."[4]

Despite the evident opposition within the GNA, most Bulgarians supported the new basic law. The National Public Opinion Center reported that 57 percent of the respondents in the latest public opinion poll approved of the Grand National Assembly in ratifying the new

Constitution, 20 percent disapproved, and 23 percent expressed no opinion. The poll also indicated that Bulgarians could support the new constitutional order even if their favorite political party might lose in the upcoming national elections. The poll showed that 67 percent of the respondents would not join any form of political protest in such an eventuality. Thirty-two percent said they would take part in protest rallies, 14 percent were willing to take part in a strike, and 7 percent in a sit-in strike. Only 3 percent indicated they would be willing to engage in direct confrontation.[5]

Within a few weeks after the adoption of the Constitution, face-saving compromises were reached on several sticking points. This made it possible for those who found fault with the new Constitution to support it. A second oath to support the Constitution became entirely voluntary when Parliament enacted a new law voiding the previous one, which had required all deputies to sign a new oath.[6] In a public address to the nation, President Zhelev went on record in support of the new Constitution; he admonished his countrymen not to engage in disruptions that had included beatings of public officials. The mayor of Sofia was among the victims, illustrating that violence is one of the things that can go wrong in such emotional times.[7] A few days later, addressing fears that a proportional election system would permanently advantage the BSP, the president expressed the hope that the new elections might be held under an improved proportional representation system and that the National Assembly would decide how to divide Bulgaria's administrative state system.[8]

Features of the New Constitution

To facilitate their responsibility to write a new basic document, the members of the Grand National Assembly appointed a constitutional committee to draft a working proposal. Ginio Ganev was appointed by the GNA to head the committee. A respected member of the assembly and its deputy chairman, Ganev was an experienced politician, the leader of the Fatherland Front, and not a person associated with extreme views. He appointed subcommittees to treat various major parts of the proposed new document. In all, fifteen complete drafts were presented to Ganev's committee. Political parties, groups of

The signatories to the July 1991 Constitution in front of the Parliament building in Sofia

constitutional law experts, and individuals, including members of the GNA and constitutional law experts acting on their own behalf, sponsored these drafts.[9] Constitution experts from Western Europe and the United States visited Sofia and offered suggestions during this period. Although their views were politely received and carefully considered, there is no evidence that any of the experts exercised dispositive influence.

A Bulgarian think tank that reviewed each of the working drafts concluded that all the drafts emphasized certain commonalities: a republican form of government; government by consent of the governed; a unitary rather than a federal government; declarations of freedom, justice, humanism, and equality; constitutional supremacy and direct application of constitutional provisions; separation of powers; acknowledgment and guarantee of private property ownership; the existence of both private and public property; a market system of economics; and state support for science, culture, and the arts. These drafts envisaged Bulgaria as independent from foreign domination, and a member of the international community compliant with international law. A few drafts explicitly mentioned political integration with Europe and the rest of the world.[10]

Central Theme and Operating Principles

As finally ratified, the Constitution of 1991 is a ten-chapter document with human rights occupying a fundamental and central theme. In the preamble, the members of the Grand National Assembly pledge "loyalty to the universal human values of liberty, peace, humanism, equality, justice and tolerance." It does so "by elevating as the uppermost principle the rights, dignity and security of the individual."

Chapter 1 of the Constitution establishes fundamental operating principles. Bulgaria is a republic with a parliamentary form of government. As anachronistic as it may seem that a discussion about monarchy versus a republic might occur in the last decade of the twentieth century, the discussion was nevertheless a lively one. There were many people, some of whom were GNA members, who sought the return of Prince Simeon, heir to the throne. His father, King Boris III, had fallen ill and died in August 1943, nine days after returning from Germany, where he had had stormy meetings with Hitler. The death certificate cites natural causes for Boris's death but many Bulgarians believe the Germans, the Soviets, or the Italians poisoned him.[11] In any event, Boris, whose burial site was desecrated in 1954, reportedly by the Communist regime, had become something of a symbol of national unity. Many sincere Bulgarians sought the return of Simeon from Spain, where he is a successful businessman. They wanted him to lead the nation in the transition period from communism to some form of democracy. Republicans became alarmed when Simeon's sister returned to Sofia for a visit in 1991; she was greeted by thousands of enthusiastic well-wishers.[12] But by declaring Bulgaria a republic, members of the Grand National Assembly blocked the rebirth of the monarchy and with it Prince Simeon as head of state. Moreover, by reaffirming the Roundtable agreement and the action of Parliament in 1990, the reference to Bulgaria as a socialist state under the leadership of the Communist Party was eliminated forever.

Legislative Power

The Grand National Assembly embedded within the Constitution Montesquieu's idea of protecting liberty by separating legislative, executive, and judicial authority. Article 8 separates the power of the state "between a legislative, an executive and a judicial branch."

Lawmaking power is vested in a single chamber body called the National Assembly (Narodno Subranie). The two hundred forty members of the National Assembly are elected for four-year terms. Any Bulgarian citizen not holding another citizenship, twenty-one years or older, and not on trial or in prison is eligible for election. Once elected, the Constitution obliges members of the National Assembly to follow their own conscience when performing their duties. Those candidates for a National Assembly seat who also hold a state post must resign upon the registration of their candidacy. In keeping with that separation-of-powers principle, no member of Parliament shall occupy another state post; if selected as a government minister, for example, a person must cease to serve as a member of the National Assembly. In these circumstances, the Constitution mandates that such persons are replaced for the period during which they function as ministers by the next person on the party slate for the National Assembly election. When such persons are dismissed as ministers they resume their parliamentary duties and their replacements are relieved as members of the National Assembly.[13]

The Constitution empowers the National Assembly to pass, amend, and rescind laws; pass the state budget bill and the budget report; establish taxes and their size; schedule the elections for a president of the Republic; resolve on the holding of a national referendum; elect and dismiss the prime minister and, on his motion, the members of the Council of Ministers; effect changes in the government on a motion from the prime minister; elect and dismiss the governor of the Bulgarian National Bank and the heads of other institutions established by law; approve state-loan agreements; resolve on the declaration of war and conclusion of peace; approve any deployment and use of Bulgarian armed forces outside the country's borders; and approve, on a motion from the president or the Council of Ministers, the deployment of foreign troops on the territory of the country or their crossing of that territory. The National Assembly may introduce martial law or a state of emergency on all or part of the country's territory, grant amnesty, institute orders and medals, and establish official holidays. The National Assembly also possesses considerable authority in the ratification of international agreements and treaties.

There are two circumstances when the National Assembly may conduct a no-confidence vote. First, the cabinet itself may request that the National Assembly take a no-confidence vote on its overall policy or on specific grounds. The assembly's motion is carried if more than half of its members present and voting cast their vote for it. Second, one fifth of the members of the National Assembly may move a reasoned draft resolution of no-confidence either of the prime minister or the Council of Ministers. In this instance, the no-confidence resolution is carried if more than half of all members of the National Assembly vote for it. If a no-confidence vote fails, Parliament may not entertain another confidence motion predicated on the same reason for the next six months. Incumbent prime ministers may use the no-confidence device as a method to secure their governments against removal during the six-month period.

Within the government itself, if the prime minister resigns, then the entire cabinet must also follow suit. The prime minister may ask for a change in cabinet ministers, but the National Assembly must approve. This constitutional mandate leaves the door open for fledgling ministers to appeal to the broader Parliament to save their jobs.

Council of Ministers and Administration

In principle, there is a separation of powers between the legislative and executive branches of government. But as one thoughtful writer maintains, there is no balance of power between them.[14] Politicians must give up their seats in Parliament when they accept a position in the Council of Ministers (Ministerski Suvet). But there is a lack of balance because the politicians in the National Assembly are in a position to control the activities of the council through the exercise of their power to conduct no-confidence votes.

The Constitution charges the Council of Ministers with the responsibility to implement domestic and foreign policy consistent with the Constitution and the laws of the country. It serves, in other words, as the government with a prime minster and other ministers with particular portfolios. It is charged with the responsibility to maintain public order and national security and to provide overall leadership over public administration and the armed forces. The council promulgates decrees, orders, resolutions, rules, and regulations.

Parliament has been slow to enact a civil service law providing working bureaucrats with the assurance that their jobs are not threatened every time a new government is installed. Indeed, there is no mention in the Constitution of the tasks of the central administration or about the status of civil servants. As constitutional scholar Tony Verheijen points out, during the first years of regime change in Central and Eastern Europe, little attention was paid to the crucial role of public administration, especially with respect to its place in regulating a market economy.[15] Verheijen offers several explanations for this condition. First, reform leaders do not trust civil servants to carry out reforms, particularly those in the higher ranks of government. In the past, these bureaucrats served the communist regimes, and it is feared that they may harbor sentiments that favor the status quo ante. Second, some civil servants are incompetent, and they find it difficult to change their habits consistent with the needs of the new era. If they are to be part of the solution and not part of the problem, they need incentives such as job security. And finally, the new political leaders are appointing public administrators, particularly at the top levels, with a view toward their political reliability and without adequate consideration for their professionalism. This state of affairs is not conducive for creating a professional bureaucracy that will openly provide feedback to policymakers in an effort to correct laws that are not working.[16]

In Bulgaria, there has been no rush to create a comprehensive civil service law. It is said that the absence of such a law has made it difficult for the Council of Ministers to exercise effective control over administration. Yet, government workers continue to be protected by the longstanding labor code that pertains to all workers—meaning those who work in industry or public administration. The enactment of a thoroughgoing civil service law would be helpful, and no doubt the National Assembly will pass legislation in the near future. However, the fundamental difficulty lies in the contemporary political situation. Political polarization and insufficient coalition building has made it difficult for politicians to bend government to their will. As there is greater movement toward democratic consolidation, then the task of the Council of Ministers to administer the government will become less daunting.

Presidential Authority

The president of the Republic (Prezident na Republikata) is the head of state. Because the constitutional framers conceived Bulgaria as a parliamentary system, presidential authority is limited, especially when compared to the powers of the president of the United States. As head of state, Bulgaria's president embodies the unity of the nation and represents the nation in international relations. A vice president is elected on the same ballot with the president for a five-year term, limited to two terms. Bulgaria is the only parliamentary republic with a directly elected vice president.

The institution of an elected head of state was unknown in Bulgaria until April 1990. Participants at the National Roundtable Talks agreed to an amendment to the existing Constitution as a way to alter the continuing one-party domination of the state by the Bulgarian Communist Party. In part, reform elements within the old Bulgarian Communist Party, by then renamed the Bulgarian Socialist Party, approved the creation of the office of the president because they believed that Parliament would elect their man, Petar Mladenov, as the first president. On April 3, 1990, this came to pass. Unexpectedly, however, as has been explained in previous chapters, Mladenov was forced to resign on July 6, 1990. After three ballots, the National Assembly reached a compromise. Dr. Zhelyu Zhelev, a leader of the UDF, was elected president. Colonel General Attanas Semerjiev, a popular leader of the BSP, was elected the nation's first vice president.[17] In January 1992, under the terms of the July 1991 Constitution, Zhelyu Zhelev won election for a full five-year term with Blaga Dimitrova as his running mate. Seven months later Dimitrova abruptly resigned, charging that the country was being prepared for dictatorship.[18]

A weak head of state may function successfully as a symbol of national unity. It provides the primary benefit of a monarchy without the regal trappings. Some also argue that a presidential system of government should be eschewed in favor of a parliamentary democracy because within presidential systems there is a tendency toward deadlock or authoritarianism. The United States is a good example of the former, and Latin America is cited in support of the latter. Evidence based on third world countries tends to support this view as well.[19]

There is, however, an obvious difficulty with an elected president in a parliamentary democracy. If parliament is the center of power there is little room for an additional locus of authority. Yet, because Bulgarians elect their president on a popular ballot there is an expectation of independent authority; but in fact the presidency possesses little institutional power. Nevertheless, Bulgaria's constitutional framers, insisting upon a separation of powers model, fused a predominately parliamentary model with some features of a presidential system.[20]

Article 98 of the Constitution specifies some of the president's most routine duties as head of state, including scheduling elections for the National Assembly and for local self-governing bodies, issuing appeals to the people and to the National Assembly, concluding international treaties in the cases stipulated by law, promulgating laws, and sanctioning changes in the borders and centers of administrative-territorial units when proposed by the Council of Ministers. At the request of the Council of Ministers, the president appoints and dismisses from their positions the heads of diplomatic missions and other international organizations and accepts the credentials and letters of recall of foreign diplomatic representatives. The president awards orders and medals and may pardon persons for their crimes.

Among the most important roles of the president is as commander-in-chief of the armed forces. Consistent with that role, the president appoints and dismisses the high command of the armed forces and awards high military ranks at the proposal of the Council of Ministers. The president heads the Consultative Council for National Security. When the Council of Ministers proposes, the president declares general or partial military mobilization. Further, if the National Assembly is in recess, the president may declare a state of war in the event of an armed attack against the country or in response to the need for urgent implementation of international obligations. The president may also declare martial law or any other state of emergency. In such cases, the National Assembly possesses the ultimate authority because the Constitution requires it to convene immediately to vote on any such declaration.

Because the president's constitutional authority in the legislative system is limited, there is little opportunity to affect the course of law making. By way of a suspensory veto, the president may return a law he or she disapproves of to the National Assembly for further debate.

However, the lawmakers may vote the law again by a simple majority. There have been notable occasions when President Zhelev has done so, as with the 1994 Judiciary Act[21] and the 1995 Amended Land Law.[22] But such actions raise questions as to whether the president should exercise this authority in light of the fact that Parliament will simply pass the law again. There are also clashes between the president and the prime minister's government over foreign policy matters, including the conditions for Bulgaria's membership in NATO.[23]

The president plays a formal role in the selection of the prime minister. After a successful no-confidence vote or a regular parliamentary election, the president must consult with the parliamentary groups when appointing the next prime minister. Article 99 of the Constitution spells out in detail the sequence of events that the president must follow.

The president first asks the candidate for prime minister of the largest parliamentary group to form a cabinet. If within a seven-day period the candidate is unable to propose a list of members of the Council of Ministers, the president must ask the candidate nominated by the second largest parliamentary group to name a new government. If, once again, the process fails to create a new government then the president asks another parliamentary group to nominate a candidate for prime minister. If all of the above consultations should fail, the Constitution directs the president to ask the National Assembly to nominate the candidate for prime minister. More drastic action is taken if this procedure fails. The president appoints a caretaker cabinet, disbands the National Assembly, and schedules a new election to take place within two months.

Local Government

Chapter 7 of the Constitution provides for the existence of local self-government and local administration within a unitary system of authority. The Constitution divides the territory of the Republic into townships and oblasts. Citizens participate in governing townships through local self-governing bodies they have elected and through referenda and general meetings of the inhabitants. Township councils and their mayors are elected to four-year terms. Townships possess the right to own property, and they have autonomous budgets. The central authority assists townships by contributing funds from the national budget and by other means. The oblast is an administrative-territorial entity that carries out regional policies and state administrative tasks in the localities and ensures that the national and local governments work together. The Council of Ministers appoints oblast governors. Finally, the central authorities of the state and their local representatives exercise oversight concerning the legality of the laws passed by local self-government authorities as stipulated by law.

The Judiciary

Chapter 6 of the Constitution provides for the establishment of the judicial branch (Sudebvna Vlast). For three years, Parliament debated from time to time the details of a judiciary act to establish the new courts as provided for in the 1991 Constitution. Crises resulting from shifting coalitions and changes in government served to distract members of the National Assembly from this task. But on July 22, 1994, it promulgated a new law on the judiciary. This system provides for regional and district courts with original jurisdiction, an appellate court for cases appealed from the district courts, and the Supreme Court of Cassation. The law also provides for military courts of first instance and an appellate level court with final appeal to the Cassation Court. The 1994 law also created an administrative court system. It provides that cases originate in the regional and district courts with final decision in a Supreme Administrative Court. As is the case in other civil law systems of continental Europe, the various prosecutory functions take place outside the court system.[24] This law also contained controversial provisions aimed at removing certain jurists. The Constitutional Court found specific provisions of this law at variance with the Constitution's tenure requirements.[25]

Chapter 8 provides for the Constitutional Court (Konstitutsionen Sud). The twelve justices of the Constitutional Court are elected or appointed for nine-year nonrenewable terms of office. The National Assembly elects one-third of the justices, one-third are appointed by the president of the Republic, and one-third are elected by a joint meeting of the justices of the Supreme Court of Cassation and the Supreme Administrative Court. Although all the Constitutional Court members are highly regarded for their professional abilities, it is widely understood that politics enter the selection process. Where constitutional courts exist such as in Italy and Germany, they are clearly understood as playing a vital role in the political life of the nation.[26]

Chapter 8 provides for a Constitutional Court with the authority to (1) provide binding interpretations of the Constitution; (2) rule on challenges to the constitutionality of the laws and other acts passed by the National Assembly and the acts of the president; (3) rule on competence suits between the National Assembly, the president, and the Council of Ministers, and between the bodies of local self-government and the central executive branch of government; (4) rule on the compatibility between the Constitution and the international instruments concluded by the Republic of Bulgaria before their ratification, and on the compatibility of domestic laws with the universally recognized norms of international law and the international instruments to which Bulgaria is a party; (5) rule on challenges to the constitutionality of political parties and associations; (6) rule on challenges to the legality of the election of the president and vice president; (7) rule on challenges to the legality of an election of a member of the National Assembly; and (8) rule on impeachments by the National Assembly against the president or the vice president.

There is no actual case or controversy requirement as pertains to the U.S. system of judicial review. Abstract review permits disputes to come to Bulgaria's Constitutional Court on the petition of no fewer than one-fifth of all members of the National Assembly, the president, the Council of Ministers, the Supreme Court of Cassation, the Supreme Administrative Court, or the chief prosecutor. If during litigation the Supreme Court of Cassation or the Supreme Administrative Court should find a law and the Constitution in conflict, they must suspend the proceeding and refer the matter to the Constitutional Court for determination. Anticipating the possibility of attempts to limit the jurisdiction of the Constitutional Court, Article 149(2) of the Bulgarian Constitution specifically states that a law may not be enacted that would suspend its authority.

The judiciary and particularly the Constitutional Court play an important role by checking any tendency by the nation to backslide into totalitarianism. More than a fifth of all the articles in the 1991 Constitution provide for human rights. Chapter 2 (Articles 25 to 61) details rights of persons and citizens in very specific terms. These rights include various well-known and universally accepted political freedoms, and prohibitions against repressive police actions. Many rights provisions are written in absolutist terms. However, as is commonly the case in modern constitutions, there are qualifications. For example, Article 39(1) states: "Everyone shall be entitled to express an opinion or to publicize it through words, written or oral, sound or image, or in any other way." However, paragraph 2 of this article limits the free speech guarantee. It declares, "This right shall not be used to the detriment of the rights and reputations of others, or for the incitement of a forcible change of the constitutionally established order, the perpetration of a crime, or the incitement of enmity or violence against anyone." This and other similarly worded qualifications require constitutional interpretation. In this context, the judicial function looms large. Article 117(1) states, "The judicial branch of government shall safeguard the rights and legitimate interests of all citizens." Moreover, to make the Article 117(1) charge meaningful, Article 117(2) of Chapter 6 declares: "The judicial branch of government shall be independent."

The Constitution is declared the "supreme law, and no other law shall contravene it." Thus, while there shall be a parliamentary government, its laws may not contradict the most basic law, the Constitution. This point is further dramatized by the Article 5(2) command that "provisions of the Constitution shall apply directly." This means that rights exist independent of and are superior to parliamentary enactments, or the executive acts of national or local governments.

Several court cases involving property expropriation serve as examples of direct application of the Constitution and the principle of constitutional supremacy. Clause 3(1) of the Transitional and Concluding Provisions of the July 1991 Constitution provides that existing laws are "applicable insofar as they do not contravene the Constitution." The old law, dating from the days of the communist regime, permitted taking of property with compensation promised after expropriation. However, Article 19(5) of the new July 1991 Constitution requires that forcible expropriation of property for state or municipal needs may only take place "after fair compensation has been ensured in advance." Relying on the direct application principle, the Bulgarian Supreme Court in several cases abolished expropriation orders because compensation was not ensured in advance. Judicial officials, therefore, need not depend on other branches of government to define rights. Rather, personal liberties and civil rights exist independent of and are superior to legislative or executive action or inaction. It is within the realm of judicial authority to define and protect these rights.[27]

Human Rights Protections

Chapter 1 "guarantees the life, dignity and rights of the individual and the creation of conditions in Bulgaria . . . conducive to the free development of the individual and the civil society." It also contains a provision that international instruments ratified by Bulgaria automatically become part of the internal domestic law. Therefore, international conventions on human rights to which Bulgaria is a party supersede any internal law. Bulgaria is a signatory to a variety of international human rights conventions including those dealing with all forms of racial discrimination and the European Convention for Human Rights and Liberties. On December 10, 1991, the National Assembly ratified the optional protocol to the International Convention on Civil and Political Rights. Bulgaria ratified the international convention in 1970, but ideological factors militated against acceding to the protocol until the current political era.[28]

Bulgaria's Constitutional Court has since affirmed a broad interpretation and understanding of Article 5, section 4 of the Constitution. It held that international law is part of the national law and takes priority over internal law.[29] Thus, Article 5 creates a further protection against the resurgence of repressive government. Although the issue generates internal disputes, there can be little doubt the framers of Bulgaria's 1991 Constitution were serious about the human rights question.

Chapter 1 of the Constitution declares all persons are "born free and equal in dignity and rights." It explicitly says that all citizens must be afforded equal treatment under the law and specifically prohibits "privileges or restrictions of rights on the grounds of race, nationality, ethnic self-identity, sex, origin, region, education, opinion, political affiliation, personal or social status or property status." This provision is something of an article of peace. It seeks to assure constitutional protection for the nation's diverse populations, including especially Turks, Jews, Armenians, and Gypsies. Bulgaria is seeking to avoid the ethnic unrest and separatist movements that currently grip several

Eastern European nation-states and many former Soviet republics. Yet, it is a matter that is difficult to resolve to the satisfaction of everyone.

In the mid-1980s, the Zhivkov regime repressed the sizable ethnic Turkish Moslem minority. The old regime forced Moslems to change their names and limited the use of other languages besides the official Bulgarian language in everyday communication. As many as 350,000 ethnic Turks left Bulgaria to escape the persecution after the Bulgarian authorities opened the border in May 1989. About half returned to Bulgaria after the Zhivkov regime fell. However, they found that it was difficult for them to regain their homes and property that had been lost, sold, or expropriated by local officials. The ethnic Turks fought back by organizing hunger strikes and school boycotts. In the end, the Turkish minority organized itself into the Movement for Rights and Freedoms, a political organization headed by the charismatic Ahmed Dogan. It has been a force in Bulgarian politics ever since.[30] The constitutional status of this organization has occupied the attention of both the Bulgarian Supreme Court and the Constitutional Court. In controversial decisions, these courts ruled in favor of MRF participation in the political process.[31] Yet, Bulgarians are emotional about the Turkish minority issue. It remains a central question challenging national unity.[32]

The Constitutional Court came to the rescue of the market economy cause when it was petitioned by President Zhelev and fifty-eight UDF members of the National Assembly. They asked the Court to declare unconstitutional the 1995 law amending the Agricultural Land Tenure Act. The law passed by the Socialist parliamentary majority over Zhelev's suspensory veto provides for the restitution of agricultural land taken for purposes of creating collective farms during the Communist regime.[33] The objection raised against the legislation was the requirement that owners wishing to sell any of the restituted land must first offer it to neighbors and to the state before it could be sold on the open market to the highest bidder. The Constitutional Court found that controversial provision of the law inconsistent with Article 17, that private property is inviolable.

Clearly, then, the Constitution imposes upon the judiciary the responsibility to safeguard rights, and grants it the authority to pursue this duty as an independent branch of government. Moreover, Article

117 of the Constitution requires that in the performance of their functions, all judges, court assessors, prosecutors, and investigating magistrates shall be subservient only to the law. Within the Bulgarian context, this means there shall be no attempt to unduly influence judges about matters before their courts.

In sum, the July 1991 Constitution of Bulgaria is a document designed to protect rights subject to the usual exceptions polities demand to guard the order and well-being of the general population. Because the Constitution reflects compromise, it is not perfectly logical in all its parts. For example, while the Constitution provides for political and religious freedom, it also limits the right of religious and ethnic groups to participate in the political process. While the Constitution establishes a parliamentary democracy, it provides for a president with some authority in the legislative process. Yet, a system of separation of powers with its checks and balances is inconsistent with the notion of parliamentary supremacy. Further, while the Constitution extols the virtues of judicial independence there is no prohibition on reducing judicial salaries, reassigning judges from one court jurisdiction to another or moving judges from one venue to another. In the brief period since the adoption of the 1991 basic document, constitutional ambiguities have been subjected to political and legal tests. There is little doubt that more challenges will be lodged in the future.

7

Interpreting Events

UPON FIRST CONSIDERATION it may seem puzzling that the creation of a new constitution should be anything but a formality. After all, participants in the National Roundtable Talks had managed to reach fundamental agreements about the nature of the new political order. Upon closer inspection, however, several differences divided the nation and its deputies. First, some members of the Grand National Assembly were monarchists or had monarchistic sympathies. They sought a return of the dead king's son, Prince Simeon, from Spain, to take his rightful place as head of state. Second, it upset some anti-Communists that former Communist leaders and members of the nomenklatura had yet to pay an appropriate price for their past misdeeds; and, indeed, some leaders of the Bulgarian Socialist Party are said to be guilty of profiting personally from the political accommodation hammered out at the National Roundtable Talks. This result, incredulous opponents of the July 1991 Constitution maintain, is confirmed by the creation of a new basic document that allows former Communist Party functionaries a place in what is purported to be a new political order. This accommodation remains a source of considerable irritation, resentment, and political conflict. Third, many think the time devoted to creating a new Constitution was wasteful of the nation's energy. Instead, Parliament should have been occupied enacting laws restoring expropriated property to private persons, converting the socialist economy to a market system, and instituting democratic reforms throughout society. By simply amending the existing Constitution, as was done in Hungary or the Czech Republic, for example, lawmakers might have saved valuable time to get on with the really important tasks facing the nation.

There was also a related matter of practical political science. How might it be possible for persons with little if any experience at parliamentary politics to function adequately in the new environment? While the former Communists had experience of a sort with parliamentary institutions, the oppositionists' main experience with democracy was in the streets as protesters.

A final difficulty faced by the proponents of a new basic document was how to promulgate any new constitution. Should the people or their representatives ratify the document? The legitimacy question was a serious one. Many thought that there had been a preexisting agreement for a referendum to be held at the close of the work of the Grand National Assembly. Indeed, such an agreement did exist. Instead, however, members of the GNA fixed their signatures to the document, putting into place the new Constitution without a vote of the people.

From the Roundtable to the Grand National Assembly

Ginio Ganev, the deputy chairman of the GNA and the respected chairman of the parliamentary committee for the drafting and approval of the Constitution, explained to me the important linkage between the Roundtable Talks and the accomplishments at the Grand National Assembly.[1]

> **GG:** I belong to those people who consider the National Roundtable a great achievement of the democratic process in Bulgaria. I need to emphasize this fact now, although until very recently I thought it was implicit. Yet, presently I see that many people are trying to deny the necessity at the time to establish such a dialogue.
>
> In your letter on which the arrangement for this interview is based, you point to something that should be described as a supreme value for the Bulgarian transition to democracy—and this is its peaceful character. The National Roundtable was one of the initial forms it has taken; that is, to sit together and discuss the problems, never mind the obstacles created by the then existing balance of forces. And regardless of all the difficulties and the circumstances

of the day, the National Roundtable was able to work out compromises and to reach decisions with long-lasting effect.

It needs to be admitted that from a juridical viewpoint it was a somewhat peculiar situation: there was a functioning Parliament, but at the same time a National Roundtable was setting up its direction and telling it exactly what to do. We should not discount how difficult this was—both from a psychological and practical point of view. At the National Roundtable it was decided that the then acting Parliament should pass without delay a couple of laws that played an important role in promoting political democracy and made real the declared liberties like freedom of speech, of political organization, of public meetings, rallies and so on. And the changes in the then existing Constitution were strongly influenced by the stand taken at the National Roundtable.

In fact it was at the Roundtable Talks that the decision to have elections for a Grand National Assembly was made. In accordance with Bulgarian constitutional and political tradition, such an assembly is called only when it is thought crucial changes in the governing of the country are necessary. . . . The political opposition stuck to this idea very persistently indeed. Originally, the Bulgarian Communist Party and the Agrarian Union—the pro-Communist one—lacked the understanding why it was important to convene a Grand National Assembly.

AM: Oh, are you suggesting that the Communists had other things in mind?

GG: Initially, they were not convinced that it was necessary to call a Grand National Assembly. Indeed, I was among the three nonparty representatives at the National Roundtable who thought it unnecessary to start the democratic changes by electing a Grand National Assembly and by enacting a new constitution. I admit that this idea was alien to me.

AM: I see. At the time you believed that it was unnecessary to create a new constitution. Did you consider simply amending the then existing Constitution?

GG: An amendment was enacted, and we did need an ordinary Parliament because we wanted to change existing legislation. That idea reigned supreme at the moment.[2] But that is not the point.

It was Mr. Zhelyu Zhelev and his circle who came up with the idea that what we need is a Grand National Assembly to create a new constitution and by this to start the overall democratic process in the country. I had many discussions with Mr. Zhelev and his people about this issue. So I know for sure who was the father of this idea. In the end, none of the Roundtable participants opposed the decision to hold elections for a Grand National Assembly that would create a new constitution. We could have gone the other way, to follow the Hungarian experience, for example: there is a working Parliament, bills are passed and the existing Constitution is constantly amended to suit the requirements of political development. That is why I used to quote the Hungarian example, as did other colleagues of mine. I pointed to the fact that there the democratic process is developing fine, that they make important laws, and the Constitution is not considered an obstacle to them. . . . So, at the end of the day, there is just one clause of the Hungarian Constitution left. Can you guess which one?

AM: No.

GG: That Budapest is the capital of Hungary!

AM: Yes, Bulgaria [as well as Romania] remains the only Eastern European nation with a brand-new constitution. This is very interesting, but can you tell me more about your personal role in crafting the Constitution?

GG: . . . Yes, indeed. I will come to that. In other words, the decision of the National Roundtable to call elections, to create a constitutional assembly and to pass a constitution is extraordinarily important for the Bulgarian democratic process. But you have asked me about my personal role in this process. At the time there were two confronting sides. If we were truly striving for democracy, it was necessary to try to invent a formula to make mutually acceptable decisions. As it so happened, there was no objection from either side that I emerged as a kind of go-between person. I, therefore, became chairman of the editorial group charged with the responsibility to prepare the texts of the decisions of the National Roundtable. And let me state openly that I felt for the first time with all my body and soul the greatest principle of democracy in its best definition: people who had not been on speaking terms at all met together and entered discussions with the goal of finding a common solution.

In this sense the National Roundtable achieved several goals: that alterations in the then existing laws created the prerequisites for democratic political and economic changes; the parliamentary way to transform the society was declared supreme; and finally, the leaders of the united opposition became public figures for the first time in their lives. The discussions at the National Roundtable Talks were covered live by the media. The people watched these proceedings and were getting used to a new scene. It was totally different from what in forty consecutive years was presented to them as inevitable. In its substance this was proof that dialogue is possible. Never mind the complexity of the situation as a whole and the different intentions of the people who gathered at the National Roundtable. Inevitably, there were many attempts to break off the work of the National Roundtable. There were attempts to impose "street democracy" (mob rule). . . .

But we had to state that the street is unable to govern. It is extremely difficult to say this openly and at the same time to keep your influence. So this is in brief my assessment about the role of the National Roundtable.

AM: Was there an idea early at the Roundtable to put the new Constitution to a vote of the people? That is, to a referendum? Was that part of the agreement reached at the National Roundtable Talks?

GG: True, such ideas were around. But we decided upon an approach that is closer to the traditions of Bulgarian constitutionalism. The first constitution of the newly liberated Bulgaria from the Turks, the so-called Turnovo Constitution [1879], was enacted by a majority of the deputies in the Grand National Assembly and not by referendum. By contrast, the [1971] Constitution of Todor Zhivkov was enacted by referendum. Our memories of the referendum for Todor Zhivkov's Constitution are not associated with democracy. Because of this, it was agreed that the new Constitution

> shall be passed by a two-thirds majority from the total number of all deputies in the Grand National Assembly; in the context of the Bulgarian tradition and the actual representation at the Grand National Assembly this meant a great number of people, because the Grand National Assembly had four hundred deputies. For a country the size of Bulgaria [nine million] there is no need for a Parliament with more than two hundred MPs. . . . The electoral law, which was passed [for the GNA election] was a relatively good one, and it promoted the so-called mixed system—a combination between the majority and proportional system.

Street Radicals and Parliamentarians

After elaborating upon the legitimacy of the Grand National Assembly, Ganev then talked about the problem of instilling a sense of parliamentarianism among the members of Grand National Assembly. That is, how might it be possible to convert stridently uncompromising street radicals to members of a parliamentary body wherein they must engage in dialogue, rule abiding, and compromise. Ganev said:

> We all came to the Grand National Assembly straight from the squares with our megaphones, so many of us believed that standing on the parliamentary rostrum is the same as speaking into a megaphone at a mass rally. But that has nothing to do with parliamentarianism. Everybody was trying to make their way to the rostrum; they were carrying letters and insisting upon reading them. . . . MPs did not speak to each other in the Parliament and so on. And as an active leader in this National Assembly, I must say that, although it was short, the experience was extremely important for the development of Bulgarian democracy. Although my efforts were not unaided by others, my personal involvement prevented the Parliament from disintegrating. There were several attempts to do this. Well, I was once asked—"Mr. Ganev, if you leave the Parliament, it will break down for sure. So, why don't you leave it?" This became a topical issue especially after the so-called Group of Thirty-Nine disaffected members, including hunger strikers, emerged. But that is another issue.
>
> But I will tell you how I used to answer: This particular

Parliament does not matter much. The important matter is the principle of parliamentarianism. The fact that the Grand National Assembly exists is important by itself. Otherwise, we could get into the bad habit of disbanding parliamentary institutions by illegal means any time it suits us.

My efforts to find some kind of modus vivendi proved successful. I prevented any issue from entry into the parliamentary itinerary that could be voted "automatically," so to speak. This is an important rule because in a divided society such as ours at that time—and it is divided still—automatic voting, passing bills with a narrow majority, is dangerous to democracy.

AM: By "automatic" you mean without discussion. Therefore, you required debate?

GG: Not only debate, but I required contact groups that would achieve some kind of understanding outside the plenary hall before the start of the official debates. Because in a divided society like ours, now and then, to put a bill to a quick vote and to pass it by a minimal majority is not democratic by definition. This is so because in the transitional period you need the largest possible support of good will and respect for legitimacy mobilized behind a law. I think that is clear, but not to all people.

AM: So one might say in your official capacity as deputy chairman of the GNA you behaved as something of a classroom teacher for the pupils of democracy.

GG: Well, I treated everyone evenhandedly; I was just an equal among equals and behaved very politely. One of the great democratic results of this first stage of our transition was that crucial bills were passed. They can make up a whole catalogue: the law for political rehabilitation and amnesty; laws to change the economic structure of the society—for the land, for foreign investments for the local government and so on. Plus the Constitution, of course. Who says there are perfect laws? There are no such laws. But the important thing is to have laws as such. In a country like Bulgaria, which just emerged from the totalitarian period, the most important thing is to get used to the idea that the state cannot be governed by the ambition of people who just want to hold power. From now on, it shall be governed by rules [laws].

AM: Right.

GG: I am more aware than many others that this Constitution could have been more sophisticated, but it is in no way a bad constitution. It is by no means a Communist constitution—I state this openly and clearly in my capacity as chairman of the parliamentary committee for the drafting and approval of the Constitution. There were sixteen projects. Each parliamentary group had its own project. Apart from these there were too many other projects, initiated by private persons and the public in general. The committee debated all issues by involving experts, and the public had full access to the discussions. We had at our disposal the most up-to-date constitutional texts. In the end, a Constitution was passed where constitutionalism in its modern form dominates as a principle: a developed parliamentarianism; a chapter for the rights and liberties is not just mentioned but is developed or fortified by the corresponding detailed legislative and court procedures. We proclaim the supremacy of the principle that in all cases where Bulgaria is a party under international law that such acts are directly applied even if they contradict the norms of the internal law. And so on. But that is another story.

The point is that the Constitution works. Even those people who were against it must read and quote from it—in accordance with their own interests, of course. That is natural. Let the Constitution be. As happens with every constitution in the world, let us prepare changes of particular provisions to better reflect developments in society. I make this extra pronouncement to point out that despite my initial opposition to the idea to create a Grand National Assembly, later I did my best to help it function successfully.

* * *

Writing a new constitution was thought an appropriate legitimating act, one that was consistent with precedent when the nation had undergone fundamental changes dating from the original Constitution promulgated after liberation from Turkish rule in 1879. Mr. Ganev's

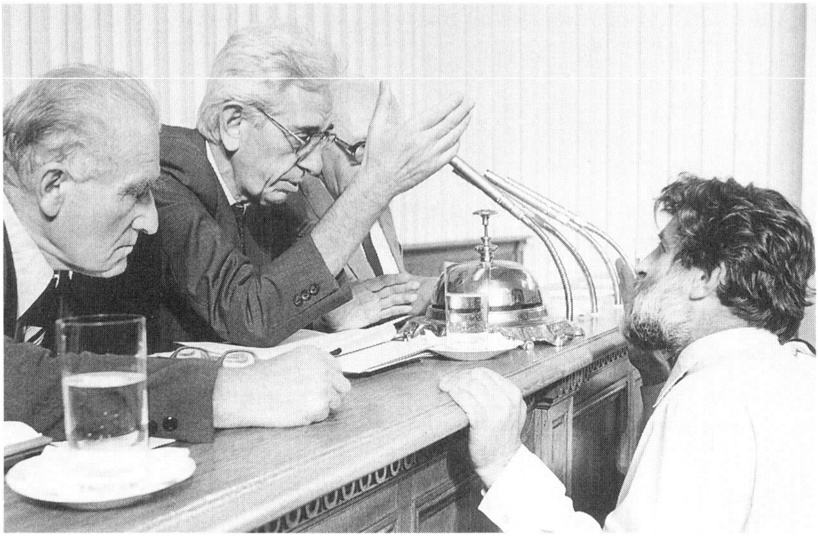

The Grand National Assembly at work. Petar Beron and Deputy Chairman Ginio Ganev hotly discuss a point of order.

observations are valuable because we learn that the idea of a Grand National Assembly that would function both as a regular parliamentary lawmaking body and as a constitutional convention was an idea of the UDF leadership. It was not an idea of the leadership of the Bulgarian Socialist Party. Oddly enough, as the GNA was completing its task, the new draft constitution created internal conflict within UDF ranks, while at the same time the BSP embraced it. It is also of particular interest to learn that Ganev understood the importance of developing democratic habits. As a leader, he insisted upon full debate preceded by careful study of all the issues involved in creating the new Constitution. This action may have aided decision makers in learning the ways of democratic institutions. Then, too, the cathartic value of robust debate should not be underestimated. It is functional because with a full airing of arguments on all sides of an issue, people may view democratic forums as legitimate expressions of their will.

Opponents of Ratification

When speaking with Ginio Ganev one is impressed with his commitment and sincerity. Yet, there are other persons of demonstrable good will who view matters differently. Not everyone who opposed the promulgation of the new Constitution did so for the same reasons—including the hunger strikers who threatened the conclusion of the GNA's work. Then too, there were ninety-one members of the Grand National Assembly that for one reason or another did not sign the new Constitution. I asked Petko Simeonov why so many deputies decided to boycott the GNA at the end of its deliberations. Besides being a founder of the UDF and a leading figure of the Grand National Assembly, at one time, Simeonov boycotted the plenary sessions. He said:[3]

> There was an artificial slowdown of the activity of the Grand National Assembly on behalf of the Communist Party, in which the conservatives began to regain their self-confidence. . . .
>
> **AM:** So, you mean they wanted to delay the ratification of the Constitution?
>
> **PS:** Well, not only to delay ratification, but to delay the work on the creation of the Constitution; they did so intentionally, by use of the procedural rules. By giving priority to the laws . . . So this delay was the reason [for the boycott]. When they left [the Parliament] I also followed suit, because I was greatly dissatisfied with the slowdown in the work of the National Assembly and with those decisions imposed by force. And when they left I was with them. But when this protest took the form of a hunger strike, when they started to proclaim revolutionary slogans, I dissociated from them and stated outright that the Constitution should be signed, because this represents a step forward. I was torn to pieces for taking this stand. Nevertheless, because of the boycott of the National Assembly the work on the Constitution actually sped up. So it played a positive role in the creation of the new Constitution.
>
> **AM:** So, it was not a matter of disagreement with the decisions made by the Grand National Assembly, of particular provisions in the Constitution; it was a matter of how rapid the process should go. Is that correct?
>
> **PS:** No. The issue originally was that the Grand National Assembly worked with great difficulty. Then, some of those who left started

to proclaim revolutionary slogans. Simultaneously, they began to explain their behavior to the people by saying that they left [the Parliament], and that they are on a hunger strike because they disagree with the [new] Constitution. But this was, so to speak, just a pretext. The heart of the matter, the basic motive of their actions, which was not stated openly, is that they disagreed with the Constitution because it is a republican one.

AM: Aha, they were monarchists, the hunger strikers?

PS: Yes, those of them who were the leaders as well as the behind-the-scene abettors. Because acceptance of the new Constitution would mean closing the door for the eventual return of the Turnovo Constitution.

AM: Oh, from 1879.

PS: Yes, of that one, which proclaimed Bulgaria a monarchy.

AM: So, they wanted to go back to the Constitution of 1879. . . .

PS: Exactly.

AM: And the Communist Constitution created in 1947 was an illegal act from their point of view?

PS: Yes, indeed.

AM: That is very interesting.

PS: They did not say "we want the tsar back," they said instead: "We do not want this Constitution, it is a Communist one"; or sometimes they said: "We want the Turnovo Constitution," which in fact meant that they also want the monarchy. But this was said under their breath.

AM: Do these monarchists believe in human rights? I ask this because much of the 1991 Constitution contains references to human rights.

PS: I doubt it. I know a thing or two about some of these people. What they wanted was the restoration, to get back to the status quo of the prewar [World War II] days.

AM: Are the proponents of monarchy young or very old people?

PS: People of all ages.

AM: Would you say they are romantics?

PS: There is nothing romantic in their motives. They seek only mercantile interests or they desire to restore their former positions in the system of power. They believe in some absurd things. For example, they call the anti-fascists bandits. They claim fascism never existed in Bulgaria. So I asked at a press conference, I appealed to the gentlemen from the UDF to kindly inform the ambassadors of the United States, Great Britain, and France that Roosevelt, Churchill, and de Gaulle were bandits and criminals. And this is true because their allies, people who fought along with them, were called these names.

* * *

Simeonov's view of the hunger strikers is not universally shared. Stefan Gaitanjiev, another UDF leader and GNA member, and later the leader of his own political party, said there are other reasons that some people took part in the hunger strikes. That is, there were hunger strikers who were not closet monarchists. Some strikers sought early elections, and some simply thought the new Constitution as it was shaping up was a procommunist document. But Gaitanjiev, an academic sociologist with the Institute for State and Law, added a most interesting possible cause that might explain the radical actions of some hunger strikers. He said they wanted to bring to a halt the work of Parliament because that body had commissioned a study that would name persons who had cooperated in the past with the secret police; they feared revealing the dossiers of former security service collaborators.[4]

Clearly, then, there is a host of possible reasons advanced for why some attempted to block the work of the Grand National Assembly. I asked Jordan Vasilev, a leader of the hunger strikers, about the justification for their action and why the leaders of the Turkish ethnic movement did not join them. He said:[5]

Well, I can give you firsthand information, I witnessed the situation, for I was an MP at the Grand National Assembly. At that moment

The Socialist side at the Grand National Assembly

they [the Movement for Rights and Freedoms] were absolutely close to us in the UDF. Our political ideas were almost identical. The most acute moment came when about forty UDF deputies came to the conclusion that this Constitution is riddled with dangerous traps. So we decided not to sign it and to leave Parliament. And because I was the initiator of this and author of the declaration of the hunger-strikers, I consulted a couple of times Mr. Dogan and some other men from the MRF leadership. Their reply was "we regard you as the right ones; the greater part of the UDF deputies, about one hundred, who said they will sign the Constitution, are wrong. Yet, it is politically embarrassing to leave the Parliament at the same time as you. We are going to wait a couple of weeks before following suit." And they did it.

AM: They did it later.

JV: Indeed. Of those one hundred deputies from the UDF who stayed and became signatories to the Constitution, you will not find any person who is in Parliament at the present moment [1993].

* * *

The opposition side at the Grand National Assembly

Politics as the art of the possible. The leader of the former Communists, Alexander Lilov, is engaged in discussion with UDF leader Zhelyu Zhelev during the Grand National Assembly.

When the work of the Grand National Assembly was complete, a large number of its members refused to sign the new Constitution. I asked Ivan Glushkov about the sources of the internal disunity within the UDF during these days. When I interviewed him in October 1993, Glushkov was the leader of the Christian-Agrarian Party. At the Roundtable Talks he served as a leader of the BZNS (the Agrarian Union or Agrarian Party, as it is sometimes called), and later he was an elected member and deputy speaker of the Grand National Assembly.[6] Explaining first that there was relative unity within the UDF during the days of the Roundtable Talks, Glushkov went on to say:

> This happened during the Grand National Assembly. A couple of months after the start of the Grand National Assembly, disunity began to show.
>
> **AM:** What were the first signs? In your capacity as a deputy speaker can you recall the first signs of disunity within the ranks of the UDF?
>
> **IG:** I believe that the first differences that became prominent had their formal cause in issues surrounding the Constitution. But the real cause was that part of the democratic forces wanted a harder, more definite and decisive stand against the Bulgarian Socialist Party. To put this clearer—this was the time when the UDF split. The divisive issue was whether it should accept some kind of "collaboration approach" toward the Bulgarian Socialist Party. The justification for this approach was to complete the work on the Constitution. But in the process it would be necessary to make more concessions. The other faction stood for a tougher stand and was against any concessions to the Communists.
>
> **AM:** Yes, but within the framework of the debate about the Constitution, how was a more rigid line manifested? What did it look like? If a person was more anti-Communist than someone else, what position would that person take on specific constitutional provisions that would distinguish him . . . ?
>
> **IG:** These differences took initially the form of sharp debates within the UDF and its parliamentary group. . . .

AM: I see, but I want to know what specific issues about the Constitution, for example . . .

IG: . . . I would say there was no specific issue around which the disagreements were concentrated. Simply the UDF, the UDF's leadership, and the hard-liners within the UDF insisted upon the inclusion of certain clauses in the Constitution. These suggestions were absolutely unacceptable to the Bulgarian Socialist Party. Finally, these disagreements took their most outright form with the decision of thirty-nine MPs, in fact there were about forty, from the UDF's parliamentary group. They decided to leave the Grand National Assembly and to go on a hunger strike. . . .

The Bulgarian Socialist Party had an absolute majority in the Grand National Assembly. But the BSP was lacking the required qualified majority (of two-thirds of the total vote) to ratify the Constitution. So if the UDF parliamentary group had stayed united until the end, the Constitution could not have entered into force. The Agrarian Party [BZNS] had sixteen votes. If, theoretically, they are added to the votes of the BSP, the overall votes would not have been enough to make up a qualified majority. And yet in the Grand National Assembly, the BZNS voted more often, I would say almost constantly with the UDF.

AM: Well, that is interesting, but I do not yet understand the specific issues they were arguing about . . . I understand the general philosophy of the opposition to the Communist Party. . . . Let me give you an example . . .

IG: . . . At the time one of the basic issues discussed was the guilt of the Communist functionaries for the last forty-five years of rule. I am not a jurist, and so it is difficult for me to create a proper formula for this. The other reason that motivated the UDF hardliners to behave so resolutely was our conviction that the Communists wanted to pass the Constitution and then to treat the Grand National Assembly as an ordinary parliament for quite a long time, where they will keep their majority.

AM: So it did, I mean, the Grand National Assembly tackled parliamentary questions.

IG: . . . The hard-liners in the UDF and two or three BZNS deputies, including myself, insisted that the Grand National Assembly disband itself right after it passes the Constitution and to have general elections for an ordinary National Assembly within a two- to three-month period. This was the substance of the demand of those from the UDF who left Parliament. They did not sign the Constitution and declared they would not be back in Parliament until the GNA makes a decision to disband itself, and to set a date for general elections in the fall.

AM: Did some hunger strikers—the thirty-nine—did they believe that a referendum should be held on the Constitution?[7]

IG: Yes, the referendum question was advanced because there had been much talk that the new Constitution was undemocratic, a pro-Communist one. So we put the issue, which was quite logical, to the National Assembly: well, we argued, if some claim that the new Constitution is pro-Communist and others maintain that it is a democratic one—although to be fair, they have not read it yet—it is wise to have a ratification referendum two to three months after the Constitution's vote in the Grand National Assembly. Let the people express their wish. That will put all the speculation to an end. But the Communists were definitely against this idea. They knew the new Constitution would stabilize their economic power established during 1990 and 1991. So the day of the Constitution's entry into force was a celebration day for them.

AM: Let me summarize your point of view and see if I have it right. The Communist Party wanted to survive into the future. The UDF—some UDF leaders—agreed to allow them to continue to exist. So an agreement was made—either formally or informally.

IG: The existence or nonexistence of the Bulgarian Socialist Party was not at the time considered an issue. The Communist Party was keen to assure for itself first of all to go scot-free for all the crimes committed during the past forty-five years; and, second, it wanted to further its existence, and by this I mean not just its survival but its good prospects.

AM: But some UDF leaders went along with this wish to allow for a peaceful transition. And there were some of you, such as yourself, who were against this accommodation.

IG: Exactly.

AM: What else could you have done, given the fact that the Communist Party, the Bulgarian Socialist Party, had the power, they had the military, the militia?

IG: Nobody questioned the peaceful character of the transition. But we considered—and I am still convinced about this—Bulgaria made a mistake by electing in 1990 a Grand National Assembly, whose task it was to create a new constitution. Even now the leaders of the UDF are unable to explain to their followers where this idea to create a Grand National Assembly originated. Actually this idea was proposed by Mr. Stoyan Ganev, who served then as an [UDF constitutional] expert. Mr. Stoyan Ganev became later a UDF leader, and the party he founded—the United Christian-Democratic Center—is still a member of the UDF coalition. During Mr. Philip Dimitrov's government [1991–92] he was appointed Bulgaria's foreign minister, and in this capacity he chaired the 1992–93 session of the General Assembly of the United Nations. Meanwhile, he went out of favor and was expelled from the UDF and from his own party. Currently, [October 1993] he is in the USA and does not seem keen to come back. Nevertheless, some UDF moderates that survived the purges so far, or those who are already out of the coalition, place their hopes in him as a "savior" of the "original" and "true" UDF. Out of the blue, during the Roundtable, sometime in the middle of the discussions, Stoyan Ganev began to promote the idea that we should have a Grand National Assembly at any cost and that its mission should be to create a new constitution. I still believe that we would have gone much faster toward democratization and market reform if we had spent our time in the Grand National Assembly creating laws necessary for the transition instead of creating the Constitution. Such laws were really essential; for example: taxation laws, laws regulating the structural changes [in the economy]—we still do not have them—or privatization laws. In other words, we should have acted like Hungary and the Czech

Republic. They kept their old constitutions and altered their provisions to such an extent, that, as the anecdote goes, the only thing left from the Hungarian Socialist Constitution is the name of the capital city, Budapest. They did not waste a year or more producing a new constitution. Some people here say it would have been fatal to carry on with the old, Zhivkov Constitution. But we could have changed a number of articles in it. Formally, it looked very democratic. We should have concentrated our efforts on changing the system, and we should have taken the power from the Communists by means of the law. And by this we would have sped up the transition of property ownership from state to private. This process is still deadlocked.

AM: You present a very interesting interpretation. . . . It occurs to me that at least one very important constitutional change was made by using the old constitutional system—that is, the Party's leading role in society. This proposal was introduced in the National Assembly in December [1989], and a month later it became part of Bulgarian law. Is that true?

IG: We should have changed many more articles in that way!

AM: Yes, I see. Let me ask another question: Are there any provisions in the current Constitution that you find obnoxious? In other words, are there any provisions you think should not be there?

IG: I do not regard it as a grave political mistake, but this Constitution has one fundamental weakness. When on the occasion of the second anniversary of the Constitution I participated in a TV program along with the current minister of justice Mr. Petar Kornajev, who was at the time a UDF (leading) member, I said that the basic deficiency of this Constitution is the lack of balance among the three powers and that their prerogatives are not clearly defined.

When we started work on the Constitution we invited a couple of times Professor Robert Baninter from France, who is a prominent constitutionalist, chairman of the Constitutional Council, and former minister of justice under President Mitterand. He drew our attention to the issue of separation of powers, placing special importance on the need for the precise prerogatives of each of the three powers. Events since the enactment of the Constitution reveal that there are a great many ambiguities, omissions, and inconsistencies in our Constitution. Almost every case involving a constitutional matter must be referred to the Constitutional Court for a ruling.

I will give you a very illustrative example to show you how far the Bulgarian Constitution is from perfection. The chapter stipulating the prerogatives of the president states there is a president and vice president. Under certain circumstances, like death or impeachment, when the president is unable to execute his functions, the vice president takes over until the end of the given mandate. But there is not a single word about what would happen if the vice president resigns from office; it does not say there would be an election for vice president—such a provision is not logical, by the way, but it should be stated clearly. When Mrs. Blaga Dimitrova resigned [as vice president], there was much speculation in the mass media and by politicians: some said that President Zhelev should resign too; others retorted: no, he has to stay until the end of his mandate; and a third view insisted that only elections for vice president are necessary. I do not think there are such stupid things in the U.S. Constitution!

AM: [Laughter] We had a similar problem until very recently. But your point is very interesting. Are you suggesting that political questions are being framed in legal terms—and this may not be good for the political life of the community. Is the political energy of the nation being sapped with these legal constitutional questions, rather than debating the substantive policy questions facing society?

IG: I want to state once more my earnest belief that if we had used that year in the National Assembly to pass, say, ten laws: for taxation, for quick privatization, for a national audit chamber, et cetera, we would have achieved more to change the system and to achieve privatization. As I already have said, the Constitution, which is the basic law of the country, does not change the system. If the system has to change this should be done by laws . . .

* * *

Ivan Glushkov, vice chairman of the Grand National Assembly and leader of the Christian Agrarian Party

Ivan Glushkov expresses a perspective shared by many of those I interviewed on all sides of the issues. Despite the painstaking care taken by those at the National Roundtable Talks to work out an accommodation between the inheritors of the former Communist Party and their opponents, suspicion and fear of the possible motives and intentions of the former Communists made cooperation among the deputies to the Grand National Assembly very difficult to achieve. Bulgarian Socialist Party leaders' support of the new Constitution was a red flag for some deputies; it served as a cue to oppose the new document. Perhaps they did so reactively, that is, without careful analysis of the specific issues. They behaved in this way because they did not want to think of themselves or for others to think of them as guilty of collaborating with the enemy. These people believed then and many remain convinced that the proper course was to severely punish the Communists for their past misdeeds. Like others I interviewed, Glushkov has some specific criticisms of the Constitution as finally ratified. But none of the criticisms are fundamental. His harshest criticism is that the GNA wasted its time by drafting a Constitution, time that could have been better spent writing new laws that might have facilitated a more rapid transition to democracy and a market economy.

Accomplishments of the GNA

Though critics may be correct that the GNA's work on the Constitution delayed efforts to legislate dramatically in important areas of public life, it is erroneous to conclude that the assembly accomplished very little. From the GNA's start on July 10, 1990, until September 20, 1991, just before the new general elections, deputies introduced more than five hundred bills in their complete or draft form. Ninety-seven of them became law, twenty-nine were withdrawn, and the rest did not receive approval from parliamentary committees or were not subjected to a vote at the plenary sessions because they were too controversial. The GNA issued another two hundred decisions, declarations, and appeals; seven of the twelve parliamentary declarations dealt with international or internal crises.[8]

Though it is true Bulgaria was slow to move to a market economy because it failed to embrace the Western economic recommendation of shock therapy, it is incorrect to conclude that the GNA did nothing with respect to this matter. The GNA enacted on January 9, 1991, the Law for Accountancy; on February 22, 1991, it took the first legal step toward the restitution of the land to its former owners with the passage of the Law for Land Ownership and of the Use of Agricultural Land. On May 2, 1991, the GNA passed the Law for the Protection of Competition. On May 16, 1991, it passed a Trade Law, and a day later it enacted the Law on Foreign Investments. On June 6, 1991, the GNA enacted the Law for the Bulgarian National Bank. And on July 19, 1991, it enacted the Law for the Co-operative Societies.[9]

The GNA passed other laws important for establishing a new political infrastructure. These include the Law for the Ministry of Interior (July 3, 1991), the Law for the Constitutional Court (July 30, 1991), the Law for Administrative and Territorial Restructuring of the Country (August 12, 1991), the Law for Election of the Peoples' Deputies, Municipal Councilors, and Mayors (August 15, 1991), the Law for the Supreme Judicial Council (August 21, 1991), the Legal Profession Law (September 12, 1991), and the Law for Electing the President and Vice-President of Bulgaria (September 17, 1991).[10]

The GNA also ratified some important international agreements. Ministers gave answers to nearly five hundred parliamentary questions in response to concerns about the government's policy. The Grand National Assembly also established a half dozen study commissions.[11]

Thus, critics must concede the GNA enacted important legislation, and by doing so, progress was made toward building a more democratic nation. Yet, it is also true, as a matter of logic, that greater progress toward a democratic and capitalist future might have been possible if the GNA had not directed its attention toward creating a new constitution. Obviously, time and energy saved in one area might be applied to another. But that conclusion assumes that the UDF reformers had the votes to bring about change. Because the BSP had a majority of the seats, such a scenario appears improbable. At the same time, one might hold the view that the new Constitution was an important step toward guaranteeing a democratic future for Bulgaria; time spent on this project was well worth the delay. Petar Dertliev is a person holding such a view. Some Bulgarians call him the father of the Constitution. My interview with him reveals a hopeful person with confidence that Bulgarians are capable of willing democracy into existence. Sitting in his office as the leader of the Social Democratic Party, we discussed a wide range of issues that surround the transition to democracy.[12]

AM: Thank you for this interview. It is a particular honor for me because it is my understanding that you are a longtime dissident.

PD: . . . Half a century . . .

AM: Half a century.

PD: . . . More than half a century. Plus ten years in prisons and camps. . . .

AM: Why do you think the leaders of the Bulgarian Communist Party were willing to participate rather rapidly in changing its leading role in the society? That is, in adopting the Article 1 constitutional amendment that eliminated the Party's leading role? Why do you think the Party was forthcoming in that respect?

PD: The Communist Party changed much during the fifty years of its rule. When they took power, they were almost entirely illiterate revolutionaries. But gradually the necessities of life made them reliant upon professional, well-qualified people for positions in the government. And because of changes in Russia brought about through Gorbachev's perestroika, the Bulgarian Communists realized that the era of communism is nearing its end, and if it is to preserve its influence it needs to adapt. . . . Of the socialist parties all around the world, formerly the so-called socialist camp, I believe the Bulgarian Communist Party was, perhaps, best able to adapt to the new social changes. It was very quick to declare its rejection of the communist ideas and adopted, at least formally, democratic and even some social democratic values. Of course, if you have lived with a totalitarian heart and mentality for quite a long time, it is not easy to become a democrat overnight. They were successful in keeping united the old hardcore Bolshevik guard, and the Party's intellectuals who know much about democracy, the market economy, and so on. This explains why they participated at the Roundtable with us, although not very enthusiastically, in the first democratic changes.

They perfectly applied in practice the English proverb: If you can't stop the train, jump on it. They realized that communism was doomed. So, they decided to get on the train and take it. And they have been successful to a great extent. In the first place the Party nomenklatura established itself among the newborn [Bulgarian] capitalists, thanks to its national and international connections and positions in the economy and in the society generally. Along with these advantages, they were allowed to adapt to the new social philosophy, and they did not oppose our demands for democratic change. Indeed, they created obstacles, some of them did not want to retreat, but this has never been a life-or-death issue. I am speaking about the period when I was one of the UDF leaders and the Social Democratic Party was a leading force in the coalition. They [the Communists] accepted many ideas of social democracy as a way of mimicry.

AM: To maintain themselves in power?

PD: To keep their influence over the poor, the common people. Because of their willingness to institute democratic reforms we agreed to work with them—without compromising—and we achieved democratic changes at the Roundtable, which were incorporated in the [new] Constitution. The documents we signed, including the Constitution itself, have no communist features at all. The Constitution is based on the example of all modern European constitutions: separation of powers and balance between them and guarantees for their proper function. Like every other human deed, the new Constitution is not perfect. Moreover, everyone has his own subjective judgment about what is good or bad about the Constitution: the president wants more power for himself, while the National Assembly wants this power too . . . But on balance, I consider this Constitution a good one. And one of the greatest achievements of the Social Democratic Party is that it was able to convince most UDF deputies at the time to stay in Parliament and to create this Constitution. There was an opposite opinion that if Communists participate in the creation of the Constitution it is undoubtedly a Communist one. But even now it is impossible to have a Constitution bypassing them because we need a two-thirds majority. But these claims against our involvement in the making of the Constitution were simply a demagogy born of party partisanship. The basic reason for such behavior was the monarchists' desire to bring the old Turnovo Constitution back.

AM: Pardon me, may I interrupt with a short question? Did the constitutional provision that was eventually drafted declare Bulgaria a republic?

PD: . . . yes.

AM: . . . and that was a deliberately antimonarchist action or was it also a matter of eliminating "the people's democracy" phrase in the old Constitution? That is, was it a two-edged sword that applied not only to the monarchy—it prohibited monarchy and at the same time it prohibited the old form of Communism? Was that the thinking in the first place?

PD: We eliminated the idea of people's democracy straightaway at the Roundtable. At the time when we were creating the Constitution, the monarchists were not brave enough to come out in the open. This subtle monarchism began to manifest its true nature only very recently. The Turnovo Constitution, which they want to restore, is a document created right after the liberation of Bulgaria from the Turks. And it represents a marvelous achievement of the Bulgarian free spirit. But it contains an internal contradiction due to the timing of its creation. On one hand, there are guarantees for basic human rights, while on the other hand, it constitutes a monarchist regime; and all three monarchs, who reigned over Bulgaria [since its liberation] infringed those particular rights. I am republican, a bloody republican. [We laugh.]

AM: Let me ask you about tactics. There were mass demonstrations in November and December [1989] and, I believe, in January [1990]. The Communist Party objected to these demonstrations. And when one reads the news reports, one gets the feeling that these mass demonstrations were orchestrated by the UDF or the opposition forces in general.

PD: You see, the public mood after the change [November 10, 1989] was very enthusiastic, and the people expected great improvement in their lives. I do not think I will ever see again such an impressive mass rally as the one I saw two days before the June 1990 election. Calling it a mass rally cannot describe it fully. It was a euphoric gathering, a festival of joy and happiness. Words are weak to express the feeling. But the immaturity of our political life, on one hand, and the communist infiltration, on the other, brought gradually a split within UDF ranks. In the end, all the founding formations of the UDF were thrown out by an internal coup.

Nevertheless, we believe that we fulfilled our historic mission. The fact is that whatever confrontation may occur or political battles that might be fought, now and forever, they [the Communists] must stay within the law. That which has happened in Russia, in Romania, or in Yugoslavia cannot happen in Bulgaria. I consider myself a patriot. Therefore, I consider it my duty to preserve tolerance toward ethnic minorities.

For example, here, in this place tonight, there will be a meeting, among others, with representatives of the Movement for Rights and Freedoms. I have prepared for the occasion a draft charter for civil peace and rights, and I believe that the twelve formations, which are going to meet together, will approve it, although with some minor alterations. The basic principles in this charter are defined as follows: patriotism means in the first place peacekeeping; the creation of a national culture mostly by the three main ethnic groups and not just by the dominant Bulgarian ethnic group; nonuse of religion for political purposes—which by the way is laid out in the Constitution; change in the national consciousness by force of any person or social group is unacceptable. You know that in 1986 there began a forceful "Bulgarization" of the Turks by changing their names. Well, you also know, perhaps, that in 1945–46 there was a similar forceful "Macedonization" [assimilation] of the Bulgarians who lived in Pirin's Macedonia to please Stalin and Tito.

AM: Yes.

PD: Currently all communist parties have changed from national nihilism to national communism.[13] They all are fiercely nationalistic, hateful of all other nations and ethnic groups. I do not think I need to clarify this point. That is why we are so proud, I am particularly proud because this Constitution has been named after me; my political opponents call it "the Dertliev Constitution."

AM: Yes, I heard that.

PD: This was a very great political battle. Many people believed that we had created the Constitution by compromising with the Communists. So, suddenly as one of the much loved leaders in the country I was denigrated as a person deeply hated by a great many people. But I consider the interests of the country superior to the interests of any one person. I have served this idea and my people for over sixty years, and nothing can make me become a traitor to the interests of this country as I understand them. It sounds too pathetic, but it is true. Now, after we [the Social Democratic Party] lost the second election [in October 1991], we are looking forward to the third one [December 1994] and hope we will be successful this time. A lot of things have changed. Many people have begun to think on their own and with their heads, not from their hearts. So I believe we will win. But whatever the outcome, I am pretty sure we avoided the worst thing that could have happened in this country. For there is nothing worse than a civil war.

AM: I do not want to divert our attention from discussing the Constitution. But you raise a very interesting issue with the declaration on civil peace that you will be proposing tonight. Is there any provision in your working document to integrate Turkish ethnic minority people into positions of political power? For example, to make more of them judges? Would such actions help to alleviate the feeling that members of the Turkish ethnic minority are out of the mainstream of Bulgarian life?

PD: Let us look at the problem from two different points of view: my personal opinion . . . and with respect to the realities in the country as they now exist. Bulgaria spent five centuries under the Turkish yoke, and it is very easy to create negative attitudes against the Turkish people. Additionally, fascists and the far right always base their propaganda on certain visual symbols like some minority groups: Jews, Arabs, etc. In Bulgaria, the group that can be exploited for such purposes is the Turks, the common people. This fact is going to be exploited by the Communists [BSP] at the next general election. Unfortunately, I suspect that the UDF may be tempted to use this cause too. The Left and the Right both will play that card.

AM: The nationalist's card?

PD: Yes. Currently, the ethnic party of the Turks [the Movement for Rights and Freedoms] balances the political life of the country, as well as in Parliament. That is why I openly say to them that in the name of the future and preservation of peace in this country that they should not push too fast to get certain rights. By the way, I regard their desire to press for rights a natural one. It is clear to me that sooner or later it is inevitable to have Turkish judges, military officers, political statesmen, businessmen, and so on. From my perspective, which I believe you also share, it does not create a problem to have a Gypsy, a Jew, or a Turk as a prime minister or president. As our greatest revolutionary Vassil Levsky used to say, "We belong to our time and it leaves its hallmark upon every one of us." We all are children of our time, and the wisdom of the politician is to know how to push things forward to the limit, while also avoiding potential collisions. It is in this context that the rights you just mentioned exist. It is my contention that we, Bulgarians, are the champions of human rights in the Balkans. You will not find such support in either Greece or Turkey, nor in Yugoslavia and Romania. Well, it is quite possible that we represent an imperfect model of a tolerant polyethnic society. Nevertheless, it functions successfully.

AM: I am reminded of the Spanish transition. Do you think Bulgaria resembles the Spanish transition to democracy?

PD: Yes, but not fully. I think the Spanish were wiser than we. Of course, they had in their history a bloody civil war—this happened at the time when I was actively involved in political life [as a youth]. In fact, in Bulgaria the great confrontations and the bloody events were, so to say, the result of foreign influence. There were atrocities, labor camps, and [political] prisons, but there was no civil war. And the curious thing was that the two organizations that suffered most from the Communist regime are the Agrarian Union and the Social Democratic Party. We are anti-Communists, but simultaneously we are for a sensible and prudent transition. The most fanatical anti-Communists now are the former Communists, because they want to make a career of being anti-Communist. Some people cannot understand why those of us who suffered and lost their comrades behave in this way. It is because, as a teacher of mine used to say, suffering makes strong people wise and breaks the weak ones. We have suffered too much, and because of this we do not want revenge to create a new wave of terror and vengeance.

AM: I mention the Spanish example because, as you know, from a theoretical perspective, one would not expect democracy to occur in Bulgaria. Theoreticians argue that you need first a middle class, you need a strong economy, you need functional political parties, and so on. But in Bulgaria you are going about building democracy differently. By creating a constitution, you are coaxing democratic or civil society into existence.

PD: I think that the thesis for the existence of a middle-class as an absolute prerequisite for democracy has at least fifty different formulations. I tried to find the true answer by asking many of my friends, economists, and every one of them has given me a different answer. It remains unclear whether being middle class requires the possession of certain material things and, if that is the case, of what kind. If you need to possess a house to qualify as middle class, then there is no other class in Bulgaria than the middle class. If the criterion is the ownership of the means of production, then there are relatively few owners.[14] Our social democratic idea is to combine two things: personal richness with the ownership of the means of production during a period of mass privatization. Namely, social privatization will turn a great many people into shareholders and owners in cooperative societies.

AM: What is your interpretation of why certain members of the Grand National Assembly participated in a hunger strike?

PD: I have two points of view. I am a doctor. So one explanation is as a doctor. The other one is that this hunger strike is just a funny or perhaps a tragic event. Because I cannot imagine that in a developed society this kind of reaction might exist. What was the reason? The reason was that the monarchists cannot declare that they do not want to have a republican Constitution. That is the first explanation. The second one: it was the involvement of KGB agents, the Bulgarian KGB. The third one: there were some Communists, former Communists, who wanted to create a good political image by presenting themselves as fighters against Communism.

AM: By claiming that the Constitution is not anti-Communist enough?

PD: But, see, one of our parties whose leaders were going on a hunger strike because of the Constitution—the Radical Democratic Party—they were very proud that by the second reading of the proposed new Constitution the document was very close to their own proposals. . . . It is all demagogy. They wanted to make political profit, but they did not succeed. Why? Because of the first law of Pavlov's dogs.

* * *

Petar Dertliev confirms the observations of others concerning the motivations of the leaders on both sides of the Communist/anti-Communist split in Bulgarian politics. First, the reform leaders within

Petar Dertliev, father of the 1991 Constitution, arguing a point in favor of the new basic law during the Grand National Assembly

the old Communist Party are sophisticated persons. They represent a new generation of leaders who, unlike most of their predecessors, are well educated and widely traveled, both within the Eastern bloc nations and in the West. They understood that with the fall of the Soviet Union and the new openness it would be impossible to hold back the democratic tide. They willingly embraced a new democratic order with the knowledge that if they were part of the process of change they had a good chance to shape events and to preserve a place for themselves in the new order. As revealed by many persons I interviewed, including BSP members, this motivation was no secret to any of the participants in the constitution-making process. Secondly, many anti-Communists were relatively unsophisticated in the ways of democracy. They were at a tactical disadvantage because many of them had no experience in parliamentary systems. They were the radicals of their day. They took their mandate directly from the masses in the streets into the committee rooms and halls of the Parliament building. Leaders such as Petar Dertliev and Ginio Ganev insisted that the exercise of creating a new constitution was an important learning experience in the ways and means of democracy.

Resulting Democratic Institutions

The post-Communist Constitution ratified on July 12, 1991, contains all the requisite features for its appropriate labeling as a democratic document. It is a republican document because proponents were able to defeat the monarchists. It allows for competing political parties, and it discards the Communist notion that one party should lead. It contains the principle of separation of powers with a strong parliament and a relatively weak president, and it establishes a strong judiciary, including a Constitutional Court designed to guard against backsliding into totalitarianism.

Though the Constitution is imperfect in several respects, especially how it treats political parties based upon ethnic or religious foundations, it contains methods for working through these problems by the trial-and-error method of constitutional politics. In the years since the ratification of the Constitution, many challenges have been met successfully; these include preserving the right of minorities to form political parties, protecting the judiciary from institutional attacks, and supporting the concept of rights in private property.

By enacting a new Constitution, Bulgarians created a basis for accepting the party class in the new order, and in the process avoided civil war. With this accomplishment, Bulgarians are in the position to avoid repeating their own history; it is a history riddled with violence and vendetta.

The enlightened self-interest of the leaders of the Bulgarian Socialist Party operated to convince them that their future survival depended upon a new democratic form of government that forced them to compete with opposing forces for the votes of the people. Given the alternative, there is little wonder that the leaders of the BSP participated in the creation of a new constitution. At the same time, opponents of the former Communist rulers sought the avoidance of civil war while also guaranteeing a democratic future. They agreed to accept the possibility that the former Communists might retain power by winning elections. In fact, after the BSP won a majority of the seats in the Grand

Josif Petrov, former dissident political prisoner and the oldest deputy (man in the white shirt), salutes his colleagues after the approval of the new Constitution by the Grand National Assembly

National Assembly, their democratic opponents resolved to continue the process of democratization. They cooperated with the BSP in drafting a new constitution, despite suffering disunity from within their own ranks. This was done with the faith that they can at some point dislodge the BSP from control of the government. Indeed, the combined anti-BSP forces did just that at the next general election, only to lose control of the government a year later and a general election the following year. Many opposition leaders who participated as GNA deputies suffered defeat at the polls. Parties led by such luminaries as Dertliev, Ganev, and Simeonov were unable to garner the requisite 4 percent of the votes necessary for seats in the National Assembly. Thus, the voters relegated some important architects of Bulgaria's Constitution to the sidelines of a political system they are responsible for bringing into place.

Finally, it is worth noting that although it may be a necessary condition, all the hard work that goes into creating a constitution will not guarantee a continuing democratic system. Bulgaria's leaders of all ideological stripes know it is necessary to work at the process by institutionalizing democratic procedures and inculcating democratic attitudes. It is a matter of coaxing civil society into a stable and vigorous existence. Ginio Ganev's insistence that "automatic voting" must be eschewed in favor of full debate manifests the importance of creating democratic habits, which in turn contributes to the legitimacy of the system as a whole. Then too, Petar Dertliev made it his business to encourage the type of dialogue necessary to create and sustain democratic habits. Long after the GNA had finished its business and governments had come and gone, the father of the Constitution convened in October 1993 a meeting of a variety of political parties and movements to discuss how the nation should in the future treat ethnic minorities. Moreover, as the parliamentary system is institutionalized and the roles of the president, the Council of Ministers, and the judiciary are better understood, the concept of constitutionalism will become more deeply embedded within the psyche of the body politic. Though this process is fraught with peril, the prospects are encouraging. In part 3 of this volume I explicate that history through the first few months in 1997.

PART III

Consolidation Politics: Parliament and Interinstitutional Conflict

We are all children of our time, and the wisdom of the politician is to know how to push things forward to the limit, while also avoiding potential collisions.

—PETAR DERTLIEV

8

Bulgaria's Parliament and Democracy as a Work in Progress

THERE IS A WIDELY shared view that democracy in Eastern Europe and the republics of the former Soviet Union is likely to be short-lived. This pessimism is borne of the political theory that, in the first place, these republics lack the prerequisites necessary for democracy. Second, the consequences of economic dislocation owing to the transition from command to market economies militate for a return to the certitude of the totalitarian days. Therefore, given their premises, the naysayers persuasively argue the movement toward democracy in this region of the world is not only theoretically impossible, it most certainly cannot be sustained. This view doggedly persists despite the reality of democracies in these places and despite the fact that in the short run these formerly communist states have survived difficult trials.

The obvious bankruptcy of development theory seems to have little impact on our collective thinking. For example, Howard J. Wiarda, in his leading textbook on comparative politics, expresses the view that while no one doubts the end of authoritarianism in southern Europe and the permanency of democracy there, we cannot be sure for Eastern Europe and Russia. He writes: "In societies lacking consensus, lacking well-established institutions, lacking civic culture, but with a plethora of severe social and economic problems, almost any outcome is possible. Uncertain and potentially violent means can yield a great variety of ends."[1] Adam Przeworski insists: "The durability of the new democracies will depend . . . not only on their institutional structure and the ideology of the major political forces, but to a large extent on their economic performance. Profound economic reforms must be undertaken if there is to be any hope that the deterioration in living conditions experienced by many nascent democratic countries will ever cease."[2] Samuel P. Huntington asks: "How long?" Just because there are free and fair elections after years without them, that does not mean democracy will endure. He asks: "Do the new systems consolidate or collapse?"[3]

The skeptics fail to consider adequately two important points. First, where there exists a negotiated agreement among the major competing forces in society, as in Bulgaria and other east European venues, democracy became a practical reality upon the consummation of the agreement to change. Second, though Bulgaria—and other similarly situated states—is undergoing difficult economic times, there is insufficient reason to conclude that Bulgarians will revert to a command economy with totalitarian controls. Rather, they are likely to continue the trend toward a market economy because there is no real alternative. The realities of international economic life require these states to find their place within the world capitalist order. The only real choice is how rapidly they are willing to progress down this path, not whether they will take such a course.

So then, Giuseppe Di Palma's orientation is preferable. The glass is not half empty. It is half full! With the forging of agreements among the dominant forces in society for democratic procedures, the transition from totalitarianism to democracy is already complete.[4] This situation is much different than where no agreement exists in the mutual self-interest of the leading factions in society—for example, a violent coup d'état or the intervention of an outside power imposing a new order. In Bulgaria, on the other hand, the participants at the National Roundtable Talks and the Grand National Assembly agreed on the rules for an enduring democracy. But is the agreement of the sort achieved in Bulgaria a sufficient condition for the maintenance of democracy? Slightly at variance with Di Palma's minimalist view, my answer is that the proof is in the practice. If Bulgarians are practicing the fine art of democracy, then indeed the consolidation of democracy is taking place. If this is the case, there is every reason to believe that Bulgarians will not backslide into the dark days of their totalitarian past.

The emphasis is on the word *practice.* Democracy is about the observance of procedural norms wherein the rules of the political game are followed. In such an environment, the process affords sets of candidates a regular constitutional opportunity to have their ideas enacted into law, and the voters may express their policy desires through elections. At the same time, rights of the losers in policy debates are respected and permanent minorities are afforded protection from the potential tyranny of the majority. With every passing day, democracy proves superior to dictatorships of all sorts. As Di Palma states: "It . . . is superior as a system to curb oppression; to reassert, as a matter of self-interest, mutual coexistence; to reconstitute a community; and to reestablish a sense of personal worth and public dignity."[5] Though the way certain crises have been resolved is cause for concern, there is insufficient justification to believe that a return to Bulgaria's totalitarian past is imminent. Admittedly, if citizens are to maintain their democracy they must work at it. The possibility always exists that democracy may be lost to forces demanding order.

New democracies should not be judged in terms of the achievement of substantive ends, including, for example, the achievement of a high standard of living and the elimination of human misery. If that is the case, few democracies around the world would pass the test. It must be granted that in democracies undergoing movement from a command to a market economy there will be unemployment, crime, and other afflictions. And in contemporary Eastern Europe, there is plenty to go around. Nonetheless, these states are democratic. Democracy is not a magic bullet: it cannot promise instant material progress. But as Di Palma puts it, "democracy has gained dramatically for delivering something else: mutual security in diversity."[6]

Since they agreed to the rules at the National Roundtable Talks and the Grand National Assembly, Bulgarians have an in-principle agreement that they will conduct their affairs in a democratic fashion. Thus, the remaining pertinent question is an empirical one: Are the principal political actors abiding by the agreement to conduct their affairs democratically? To discern the answer, it is necessary to investigate whether government institutions are performing in a democratic fashion. If the political institutions display democratic attributes and not antidemocratic tendencies, we can say that Bulgaria is a practicing democratic state and that Bulgarians are living by their democratic agreement.

The legislative arena is the centerpiece of parliamentary democracy. It is the locus of competition among various forces in the struggle for power. Therefore, it is worthwhile to investigate first the practices of Bulgaria's Parliament. Then, in a separate chapter, I investigate how other government institutions, most particularly the Constitutional Court, correct the policymaking institutions when there are impermissible transgressions of constitutional boundaries of authority. I assume that in any democracy with a written constitution there will be conflicts among the various political authorities about the exercise of power. Because the Constitution manifests the principle of separation of powers, there is every reason to anticipate interinstitutional conflict among the various branches of government. Moreover, because Bulgaria's July 1991 Constitution expressly declares its support for human rights, and because the rights of individuals and of the community will at times conflict, how Bulgarians are resolving those issues is central to answering the question. What is revealed in this part of the book are the workings of a democracy put to the test. It is not a perfect picture of efficiency and good order. But democracy everywhere is anything but tidy. The Bulgarian experience is no exception.

Parliamentary Structure and Organization

Bulgaria's July 1991 Constitution vests lawmaking power in a single chamber body called the National Assembly (Narodno Subranie). Consisting of 240 members elected directly by the people through a system of proportional representation, Parliament conducts its business in the picturesque center of Sofia at Narodno Subranie Square. The Parliament building itself is a handsome, architecturally eclectic, rectangular structure located near the imposing National Cathedral and the country's most prestigious university.

Members of the National Assembly may form parliamentary groups by party or political affiliation. The rules of the National Assembly originally required that with certain exceptions at least twenty members are necessary to form a parliamentary group. Later this number was cut in half. At the end of 1995, the number was reduced again to permit parliamentary groups of no fewer than seven members.[7] The National Assembly sits in permanent session but takes time off three times per year. It does not sit during the Christmas holiday season from December 22 until January 10, for ten days during the Easter holidays, or during the month of August. It normally sits on Wednesdays and Thursdays from 3:00 P.M. until 8:00 P.M. and on Fridays from 9:00 A.M. until 1:00 P.M. National Assembly sessions are held in public, excepting circumstances involving important state interests. Though members of the public may be admitted to the building, they require a special pass to do so and must clear armed police and metal detectors. The media are present during sessions, and Bulgarian radio and television frequently carry live broadcasts throughout the country. Private sessions are held upon a motion of the chairman of the National Assembly, upon agreement of one-tenth of the members of Parliament, or upon a request from the Council of Ministers. After listening to the justification for the motion, the National Assembly then takes a vote to decide whether a private session should be held.[8]

The chairman of the National Assembly is elected by a secret ballot on the nomination of any member of the body or by a parliamentary group. The chairperson's formal powers include announcing and assigning bills and other motions to appropriate committees; ensuring that the committees and members of the National Assembly are afforded appropriate working conditions; adopting standing orders for the premises of the National Assembly; administering the budget of the National Assembly; authenticating by his signature the verbatim records of the National Assembly sittings; determining the seating arrangements for the members by parliamentary groups, for the members of the Council of Ministers, and for the president and the vice president; administering the rules of the National Assembly; determining the schedule of positions; and appointing and dismissing the staff of the National Assembly. Assisting the chairman of the National Assembly in the performance of duties is an advisory body consisting of the deputy chairman, the parliamentary group leaders, and the chairs of the various legislative committees.

There are both standing and special committees of the National Assembly. The eighteen standing committees are the Legislative Committee; the Economic Committee; the Budget and Finance Committee; the Administrative Division and Local Government Committee; the Foreign Policy Committee; the National Security Committee; the Labor and Social Security Committee; the Human Rights Committee; the Committee on the Political Parties' Revenue, Expenditure and

Property; the Agricultural Committee; the Committee on Culture; the Committee on Education and Science; the Committee on Religious Affairs; the Committee on Radio and Television; the Environmental Committee; the Health Care Committee; the Youth, Sports, and Tourism Committee; and the Complaints, Suggestions, and Petitions Committee.[9]

No member may belong to more than two committees simultaneously and no member may be a chairman or deputy chairman of more than one standing committee. One is assigned standing committee membership based on proportional representation of the parliamentary groups. The leaders of each of these committees are designated by the members of the National Assembly on an open ballot on the motion of the chairman of the National Assembly in consultation with the leaders of the various parliamentary groups. Each standing committee may contract for expert services to conduct studies and to aid in its task performance. Moreover, the standing committees may create subcommittees and working committees. The Legislative Committee has the special responsibility to consider all bills introduced in the National Assembly and to render an opinion on their compliance with the Constitution.

On those Fridays when the National Assembly is in session, each member of the National Assembly has the right to address no more than two questions at the same sitting to the prime minister or to other members of the Council of Ministers. Notice of the questions is given forty-eight hours in advance. Ministers must answer the questions put to them within fourteen days of their submission. This may be done either orally or in writing. After the question has been answered by the minister to whom it was directed, the asking parliamentarian is entitled to ask two supplementary questions. The answer is undebatable, meaning no reply may be made on it. The member, however, is granted two minutes to indicate whether he or she is satisfied with the response.

Individual deputies lack the staff and research facilities to act independent of their parliamentary group. Also, because Parliament lacks a sufficiently large staff of its own it is in a relatively weak position to challenge the information provided to it by the executive and the bureaucracy. There is no tradition of holding public hearings on pending legislation, and little public discussion about pending legislation, including visible interest group activity of the variety often observed in Western democratic legislatures. Thus, members of Parliament perform their representative function through the medium of parliamentary groups. Within these groups the struggle over issues is negotiated, after which members are expected to dutifully follow the party line regardless of their own views. This is the case despite the constitutional mandate of Article 67(2) that requires deputies to represent their own convictions.[10]

Socialist Party Hegemony

On November 17, 1989, the National Assembly was still safely in the hands of the Communist Party. It elected Petar Mladenov, then secretary general of the Central Committee of the BCP, as president of the State Council of Bulgaria. He replaced Todor Zhivkov, the longtime dictator. In short order, the cabinet underwent a shake-up, replacing several key members. But these changes were criticized as not going far enough. Critics from within and outside the Communist Party called for radical changes, including the abolishment of Article 1 of the Constitution that granted the Communist Party the leading role in society. BCP functionaries hotly debated this matter, and there were several leadership changes in the months following Zhivkov's ouster. For a short period, Georgi Atansov replaced Mladenov as chairman of the Council of Ministers, and Andrey Lukanov succeeded him in early February 1990. Anticipating the inevitability of a multiparty system, the new leadership, anxious to align itself with the forces of change, moved to eliminate the Party's political monopoly. The Politburo and the Council of State also disbanded the Party's propaganda agency within the armed forces.[11] Leaders of the Bulgarian Socialist Party are quick to point out that their party introduced and had legislation enacted to encourage fundamental changes in Bulgaria's economic life. Nora Ananieva, leader of the parliamentary group and member of the Supreme Council of the Bulgarian Socialist Party and a former deputy prime minister, made this point during an October 1993 interview with me.[12] She asserts that the economic program of the Bulgarian Socialist Party was a serious attempt at economic reform. Ananieva said:

This is the so-called Program Lukanov. It was rejected in Parliament not because of its content but because of Lukanov, and because of the former Communist Tomov [Alexander Tomov, then deputy prime minister, responsible for the economy]. Now he is the leader of the intellectually influential centrist Civic Union for the Republic [GOR]. It openly split with the BSP a couple of months ago, but it kept at the same time its parliamentary presence as a separate group. But Program Lukanov was quite good. Today, most of its ideas are the basis of the whole economic reform. If you now read this program three years after it was first presented to Parliament you will see that the whole economic and financial strategy is contained there. We first proposed financial stabilization entailing monetary steps. It was followed by new economic reforms and then privatization. That is why we, the majority party in the Grand National Assembly, voted for not only the new Constitution but also the Law on Privatization. This law was followed by the Foreign Investments Law. . . . and then we proposed agrarian reform that provided property restitution. . . . All of these changes were consistent with our principles. Our ideology was oriented in new directions; but maybe we were coming back to the roots of the Party. Because, you understand, the Party was founded as a social democratic party.

AM: You are saying the party is coming back to what?

NA: Yes, that is very strange. It is coming back to its roots. . . . That is why the Socialist Party has 250,000 members. Within the Party there is a Left, a Center-Left, and a Right. Today in Bulgaria there are four communist parties. All four are official legal entities with papers. But they are not in Parliament! So, if somebody wants to stay with the old ideology and dogma—for example, proletarian dictatorship, leading role of the Party with one-party system, democratic centralism, and centrally planned economy—he has a home in one of the communist parties. That is why we have now 250,000 members in the party. One fourth of the party comes from the former Communist Party. A third of our party are persons who joined after the change. A third of our membership is new. You see all this mixture creates places for different personalities. For example, we have in our parliamentary group Professor Stefan Stoilov, who was

Nora Ananieva. As a member of the Grand National Assembly she was a member of the commission for drafting the constitution. As a leading member of the BSP she has served in a variety of capacities in Parliament.

minister for economic reform in our government. As a professor he was one of the first in Bulgaria to write on the necessity to create a market economy. One of his collaborators was Mr. Ventzeslav Dimitrov from the other side; he is an influential UDF member of Parliament and is currently chairman of the Economic Committee of the National Assembly.

* * *

While it may be true that there is diversity within the former Communist Party, there is ample reason to believe that there are numerous divisions within the ranks of the opposition.

By May 7, 1990, no fewer than fifty-six political parties and movements registered for the national election that was held on June 10 and

17, 1990. These parties included spin-offs from the old Communist Party and many so-called democratic parties with a variety of platforms for changing Bulgarian society.[13]

During Roundtable negotiations, BSP leaders pushed for early elections, ostensibly to hasten reform. Yet, this was also a tactic to capitalize on its political strengths. At first UDF forces resisted this suggestion. Finally, however, it acceded to the wishes of the former Communists—but there is evidence that it also complied with the desire of the official representative of the United States government, Secretary of State James Baker.[14]

To the consternation of the many political novitiates in the opposition, the Bulgarian Socialist Party won the election. In electoral terms, the BSP profited from the mixed electoral system. While it received 47 percent of all votes, it obtained 57 percent of the seats in the National Assembly. There was a sizable divergence between the votes in the large cities where the UDF had its greatest strength and in rural Bulgaria where the former Communists were still strong. Because the BSP was the best organized party, it could garner more seats in the single-member districts than its competitors. Nevertheless, there was also bad news for the BSP. In all thirteen districts where there were runoffs, UDF candidates defeated their BSP opponents.[15]

For the second time since the ouster of Todor Zhivkov, the leader of the Bulgarian Socialist Party and chairman of the Council of Ministers, Andrey Lukanov, was called upon to form a government. Once again, he headed a one-party government. Although Lukanov appealed for a cabinet consisting of representatives from the other political forces, opposition forces refused to join his government. They claimed that the Socialists were too reluctant to accept radical change. There was also a widespread belief that the Socialists had no intention of dismantling existing totalitarian structures.[16]

Consequently, Lukanov's government closely mirrored the previous one. But the prime minister insisted that his government would not be a partisan one. Instead, his government would be guided by the desire to seek national consensus. Lukanov's tenure was short-lived, lasting just a few months before falling on November 28, 1990. Parliamentary and public forces, including the major trade union organizations, created a situation in which the Lukanov government found it difficult to function. The Socialists faced criticism for the activities of the late totalitarian regime because many anti-Communists demanded retribution for past misdeeds. The severe economic conditions common to all of Eastern Europe at the time were also central to the collapse of the Socialist government. Politicians of all persuasions, including Lukanov, thought that a new government, enjoying the support of all the national political forces, was necessary at this juncture.

On December 7, 1990, President Zhelyu Zhelev proposed to the Grand National Assembly a new prime minister. A lawyer of high standing and without a party affiliation, Dimitar Popov was thought an appropriate person to form a coalition government. Many in the Popov cabinet had not served in government before as head of a ministry. Popov named as deputy prime ministers a member of the BSP, a member of the Bulgarian Agrarian Party, and a UDF politician. The task was monumental.

The Grand National Assembly, together with the government, was charged with the responsibility of tackling the nation's problems, including the transition to a market economy, while simultaneously devising a new constitution. As noted earlier, some politicians believe that because constitution-making so preoccupied the attention of the Grand National Assembly, it unduly sacrificed progress toward privatization of the economy and solving the nation's other problems. Yet despite protests, walkouts, and hunger strikes, the Popov government managed to remain in power until after the promulgation of the new Constitution in July 1991 and the successful parliamentary elections held in October 1991.

Meanwhile, the fragile UDF coalition composed of parties and movements with different agendas and flamboyant leaders underwent a crisis. The accusation was made that its charismatic leader Petar Beron was an informer for the secret police in the days of the old regime. The charge came from the forceful leader of the Podkrepa Labor Confederation, Dr. Konstantin Trenchev. Many persons believe that this charge was inaccurate and grossly unfair to the biology professor and respected progeny of a famous academic family. Only a few UDF notables came to Beron's defense, and the result was the effective retirement from politics of one many believe to be a gifted leader. The UDF leadership role then went to Philip Dimitrov, a relatively obscure lawyer in his thirties but a person of enormous energy, passion, and considerable intellect. Dimitrov stressed a desire to hold parliamentary elections as early as May 1991.[17]

UDF Victory

Elections for the new Parliament were held in October 1991. For the first time since World War II, when the Communists seized control of the government, an opposition won an election. Abandoning the mixed system of representation under which the Grand National Assembly was elected, the new election law provides that only parties receiving at least 4 percent of the votes are entitled to representation in Parliament and allots all seats based on proportional representation.

Although thirty-eight parties and coalitions registered for the 1991 parliamentary elections, only three succeeded in entering the National Assembly. The UDF received 34.36 percent of the votes and 110 of the 240 seats. The BSP received 33.14 percent of the votes and 106 of the parliamentary positions. Finally, the Movement for Rights and Freedoms received 7.55 percent of the votes and 24 of the legislative seats.[18]

One result of the 4 percent rule is that the nation was deprived of some of its most gifted leaders. Some losers were instrumental in the National Roundtable Talks and played key roles in the creation of the July 1991 Constitution. This includes Dr. Petar Dertliev, leader of the Bulgarian Social Democratic Party and a person often spoken of as the father of the Constitution. Also defeated were thoughtful public figures such as Petko Simeonov, the leader of the Liberal Party; Milan Drenchev, the head of Nikola Petkov Bulgarian Agrarian Party; and Ivan Glushkov of the Christian-Agrarian Party.

The October 1991 parliamentary election results signaled the rise to political prominence of the Turkish ethnic party, the Movement for Rights and Freedoms. It figures heavily in the ability of the two major parties to form a government. The BSP hoped to keep the MRF off the ballot for the October elections. Its supporters claimed that Article 11(4) of the Constitution forbids political parties of an ethnic, racial, or religious nature. In a series of judicial opinions, the courts permitted the Turkish ethnic-based political organization to remain on the ballot and to participate in the elections.[19]

There was good reason for the BSP to fear the influence of the MRF. The Zhivkov regime attempted to abolish the names of the Gypsy minority in the 1960s and the names of the Rhodope Turks in the 1970s. In the 1980s there were attempts to prohibit the use of the Turkish language in schools and other public institutions, and many ethnic Turks left Bulgaria fearing persecution. This led to the creation of the National Turkish Liberation Movement in 1985. Subsequently, many of its leaders went to jail, including Ahmed Dogan. MRF officials claim that its activities were one reason that the totalitarian regime fell in November 1989. It turns out that the BSP fears were warranted, at least with respect to the creation of the new government after the October 1991 elections. Dogan's parliamentary forces supported the election of a UDF government.

Despite the UDF victory, Philip Dimitrov's government suffered not only BSP opposition but, within a year, serious fractures within UDF ranks. "Center-oriented parties" gradually reappeared within the National Assembly. Various deputies from the three parliamentary groups initially declared themselves independent and then started establishing organizational structures for their own "independent" parties. The UDF had twenty-nine defectors, while the more disciplined BSP and MRF had far fewer. Because of these defections and the attendant lack of party discipline, the UDF lost its parliamentary majority, and the BSP actively supported the clamor for a new cabinet.

I conducted an interview with Stefan Savov, who was the chairman of the National Assembly during the period of the Dimitrov government.[20] When I interviewed Stefan Savov in 1993 he was the floor leader of the UDF and the leader of the Democratic Party in Parliament. I asked this dignified gentleman in his late sixties to explain the sources of factionalism within the UDF. Savov said:

> The first split, or I should put it rather differently, the first big purge in the UDF occurred because of the ratification of the Constitution. . . . This happened during the Grand National Assembly. Then people like Mr. Dertliev, Mr. Drenchev, Mr. Petko Simeonov, who were in fact among the grand figures of the UDF, made moves which led practically to collaboration with the Communists. And they were punished for this political blunder simply by not being elected in the last general election; they received too low a percent of

the votes [below 4 percent], so they could not enter the Parliament. Actually the group that had left the Grand National Assembly—this was our group, the hunger strikers—won the elections by a vote of 35 percent. Now, during the term of this National Assembly there has been, if I may say so, a second dismissal and further division in the UDF. A second splinter group of about twenty-five people emerged in the UDF after our government had been toppled from power. It needs to be pointed out that these were mainly representatives of one very peculiar and ludicrous organization, the so-called Social-Liberal Party. It was created under the name of the Alternative Socialist Party (ASP). It was formed not only by former Communist members but also by secretaries of the former Communist Party.

Well, I would not say there are currently no problems in the UDF. But do not forget there are sixteen parties and other organizations and movements in the coalition. We share many common ideas that unite us in the fight against communism and for democracy. But we also have natural differences. For example, there is a Social Democratic Party in the coalition; it is somewhat left-wing. There is the Democratic Party led by me. It is very close ideologically to Christian-Democratic and Conservative Parties in the West. We are even a member of the International Organization of the Conservative and Christian-Democratic Parties and of the European Democratic Union. . . . In general, I regard our internal divisions as typical for the underdeveloped democracies. But it is also a result of a certain "bad blood" in our national character. It manifested itself even when we had a period of democracy in our political life. The problem is that there are always too many overambitious people who are keen to become leaders. And, of course, this also leads to disunity, friction, and infighting.

AM: As we say in America, there are too many chiefs and not enough Indians.

SS: Yes, that is it! As a friend of mine cracked a joke about another friend of ours: "His party is comprised of himself, his wife, and . . . his briefcase."

AM: Yes, I have that impression. The question of internal disunity is important because theoretically your opponents—the Socialists, namely, the former Communist Party—are in a position to exploit this disunity.

SS: I think, Professor Melone, they do not just exploit certain opportunities, they inspire disunity. The Communists are renowned masters at this.

AM: They are able to create it? Do you mean by persons within the organization . . . or sympathizers?

SS: By using infiltrators, by suggesting certain ideas. The Communists are very tricky; they are masters of conspiracy.

AM: How about turning this analysis on its head, upside down? There are reasons to believe disunity exists within the Communist Party. There is the reform wing led by Lukanov and others and then there are hard-liners. Have the leaders of the UDF tried to exploit that difference?

SS: It is very difficult for us to exploit differences within their ranks. Of course, there are many differences within the Socialist Party. I will give you an example. A month ago we put to a vote at the National Assembly a moratorium on the privatization of the military-industrial complex. There are a great many modern factories in Bulgaria able to produce weapons. Presently in Bulgaria there exists a real Mafia and Mafia-style structures. These people are rich enough and eager to take a chance with privatization to buy those factories. We, therefore, proposed a three-year moratorium. And something very interesting happened. We of the UDF voted with the hard-liners from the Communist Party who supported us. While Mr. Lukanov, who considers himself a liberal, . . . joined forces with the UDF splinters against this moratorium. I believe Lukanov is up to his neck in a number of affairs connected with the smuggling of Communist Party money abroad.

So, there are ways for differences within the Socialist Party to show up. . . . But you need to know I am one of the very few people left from my generation. I had the benefit of knowing what the

> democratic life was like before the imposition of the Communist regime. I come from a family with a political pedigree: my father was a minister in one of the last governments during the second World War and an MP. My grandfather was elected ten times to Parliament; and so on and so forth. Let me tell you: to be a professional politician in Bulgaria is a very risky affair. I have documentary proof that four of the five generations from my family that were involved in politics professionally—some of them as early as the era of the Turkish yoke—have spent part of their lives in prison, including myself. My father was in fact killed by the Communists; he suffered two heart attacks in prison and was sent to a labor camp in Belene. I am saying all this to illustrate that there are few people in the UDF who have the required political experience. It would be fair to admit that we are now in the process of learning the trade of politics. This is the case because during the past forty years there has been no chance whatsoever for normal political life.

* * *

Amidst the disunity and inevitable confusion there were calls for a government of experts that might deal with the nation's problems in a nonpartisan way. And there developed a growing consensus for preterm general elections. Dimitrov's government managed to survive its first no-confidence vote on July 24, 1992. The MPs of the ruling UDF in cooperation with the members of the MRF unanimously voted against the no-confidence motion sponsored by the BSP.[21] Yet, there were perceptible cracks in the UDF armor. A representative of the MRF proclaimed that the UDF should not take its support for granted; it demanded that progress be made toward democratization of Bulgarian society. Further, Stefan Savov, the UDF chairman of the National Assembly, barely survived a vote to oust him from that position.[22] On September 17, the MRF made a motion for his early dismissal. At the same time, President Zhelyu Zhelev, an original UDF leader, expressed dissatisfaction with the UDF leadership in the National Assembly. The rift between the popular Zhelev and members of his own party in Parliament not only became a matter of disagreement about policy and tactics, it also became personal.[23]

In a wide-ranging interview, I asked Philip Dimitrov about the prob-

Andrey Lukanov (left) and Stefan Savov (right) enjoying a cordial moment together. These fierce political opponents, each with a political pedigree, had family members suffer from Fascist and Communist regimes, respectively. They have been unanimous in one thing: the vicious cycle of political vendetta in Bulgaria's history must be broken once and for all.

lems he had with retaining the support of the Turkish minority party and the difficulties he had with maintaining cohesion within the UDF. Sitting in his office at 134 Rakovsky Street, almost one year after his removal as prime minister, Dimitrov said:[24]

> The Freedoms and Rights party of Dogan was endorsed by the UDF. And that is the reason we never competed with them in some regions of the country and we entered into the Parliament with the idea that we had a [working] majority.
>
> **AM:** I see. . . .
>
> **PD:** And this was something that was pretty well understood by the Turkish and Moslem people in the country. That is the reason for their tremendous disappointment today with the activities of their representatives in Parliament.

AM: But since then, of course, the MRF has split with the UDF. I mean, it has gone its own way, and this has caused grave problems with the coalition.

PD: It has not gone its own way. It went the way of the Communists, and this is something that should be absolutely understood. Otherwise, the entire picture of the Bulgarian political situation as it presently exists is absolutely distorted. The point is that, with . . . many excuses, the Movement for Rights and Freedoms as well as the MPs who left the Union of Democratic Forces—both of them inspired by the tremendous efforts on the part of the president [Zhelyu Zhelev]—practically joined the Communist Party in Parliament. You will see if you go through the votes . . . there is a stable majority of 140 or so. Therefore, on all critical points they are voting with the Communists. So, I ask, what sort of going their own way is it?

AM: Well, my only point is that they [MRF] shifted from one allegiance to another presumably in their own self-interest, as they see it.

PD: I would not say that is in the best interest of the Turkish minority. And I hope that the Turkish minority now understands this pretty well. . . .

* * *

The justifications for UDF conduct offered by Stefan Savov and Philip Dimitrov notwithstanding, there is at least one other interpretation of events that requires attention. In a book published in 1994, Charles Moser of the Sofia-based Free Initiative Foundation formally expressed the view of many others with whom I have spoken. Moser is critical of the UDF because of the commission of what he calls "cardinal sins."[25]

First, the UDF expected members of its parliamentary group to take instructions from the UDF's National Coordinating Council (NCC) in the same way that the old Politburo once gave instructions to the BCP organization in Parliament. Predictably, some UDF members

Philip Dimitrov, controversial prime minster of the UDF government, 1991–92

resented this transmission belt theory of representation; it smacks of the old Communist system they were pledged to dismantle.[26]

Second, Moser argues that the UDF leadership took its coalition partner for granted. They believed that the MRF had no place to go because of the known history of Communist persecution of the Turkish minority in Bulgaria. Instead, Dogan's party was willing to negotiate with the BSP, skillfully playing the middle role in the delicately balanced parliamentary system.

And third, Moser points out the obvious fact that UDF leaders found it hard to accept internal criticism. Those who disagreed with the leadership were sometimes spoken of as traitors, and there were purges that led to a reduction in its parliamentary group of more than 30 percent. The UDF became less a party of the big tent, to use the American metaphor, and more a party of the ideologically sound.[27]

These negative stylistic traits of the UDF leadership do not speak well for building parliamentary government. Moser's keen observations apply not only to when the UDF was in power but also when it was placed in the role of the loyal opposition.

Government of "Experts"

Late in October 1992, the Dimitrov cabinet resigned under strong pressure from both the BSP and the MRF. On November 20 the National Assembly repelled an attempt to reinstate Philip Dimitrov as prime minister. The vote was 124 against and 104 for his return to power. The BSP then attempted but failed to form a government. This was followed by attempts within the UDF to propose a candidate for prime minister that the MRF could abide. Finally, the MRF proposed Lyuben Berov, a professor of economics, as the new government leader. Ahmed Dogan explained to the National Assembly that Berov's academic background made him well suited for the task of putting together a competent government to deal with the nation's serious economic problems.[28] Berov later reported that the MRF did not ask for any cabinet positions in return for its support.[29]

Berov proposed a government of so-called experts. The leadership of the BSP expressed a willingness to support Berov, but Philip Dimitrov objected. In the end, 23 of the 110 UDF members of Parliament bolted party ranks to support Berov, and with the support of the BSP and the MRF, Berov was elected prime minister on December 30, 1992. The small group of UDF parliamentarians that had defied Dimitrov later formed a separate parliamentary group, the New Alliance for Democracy.[30]

While criticizing Dimitrov's government for making mistakes, Berov expressed his commitment to the program of the previous government. He lauded the UDF because it was the political force behind the transition to democracy and a market economy. Nonetheless, Philip Dimitrov denounced the Berov government for distancing itself from UDF policies. He also announced that the UDF would act as stiff opposition to the government in Parliament.[31]

Thus, from the very beginning, the UDF viewed Berov's government with great suspicion. The government was subjected to a no-confidence vote after sixty-nine-year-old UDF floor leader Stefan Savov was beaten by police in front of the Parliament building. Many believe that the incident was entirely accidental. The BSP floor leader Nora Ananieva said that the UDF leadership used this incident because it wanted to destabilize the government and that the UDF action was irresponsible. The New Alliance for Democracy also issued a statement condemning their former UDF colleagues. The MRF called for a thorough investigation.[32]

By late June 1993, the Berov government found it necessary to make some cabinet changes. Though the government was able to win parliamentary endorsement of these changes by a 126 to 84 vote, the UDF group voted against the cabinet because the changes were the result of bargaining with the BSP. The UDF leadership declared that the parliamentary group would boycott the plenary sessions as a sign of protest and that it would only take part in meetings of parliamentary commissions and in voting on certain laws dealing with dismantling the totalitarian system of the past.[33] Moreover, it expelled from its ranks Marin Todorov Dimitrov, who was relieved of his post as minister of science, education, and culture in the Berov cabinet.[34]

The boycott action also increased tension between the UDF leadership and President Zhelev, the former UDF leader. He condemned the boycott as a serious mistake that would only heighten tensions, and pleaded that greater tolerance was required. Viewing him as something of a traitor to the prodemocracy cause he once championed, some UDF activists demanded Zhelev's resignation.[35] This schism was never repaired and was a factor in Zhelev's failed bid for reelection in 1996.

Socialists Back in Power

In July 1993 the UDF called for early general elections. Dimitrov argued that since the start of the boycott of plenary sessions on June 23, the National Assembly was functioning without adequate representation. As it presently functions, Dimitrov pointed out, Parliament makes decisions without a quorum and MPs vote using absent MPs' cards.[36] Nothing came immediately of this suggestion for early elections. Yet, it was plain that the Berov government would continue to have difficulties maintaining power.

MRF leader Dogan complained publicly that the Turkish ethnic movement was tired of balancing parliamentary forces. Its aim was to prevent political dominance by either of the two large political forces, the BSP and the UDF. For a year following the parliamentary elections in 1991, the MRF aligned with the UDF. When relations between the MRF and UDF became strained, however, Dogan's forces then supported the nonpartisan government of Berov; it did so in concert with the BSP and the UDF breakaway faction, the New Union for Democracy. Remaining true to its original position, the MRF through Dogan expressed concern that if it became clear that the BSP had gained control over the government and Parliament, the MRF would react negatively.[37]

By November 1993, the UDF had initiated four no-confidence votes in the Berov government. But each time the government survived, although its support in Parliament continued to erode. One appealing explanation for the survival of the Berov government is that no single party wanted to take control of the government because of the difficult economic and social problems facing the country. No party wants to be blamed for failure. Indeed, the Berov government carried on until the National Assembly accepted its resignation on September 8, 1994, by a vote of 219 to 4 with 1 abstention.[38]

Under the terms of the Constitution, Parliament has three chances to form a government. If it is not possible to form a new government, the president must appoint an interim cabinet and call elections within two months. President Zhelev first met with BSP leaders. The BSP declined the opportunity. Its leaders said that while they were not afraid of governing the country, Bulgaria needed instead a strong and resolute government. They said this would be impossible with the current partisan configuration of parliamentary seats.[39] Perhaps, too, BSP leaders were aware that public opinion was beginning to swing in their direction. The results of a public opinion survey released to the press on September 29 indicated that the BSP was in a good position to win a majority of the parliamentary seats.[40]

Zhelev then turned to the most vociferous opponent of the Berov government. The UDF coalition was divided on the issue because some favored the strategy of new elections. On September 21, the UDF rejected Zhelev's offer to form a new government.[41]

President Zhelev turned finally to a small centrist group, the New Choice Party. On September 29 this group proposed former defense minister and presidential adviser Dimtar Loudzhev as prime minister. Loudzhev looked for coalition partners. But the two major forces remained in support of early elections. This decision forced the third parliamentary election since the downfall of the Zhivkov regime, and it tested again the resolve of Bulgarians to proceed along a democratic path.[42]

General elections were held on December 18, 1994. The Bulgarian Socialist Party gained eighteen additional seats, giving it an absolute parliamentary majority. It formed a parliamentary group with left-wing Agrarians and Ecologists called the Democratic Left.[43] The Union of Democratic Forces lost forty-two seats and the Movement for Rights and Freedoms lost eight seats, or 33 percent of its seats. Two new parties gained access to Parliament by obtaining the requisite 4 percent of the popular vote: the Popular Union won nineteen representatives in Parliament and the Bulgarian Business Bloc acquired thirteen seats.[44]

Zhan Videnov, a thirty-five-year-old economist, was elected prime minister on January 11, 1995. This time the BSP was able to form a coalition government. In the cabinet, Videnov named representatives of the Alexander Stamboliiski Bulgarian Agrarian Party and the Ecoglasnost Political Club.[45] During its first six months the Videnov government enacted eighty-two laws and ninety-six resolutions. Videnov's government centered its attention on economic matters designed to deal with production problems and reform. The Securities, Stock Exchanges, and Investment Companies Act and the National Accounting Office Act are regarded as the most important. His government also sought the repeal of what was described as repressive and restorationist legislation while the UDF was in power from November 1991 to December 1992. Videnov's government engineered a new criminal procedures act and a central administration for dealing with organized crime. The National Assembly also enacted a number of laws that would govern the procedures for local elections held during the fall of 1995.[46]

As democratic theory presupposes, when governments fail to satisfy public demands it is likely that specific support for incumbent institutional actors will wane. In 1996, Bulgarians experienced a serious grain shortage, rampant inflation, banking irregularities, growing crime, and a dispute about the military's role in the NATO alliance. These problems and issues contributed to the serious weakening of Videnov's Democratic Left coalition government. Attacks from the UDF and other opposition parties intensified during 1996, and within the BSP itself some party leaders became critical of their own government.

On January 11, 1996, the Videnov government survived a no-confidence vote by a 130 to 105 margin. Five Socialists voted against the government, and ten deputies affiliated with other parties supported the government.[47] At the end of January, appeals to constitutionalism were used to demand the resignation of Blagovest Sendov as chairman of the National Assembly. Because he expressed to Russia's president Boris Yeltsin that Bulgaria should not become a member of NATO, leaders of the UDF, the MRF, and the Popular Union castigated Sendov. They objected that because Sendov had expressed his view of NATO without the approval of Parliament he violated the Constitution. But by a vote of 124 to 92, the motion for dismissal failed.[48]

By spring 1996, the Democratic Left government of Zhan Videnov drew fierce criticism from the parliamentary opposition, trade unions, President Zhelev, and quarters within the ruling BSP itself.[49] Though there was talk about another no-confidence vote, the UDF indicated that it would instead seek early parliamentary elections as a method for toppling the cabinet.[50] Interestingly, however, a Gallup poll showed that at the time, Foreign Minister Georgi Pirinski was the most popular politician, followed by Prime Minister Zhan Videnov; BSP critic President Zhelyu Zhelev ranked third in the poll.[51] That same survey also indicated that the public gave Parliament low marks. During this period, President Zhelev called for an overhaul of the parliamentary system, arguing that a strong presidency was needed to get the country out of its present crisis.[52] He said that amending the Constitution was necessary because, without a strong government headed by a president with sufficient executive power, the current political and economic chaos would most likely result in a return to dictatorship. Zhelev argued that changing the political system from a parliamentary to a presidential republic would prevent that dire possibility.[53]

On May 28, 1996, the UDF announced plans to file another no-confidence vote against the Socialist government. At the same time, BSP members successfully pressured Videnov to reshuffle his cabinet. He acquiesced in part by sacking the agriculture minister, the industry minister, and the culture minister.[54] Yet, BSP power brokers, former prime minister Andrey Lukanov and the former BSP chairman Alexander Lilov, criticized these moves as "inadequate, partial, and insufficient."[55] To make matters worse for the government, the two largest unions, the Confederation of Labor Podkrepa and the Confederation of Independent Trade Unions, organized mass demonstrations against the government.[56] Despite the rhetoric, however, on June 12 the Democratic Left government survived its third no-confidence vote by a margin of 99 for and 135 against.[57]

Without question the economic and social problems facing Bulgaria during 1996 were real. But these problems alone do not explain the difficulties the Videnov government encountered from the opposition in Parliament. The presidential election held on October 27, 1996, was an additional factor in the political environment. First, Zhelyu Zhelev sought reelection, but he failed to win the support of the UDF coalition he once headed. Stemming from Zhelev's quarrels with the Dimitrov government, the UDF backed and, by a 65 percent margin, the voters selected Petar Stoyanov in the primary election held on June 1, 1996.[58] Second, the election commission denied Foreign Minister Georgi Pirinski, Bulgaria's most popular politician, a place on the October ballot for president of the Republic. As I explain fully in the next chapter, the Constitutional Court ruled that under certain circumstances persons not born in Bulgaria are ineligible to become president. (Pirinski was born in New York City.) Seven weeks prior to the general election, the BSP selected a much weaker candidate than Pirinski, the former vice presidential candidate on the Pirinski ticket, Culture Minister Ivan Marazov.[59]

Thus, BSP leaders clearly sensed danger.[60] At the end of a twenty-two-hour closed-door meeting of the BSP Supreme Council and BSP members of Parliament held on November 12, 1996, Zhan Videnov was given a vote of confidence by a slim 87-to-69-vote margin. It was clear that many party leaders, including Georgi Pirinski, were dissatisfied with the Videnov government.[61] Finally, the intraparty showdown took place at the Forty-second Extraordinary Congress of the BSP held December 21–24, 1996. Zhan Videnov tendered his resignation as party leader and the resignation of his entire cabinet. A thirty-nine-year-old member of Parliament, historian Georgi Purvanov, was named the new party leader. The BSP assumed another Socialist-led government would be formed sometime in January 1997.[62] The Videnov government was in office for two years, a longer tenure than that of any of its six predecessors. Moreover, at the beginning of 1997, the BSP stood a good chance to retain its parliamentary control for at least an additional two years, when the next general elections are scheduled. Nevertheless, parliamentary government continued to be put to the test. Outrageous inflation, bread shortages, banking and currency crises, poor health care management, and soaring crime rates created public pleas for positive government action. Given these wretched conditions, would responsible leaders continue to insist upon democratic procedures as an act of political *will*?

Constitutional Crisis

On January 3, 1997, opposition forces in the National Assembly composed of deputies of the Union of Democratic Forces, the Popular Union, and the Movement for Rights and Freedoms introduced a draft resolution titled "Declaration on National Salvation." Deputies debated the issue for five hours while the people of the nation heard it broadcast live on radio and television. The proposed declaration had three demands: first, the appointment of a new governing board of Bulgaria's National Bank; second, the commencement of negotiations with the International Monetary Fund on the creation of a currency board; finally, and most important from the point of view of compromising regular constitutional processes, the Declaration on National Salvation called for the immediate dissolution of Parliament and setting a date for early general elections.[63]

The Socialists and their parliamentary allies had a legitimate claim to resist the last demand contained in the declaration, and they had already pledged to work toward a parliamentary consensus on the first two points. With the resignation of the Videnov government, the Democratic Left had the constitutional right to remain in power unless one of two events occurred: the BSP failing to obtain the necessary votes in the National Assembly to put a new government in place or a new BSP prime minister losing a no-confidence vote. From any perspective, neither scenario seemed likely. Thus, the BSP was likely to stay in power unless they were forced by other means to relinquish their authority. In fact, their opponents used mass demonstrations and other irregular tactics in an unabashed effort to dislodge the Democratic Left coalition from power.

The same day the National Assembly debated the Declaration on National Salvation, opposition forces participated in a mass rally and protest march organized by the powerful trade union amalgamations: the Confederation of Independent Trade Unions in Bulgaria, the Podkrepa

Confederation of Labor, and the Promiana (Change). It is reported that protesters shouted slogans: "Communists ruined Bulgaria," "A new socialist government will bury Bulgaria," and "Elections, Elections!" The protesters finished their march in front of BSP headquarters. Some hurled stones and eggs at the building, smashed windows, and broke through protective railings. More than one hundred policemen were called to guard the building, and one officer was wounded in the head when a stone was thrown. When asked about the street violence, BSP leader Georgi Purvanov said, "We shall not give in to the street pressure, not because we stubbornly want to keep the power, but because we do not see a real alternative to preserve the stability of the institutions."[64] But this incident was only the opening salvo in a series of shots that would batter and test the durability of democratic institutions.

Within Parliament, Yordan Sokolov, the UDF floor leader, said that the UDF might do more than ask the people to express disapproval for the Socialist government by demonstrating in the streets. He explained that the UDF reserves to itself the option to walk out of the National Assembly if the Democratic Left majority does not accept demands for early parliamentary elections. Stefan Savov, onetime chairman of the National Assembly and now cochair of the Popular Union, stated that no matter who might head a second Socialist cabinet, that person will be unable to cope with the situation. And MRF leader Ahmed Dogan said, "I am convinced that a new cabinet of the Socialist Party will be a Cabinet-Kamikaze and whomever the new prime minister may be, he will be a victim."[65]

By January 6, 1997, the protests that began in Sofia spread to the city of Plovdiv where the UDF mayor addressed more than thirty thousand people. Mayor Spas Garnevski is reported to have said: "If we have to die, we'll die on the squares."[66] Protests then spread to other cities. Especially in Sofia, protestors mimicked tactics employed by demonstrators in Belgrade, where for weeks demonstrators flooded the streets protesting the official nullification of election results in Serbia. In Sofia, workers, students, and others conducted mass demonstrations for seven straight days. Clearly exemplifying the role modern media can play as facilitator of demonstration effects, student street demonstrators in Bulgaria borrowed many of the gestures of their Serbian counterparts; in a festive mood, they walked in circles like chained

"Two years of total failure"

prisoners, flashed the V for victory sign, and joked with the police.[67] However, on Friday, January 10, 1997, there was serious violence. Demonstrators surrounded the Parliament building, breaking windows and trapping deputies in the building. Almost one hundred people were injured when, in an effort to free the trapped parliamentarians, police fired guns and waved batons to break through the demonstrators' lines.[68] By the following Monday, the BSP agreed in principle to early elections. Yet, this expression did not satisfy their opponents.

Consistent with constitutional rules, BSP leaders sought to form a new government. Suggesting compromise with their vociferous opponents, they sought to retain power for only one of the two remaining years left on their mandate. The UDF alliance, however, insisted that elections be held sometime in the summer, eighteen months before the expiration of the four-year term of office.[69] Article 99 of the Constitution requires that the president ask the candidate of the largest parliamentary group to form a cabinet. During his last week in office, however, President Zhelyu Zhelev refused to carry out his constitutional responsibility as prescribed. Although he consulted with leaders of the smallest parliamentary group, the Bulgarian Business Bloc, and with the Confederation of Independent Trade Unions, Zhelev claimed it would be inappropriate to ask the BSP to form a government because the country was being swept by demonstrations for early elections and the opposition had walked out of the National Assembly. Indeed, on Wednesday, January 15, the first day of the winter session of the Thirty-seventh National Assembly, only 123 of the 240 members of Parliament were present in the debating hall: 119 members of the BSP-dominated parliamentary group of the Democratic Left and 4 members of the Bulgarian Business Bloc. The opposition UDF, the MRF, and the Popular Union continued the boycott they had begun on Friday, January 10, because the Democratic Left refused to put to a vote the Declaration on National Salvation.[70]

Meanwhile, president-elect Petar Stoyanov met with Socialist and UDF leaders in an effort to resolve the impasse.[71] After his inauguration on January 22, and consistent with his constitutional responsibility, President Stoyanov on January 28 gave the BSP the mandate to form a new government. But he urged the leadership not to accept it. Instead, he asked the Democratic Left coalition to agree to early parliamentary elections. He also urged the UDF-led opposition to end its boycott of Parliament.[72] On February 4, 1997, after a month of mass demonstrations and random acts of civil disobedience, President Stoyanov successfully brokered an agreement. The Socialist Party leadership agreed to return the mandate to form a new government and to hold general elections in April. It was also agreed that, pending the outcome of those elections, President Stoyanov would appoint a caretaker government.[73]

Sofia's youthful mayor, Stefan Sofiyanski, was named on February 12, 1997, to head the caretaker government. This government was warmly received by the international community, and Sofiyanski and his colleagues enjoyed wide public support leading to the new elections conducted on April 19, 1997. As anticipated, the UDF did well: it captured over 52 percent of the vote and 137 of the National Assemby's 240 seats. The BSP fell to 58 seats, while the Union for National Salvation won 19 seats, the Euro-Left Party took 14 seats, and the Bulgarian Business Bloc won 12 seats.

Does the successful demand by the UDF and their allies for early elections represent a rejection of the agreed-upon rules for the establishment of parliamentary government and democracy generally?

The anti-Democratic Left forces violated the specifics of the democratic agreement as laid out in the 1991 Constitution. Elections for Parliament were not scheduled for two years. The BSP was able to put together a parliamentary majority, thereby satisfying constitutional requirements. Nor could the UDF win a no-confidence vote. No doubt the demonstrations, acts of violence, and the walkout in Parliament were all irregular and extraconstitutional tactics. In this sense, the anti-government forces' behavior was inconsistent with the development of stable parliamentary government. They had repeated their own history: both at the Grand National Assembly and in the regular National Assembly some factions within the UDF failed to fulfill the expectations of how a loyal opposition in a democratic political culture should conduct itself.

Despite the dysfunctional aspects of this particular set of events for the creation and maintenance of norms supportive of the regular conduct of parliamentary government, there is no evidence that any of the principal participants displayed nostalgia for the totalitarian days. The infliction of bodily harm by the police against demonstrators is the first in the post-Communist era. It was the type of confrontation that General Semerjiev studiously avoided during the potentially unstable period of the National Roundtable Talks in 1989 and 1990. But the use of force in this case does not support the conclusion that the police state has been or will soon be reinstated in Bulgaria. Although violence is unprotected expression, the people's right to peacefully demonstrate is constitutionally guaranteed. There is no in-principle reason that citizens may not be mobilized to petition for a change in their government. No one doubts this constitutional truism. BSP opponents seized the moment of severe economic bad times to wrest control of the Parliament and government. It had won the presidency just a few months earlier. It seemed to them that citizens would support new parliamentary elections, the results of which would produce a government willing and, they hoped, able to deliver on the unfulfilled promises of democracy. While this may be asking too much from democracy as a set of procedures, because the BSP had failed to produce material progress and community well-being, many Bulgarians felt that change was necessary. The change sought is consistent with the goals of the democratic regime created in the aftermath of the November 1989 coup d'état. Although the irregular actions of the UDF and their allies are troubling, such conduct does not represent a rejection of the basic agreement: that all factions in Bulgarian life should coexist within the framework of electoral competition.

President versus Parliament

President Zhelev laments the staying power of the BSP. He argues a constitutional amendment is needed that would grant to the president the authority to dissolve Parliament or appoint the prime minister. In this way, so the argument goes, failed governments would be more responsive to popular will. Zhelev's criticism is part of his larger plan that Bulgaria become a presidential system. Though such ideas merit study, Bulgaria's history of authoritarian leadership would seem to argue against concentrating power in the hands of a single figure. Moreover, there is considerable evidence that presidential systems tend to suffer from either deadlock or dictatorial tendencies.[74]

Whether the current president, Petar Stoyanov, will eventually come to the same conclusion as Zhelev is difficult to predict. There is little doubt, however, that Zhelev's view is borne of experience.

President Zhelev openly clashed with the Socialist-dominated National Assembly over a number of laws. He exercised the power of the suspensory veto on several occasions, and each time Parliament overrode Zhelev's action. A disagreement of considerable constitutional importance involved the amendments to the Agricultural Land Tenure Act. President Zhelev won the case in part when the Constitutional Court ruled that a provision of the law requiring landowners to offer their property for sale to municipalities and the state before offering it to other buyers is a violation of the constitutional principle of the inviolability of property. The Court also struck down a provision of the new law that restricted the rights of former owners when their land had been improved upon. Other provisions restricting the rights of property owners were likewise invalidated by the Constitutional Court.[75]

When the UDF was in power under the leadership of Philip Dimitrov, President Zhelev had expressed disapproval of his own party. However, the conflict with the BSP government of Zhan Videnov took on a sharper adversarial tone. In large part, this controversy is due to the personalities and policies of the principal antagonists. Yet, it is also a result of the somewhat awkward position of the presidency within the institutional framework of separation of powers.

For most of their first year, President Zhelev accused Videnov's Socialist government of attempting to bring back communism; he referred to it as re-communization. The president claimed that the BSP was up to the old Communist Party practice of dividing people to get their own way. In the interest of democracy, Zhelev argued, the BSP should seek compromise and mutual understanding with all the state institutions controlled by different political forces. At the same time, Zhelev was heavily criticized for vetoing acts passed by the National Assembly. His actions are said to evidence a disrespect for the will of the people, because, after all, the Socialist government was elected by the people. His rejoinder is rooted in electoral politics: "I could ask the BSP the same question: Why is it not respecting the vote of the people who elected me? The people who voted for me exceed those who voted for the BSP and its Government by 600,000 [votes]."[76]

Consistent with the re-communization theme, the president and the government also battled over the leadership of the armed forces. In late 1995 the Council of Ministers attempted to shift military personnel from one assignment to another. The president accused the government of seeking to repoliticize the army by attempting to regain control over its personnel.[77]

Zhelev's activity in Bulgarian politics was at the constitutional fault line between the Parliament and the president. Besides employing the court of public opinion, the president's most potent weapon against the Socialists is the use of his constitutional right to petition the Constitutional Court. In 1995, it declared no less than six parliamentary acts or parts thereof null and void. As a reaction against various decisions, court-curbing measures were taken by the National Assembly against the Court. In an address to the National Assembly on the fourth anniversary of the Constitution's adoption, the president was jeered when he said, "Calls for a war against the Constitutional Court are calls for war against the Constitution itself."[78]

The Socialist government responded to Zhelev's criticism in strong terms. Prime Minister Videnov charged both Zhelev and the Constitutional Court with attempting to obstruct the rule of the Democratic Left. He said Zhelev "behaves more like a candidate 'for' opposition leader than as . . . a head of state," and the Constitutional Court "behaves like an alternative parliament."[79] Continuing to act out the drama with considerable bravado, Zhelev strongly endorsed the winning anti-Socialist candidate for mayor of Sofia in the November 1995 runoff. Subsequently, fifty-six Socialist MPs played their part by taking him to the Constitutional Court. They argued unsuccessfully that Zhelev had violated Article 92(1) of the Constitution that the president "Shall embody the unity of the Nation." In what will not be the final curtain call, the Court accepted the argument that although the president embodies the unity of the nation, the Constitution also mandates political functions under the rubric of "Head of State." As such, the president is entitled under the Constitution to express political attitudes.[80]

In the next chapter, I explore in greater detail the role of the judiciary and its conflicts with other institutions. For now, however, it is fair to conclude that the six years following the transition to democracy were marked by interinstitutional conflicts. If these institutional boundary-defining battles were not entirely predictable, they are certainly understandable. Boundaries of political authority are often ambiguous and uncertain in systems featuring separation of powers. Lines of authority need definition. Given this situation, political parties behave as might be expected. Party leaders try to capture government institutions and define institutional authority with the goal of shaping public policy consistent with their own designs. Opponents often yell foul. They charge that the other side has transgressed institutional norms, as indeed, sometimes they do. Yet, this behavior is not too different from what political actors experience in other constitutional systems, including the United States. Often constitutional arguments are really about something else, including a concern over whose ox is being gored.

Democracy as a Work in Progress

When the strongman communist regime of Todor Zhivkov fell on November 10, 1989, after forty-five years of one-party dominance, the Bulgarian Communist Party possessed a constitutional monopoly on political power. At the time, there was little reason to expect the rapid development of strong competing political parties capable of organizing public discourse and laying the groundwork for effective government. Yet, the events occurring between the November 1989 peaceful coup d'état and the collapse of the most recent government at the end of 1996 evidences the commencement of a durable but not always responsible party system. The creation of the Union of Democratic Forces represents a powerful, though at times unwieldy, counterforce to the politically sophisticated former Communists, now calling themselves the Bulgarian Socialist Party. During this six-year period, a third party—the Movement for Rights and Freedoms, a primarily Turkish ethnic organization—often played a broker role between the two major parliamentary forces. Not only did the MRF help to take the rough edge off the dysfunctional bipolarized party politics caused by the two major groups in Parliament, but the mediating role played by the MRF helped to mollify ethnic tensions in Bulgaria.[81]

The political parties in Parliament are functioning to organize debate and educating the public about the issues at the national level. Yet, they are doing more for the consolidation of democracy. The elections held for local officials throughout Bulgaria in October and November 1995 illustrate the successful functioning of the party system in another important respect. The parties in Parliament have integrated the population in the political system by extending their influence throughout the nation. Parties have done so by articulating local issues within the context of the national debate. Generally reflecting their influence in the National Assembly, the prominent national parties demonstrate similar support at the local level. With a voter turnout rate in the 55–60 percent range, the BSP received 42 percent of the vote in the first round of the local elections, the UDF won 24 percent of the votes, the People's Union (NS) gathered 13 percent, the MRF won 9 percent, and the Bulgarian Business Bloc (BBB) received 6 percent of the total vote.[82] Bulgarian political leaders also displayed the ability to forge tactical alliances—in this case against the dominant BSP. The leaders of the UDF met with the People's Union and the ethnic Turkish movement MRF to establish a nationwide strategy for the runoffs held on November 5. In some places, including Sofia, the NS withdrew its candidates in favor of the better-situated UDF candidates.[83]

The National Assembly is a raucous yet fragile institution. Party unity, particularly of the UDF forces, exhibits serious fractures that bring into question the long-term viability of parliamentary democracy in Bulgaria. Yet, given the perseverance of Bulgarian politicians in and out of the National Assembly a negative prognosis is at this time premature and unwarranted. Indeed, there is justification for guarded optimism. Realism, however, demands that positive conclusions be tempered with the knowledge that the creation and maintenance of democratic institutions is anything but an automatic process.

Legislative systems everywhere require a modicum of trust and respect among their participants to carry on their daily business in a fruitful manner. The transgressions of the past make it difficult for many Bulgarians to accept a working relationship with the former Communists, because they believe that adequate retribution has yet to take place. Yet, the genius of the National Roundtable Talks is that it provided for accommodation without repeating the regrettable cycle of bloodshed and vendetta central to Bulgaria's political history. To be sure, self-taught lessons in democracy are not always well-understood while participants in the process are experiencing them. Certainly, boycotts by parliamentary groups do not speak well for the institutionalization of democratic rules of the game. It may be that the concept of a loyal opposition is not yet fully appreciated.

Moreover, the constitutional and political crisis of December 1996 and early 1997 provides evidence that democratic consolidation remains problematic. On one hand, the BSP concession for early elections violates the regularization of parliamentary processes, and to that extent the agreement sets back the cause of parliamentary government and of a law-governed state. But ironically, at the same time, the agreement among the competing forces signifies the resiliency of democracy. Rather than imposing authoritarian measures on the population and the suppression of their opponents, the incumbent Socialist government agreed to give up power. It succumbed to the demands of the opposition for testing their legitimacy at the polls. This is, after all, a democratic response to crisis. If the BSP had responded with draconian force, it might be concluded that Bulgaria had reverted to its authoritarian and totalitarian ways. But the Socialist response was one of reconciliation and a willingness to take their chances at the polls. In this sense the competing forces reaffirmed the most basic principle of the original Roundtable agreement. They would take their chances with democracy as a direct reflection of the will of the people.

When all is said and done, the National Assembly is performing its legislative functions, albeit at times imperfectly, while integrating the various social, economic, ethnic, and political cleavages that threaten national unity. Continuing economic hardships for the population at large make the task all the more difficult. Nonetheless, political parties regularly compete and, in the process, define areas of agreement and disagreement. There has been not only interparty competition but turnover in power. The Bulgarian Socialist Party won control of the first free elections in the post-Communist era with its victory at the polls in June 1990 for the election of a Grand National Assembly. The voters turned the former Communist Party operatives out of power in October 1991, with a plurality of the parliamentary seats going to the Union of Democratic Forces led by Philip Dimitrov. Then, in December 1994, the Bulgarian Socialist Party regained an absolute majority in Parliament. In the April 1997 elections, the Socialists once again lost power to their parliamentary opponents. As Samuel Huntington correctly argues in a work of great heuristic value and timely importance, anti-incumbent and antiestablishment responses by voters are classic democratic reactions to policy failure and disillusionment.[84] Selecting rulers is at the heart of democracy, and the willingness of Bulgarian leaders to turn over power to their opponents is a sure indicator that democracy in Bulgaria is becoming an institutionalized way of conducting public affairs.

The very existence of Parliament may be helping to produce attitudes among relevant publics and elites that the constitutional system adopted by the Grand National Assembly in July 1991 has earned their support and that democratic institutions have a moral right to exist. In this sense, the democratic regime is made more secure by a functioning though imperfect legislature.

9

The Struggle for Judicial Independence

IT IS FAIR TO CONCLUDE tentatively that Bulgarians are practicing the art of parliamentary government sufficiently well to be labeled democratic. Yet, there is more to democracy than this. An important feature of constitutional democracy is the procedural mechanisms for insuring that political actors play within the rules of the game. Within this context, a major role of the judicial institution is to correct the other government institutions when they fail to honor constitutional mandates and guarantees. The judiciary's fundamental goal is to aid society in the avoidance of backsliding into the totalitarian abyss. In the modern lexicon of east Europeans, the role of an independent judiciary is to insure a law-governed state. I identify in this chapter the problems and prospects of an independent judiciary in Bulgaria since the adoption of the 1991 Constitution. The evidence illustrates an aspect of the consolidation of democratic institutions that is central to the creation of a law-governed state. Legal professionals find it necessary at times to protect judicial institutions in the struggle for visibility and independence.

As Carl Pinkele aptly points out, the intention of authoritarian communist regimes was to "dejudicialize and to deprivatize" political conflict.[1] Conflict resolution in such a system took place within the parameters of party or state bureaucracies of which the judiciary was an integral but dependent part. Given this historical context, the rule of law concept has an important operational consequence. It is a way to remove political and interpersonal conflicts from the domination of party or bureaucratic structures with a specific ideological content. It would be a mistake, however, to assume that within the new so-called democratic order, decision makers will resolve conflicts without ideological influences. Legalism is a subtle yet pervasive ideological influence. Legal absolutists often express this view in terms of neutral principles and objective rules. This view promises the attractive advantage of equal treatment for equals. It fails, however, to explicitly address questions of substantive justice, the answers to which the former socialist legal system purportedly resolved in favor of the working class. By officially depoliticizing dispute resolutions with the hope of resolving them, to use Tocqueville's characterization of nineteenth-century America, "into judicial questions,"[2] legal professionals are in an ideal strategic position to give meaning to the law's content. This point is especially significant given the contemporary worldwide phenomenon of converting political issues into judicial questions.[3]

The Constitution and Judicial Independence

As an alternative to the old totalitarian ways, legalism as an ideology could serve to move society toward greater observance of democratic values. This idea presupposes that today judges in Bulgaria should enjoy independence that judges in the past were not free to exercise. One private attorney expressed the view of many when he said: "Judges have been viewed by the public as part of the old regime."[4] Yet, most of the jurists I interviewed suggested that it is probably inaccurate to label the former Bulgarian system as telephone justice. A judge who had served during the old regime and under the new system summarized the viewpoint of many of those I interviewed. He said:

> I would say there wasn't a need for telephone justice, since the justice before, under the Communist rule, dealt only with insignificant questions. In fact, those from the Communist nomenklatura were not afraid of justice, since they were out of the system of justice, of the system of courts. And that's why I say that the telephone calls were very, very rare and were for some insignificant cases. . . . I remember only one or two times a party leader called me and said: "Well, there's a civil lawsuit of this guy, he's a good guy; see whether you can do something!" But you know, all these issues were insignificant, because they [the Party nomenklatura] were not afraid of justice;

> they were outside of justice . . . there was no reason for telephone justice.

No person I interviewed denied that telephone justice was occasionally practiced. It is likely, however, that because judicial officials were members of the nomenklatura, they shared political attitudes with other officials; and, furthermore, they viewed themselves as bureaucrats and not independent actors outside the governing system. Therefore, it was usually unnecessary for Party leaders to pick up the phone to suggest what might be favorable dispositions of cases. In most instances, the judges knew what was expected of them.

The framers of the 1991 Constitution understood that if the ideal of an objective rule-oriented judiciary is to take root, it would be necessary to create an independent judiciary. Consequently, they incorporated into the basic document institutional mechanisms to assure judicial responsibility in the protection of newly established democratic processes and institutions.

The establishment of the Supreme Judicial Council (SJC) is an integral part of Bulgaria's constitutional scheme to guarantee judicial independence. Yet, the idea for such an organization to aid in the selection of judges has a precedent. Bulgaria first established a judicial council in 1910; it was a consultative body to the minister of justice on personnel policy. When the Communist Party came to power after World War II, it dissolved the judicial council in favor of Party control over judicial appointments. Article 129 of the July 1991 Constitution provides that the SJC shall elect, promote, demote, reassign, and dismiss justices, prosecutors, and investigating magistrates. This council consists of twenty-five members. Eleven members are elected for five-year terms by the National Assembly; they may not be immediately reelected upon the completion of their terms. Eleven additional council members are elected by bodies of the judicial branch. Also among the council are three ex officio members that include the chief prosecutor, the chair of the Supreme Court of Cassation, and the chair of the Supreme Administrative Court. The minister of justice serves as chair of the meetings of the Supreme Judicial Council, but this person has no voting privileges. On September 10, 1991, the National Assembly enacted a law intended to make council members as independent as possible. It specifies only three circumstances when members of the judicial system may be relieved of their duties before the end of their terms: retirement, the enforcement of a prison sentence, or because of a disability lasting more than one year.[5]

A separate budget for the judiciary is an additional constitutional measure to support its independence. Under the provisions of Article 117(3) the Supreme Judicial Council submits a separate budget for the judicial system to the National Assembly. In this way, the judiciary is not dependent upon the consent or largesse of the Council of Ministers; the Supreme Judicial Council need not secure in advance approval from the Finance Ministry of its budget requests laid before the National Assembly.

Life tenure is unavailable to Constitutional Court justices; it is available, however, to jurists in the ordinary law courts. As such, life tenure for most Bulgarian judges is another constitutional guarantee supporting the goal of judicial independence. After the third year in office, judges, prosecutors, and investigating magistrates are removable for three reasons—retirement, serving a criminal sentence, and disability as specified under Article 129(3) of the Constitution. For those judges holding office since before the adoption of the new Constitution, the applicable constitutional section was clause 5 of the Transitional and Concluding Provisions. These judicial officers who served under the previous regime were removable solely within three months of the formation of the Supreme Judicial Council, and only if the council found they lacked professional qualifications, meriting their dismissal.

The council promulgated regulations for the review of the judges held over from the old regime. Each judge found unacceptable had the opportunity to file written objections with the council. Within this procedural framework, the SJC reviewed the credentials of eighty-three legal professionals and dismissed forty-four from the judicial system. This number includes twenty-three judges, or about 2 percent of the total of all Bulgarian judges. Eighteen, or 3.2 percent, of the public prosecutors were dismissed, and three, or less than 1 percent, of investigating magistrates were removed by the actions of the Supreme Judicial Council. Seventy-seven persons voluntarily retired, and 243 persons left the system without explanation.[6] Although it is difficult to know with certainty, evidently the large number of persons who retired voluntarily or left the system without explanation must have included those who felt that self-removal from the scene was better than the alternative. Then, too, some may have left the bench without fear of reprisal for past misdeeds. Instead, they may have answered the call to the greener pastures of private law practice that the transition to democracy and a market economy promise.

Fear of Political Interference

How confident can Bulgaria's judges be that the Constitution provides mechanisms for their independence? Despite the constitutional powers of the Supreme Judicial Council, is it naive to rule out the potential for the politicization of that body? Can the National Assembly undermine the life tenure guarantee? Is it possible that politicians may punish judges for their unfavorable rulings?

My informants warn that politics will continue to motivate some judicial appointments. According to one judge, campaigning for positions on the Supreme Judicial Council goes on both in the National Assembly and among legal professionals, with some judges chosen for ideological reasons, specifically, that they do not harbor communist sympathies. The 1991 Constitution does not contain any criteria for judicial selections, and several legal professionals confirm that the council does not have objective criteria. These jurists believe that without guiding criteria some members of the judiciary will continue to be chosen for political and ideological reasons. They lament that because professional qualification is not always the sole factor in determining appointments, the belief that the judicial branch is an objective and neutral forum for resolving conflicts may be undermined.

Most legal professionals I interviewed at all court levels expressed some fear that events may unfold to frustrate constitutional protections. One Supreme Court justice was particularly adamant about the vulnerability of the judiciary to interference by sister government institutions and other political and economic interests. Prophetically, when I interviewed him, in 1993, he said that political officials would try to intimidate the judiciary; he feared that the opponents of judicial independence might try to interfere with the life tenure of judges guaranteed in the July 1991 Constitution. The politicians, he exclaimed, might attempt to interfere with the activities of the Supreme Judicial Council, a body created under the Constitution to oversee the fair workings of the judicial system. He said:

> There is a trend, especially in the executive branch of the government to influence the courts, and sometimes they find supporters in the mass media. I wouldn't say it's rare even for the American democracy, but it's also a question of habits, and from the viewpoint of the judge it's also a question of morality and dignity. . . .
>
> But I think that because we have done the first step, we can do the next. I mean now the judges are elected for life, appointed for life by this special body—the Supreme Judicial Council. . . . But I am afraid they'll try to politicize the program in the adoption of this law [the judiciary act]; I am afraid that they'll try to change . . . the staff of the Supreme Judicial Council, change the personnel of the Supreme Court, and the politicians will try to influence [courts] by making personnel changes in all the bodies of the judiciary . . .

After probing the justice with additional questions, I discovered that he was especially concerned about the possibility of legislatively moving judges from one court to another. Under the Constitution, it is theoretically possible, for instance, to move a judge from the Supreme Court in the nation's capital to a regional court in the hinterland. This has not happened as of the end of 1996, but it is possible. The important point is that a lack of protection could wear on judges' resolve to render decisions free from fear of political retaliation.

Some legal professionals I interviewed believed attempts to diminish or interfere with the judiciary were a real possibility because some politicians fear the potential influence of the judiciary. But why? One explanation seems particularly perceptive. It draws our attention to the motivations behind the accommodations worked out for the transition to democracy between the functionaries of the former Communist Party and their democratic opponents. It is the view that the former Communists do not want a strong judiciary. At this early moment in the post-Communist era, they have an opportunity to make a large amount of money by employing money laundering and other illegal schemes. Legal chaos is their ally, the argument goes, and therefore the former Communist Party functionaries resist an independent judiciary capable of enforcing the law. Perhaps, after these profiteers are secure in their ill-gotten gains, they will then cynically argue, consistent with their self-interest, for a strong judiciary.

The uncertainty associated with what the future structure and organization of the judicial system may become was on the minds of all the jurists I interviewed and spoke with over the years. They conveyed a sense of being watched by others. One Supreme Court justice put it this way: "This situation is indirect, you understand . . . it indirectly reflects upon the brain of the judge." Delivering judicial opinions that elected officials of government find unacceptable could result in setting back the cause of an independent judiciary and a "rule of law" state.

Given this concern, there is little reason to expect bold decisions from the ordinary courts. Yet, there is no suggestion that Bulgarian jurists exhibit an unwillingness to confront thorny political issues. For example, a three-judge panel of the Supreme Court ruled in favor of the right of the Turkish minority party to register for participation in national elections. This was a courageous but carefully crafted opinion, placing the judiciary on the side of political freedom and against popular sentiment.[7]

There is a more optimistic assessment of the state of judicial independence in Bulgaria. Thanks to the control imposed by the Supreme Judicial Council on the selection of judges and by the more careful scrutiny given applicants for judgeships because of a new system of competitive examinations, the quality of those acceding to the bench is improving. A supervisory judge said, "The courts secure independence not only thanks to statutory rights, but also by the selection of the candidates. And thank God we have currently a lot of capable young people in the profession."

Fear of financial strangulation is a real one for any judiciary that charts an independent course. In a system of separation of powers, the duty of legislative authorities to authorize government spending may result in subservience by other branches of government. By statutory enactment, the Supreme Judicial Council asks the National Assembly for funds on behalf of the judiciary. Yet, this has not resulted in the third branch of government being absolutely independent from the others and has occasioned two opinions of the Constitutional Court.

The Supreme Judicial Council drafts a budget for the judiciary. This draft then goes to the Finance Ministry and, according to a ruling of the Constitutional Court, the Council of Ministers has no right to cut recommendations proposed in the draft budget. The Finance Ministry introduces the draft budget to the Parliament with no alterations. In the end, it is the responsibility of the National Assembly to approve a budget with alterations in the original budget as it sees fit. Of course, there is no guarantee that the judiciary will get what it needs or wants.

Almost all the legal professionals with whom I have spoken express the view that the judiciary is underfunded. Judicial salaries are low, the support staff and equipment are inadequate, and the workload is heavy. Judges share offices and use antiquated typewriters to prepare draft opinions and memoranda. Since other institutions are also underfunded, all agree the judiciary is not a particular target for ill-treatment. Yet, this matter bears close scrutiny. Sometime in the future, the National Assembly could use its budgetary authority to send the judiciary a political message. On the other hand, it is possible to make matters better by expending court fees differently from the present practice. One judge suggested that if the Ministry of Justice and the penal system were not part of the budgetary process, the judicial system could finance itself through court fees alone. Fees are the most secure source of income for the government because they are paid in advance. This is not so in the trade sector of the economy, where taxes are paid after the transaction and therefore subject to nonpayment.

Although it is possible to improve the fiscal management of the judicial system, there is no doubt that the fundamental task of the Supreme Judicial Council is difficult to manage. Council members may work hard to identify well-qualified persons to occupy positions within the judiciary, but sometimes conditions beyond their control frustrate their best efforts. I asked an important figure of the Sofia District Court about the role of the Judicial Council in selecting judges. This person is also a proud member of the Supreme Judicial Council. He worries about the recent trend resulting from the transition to a market economy. The greater emphasis upon private property and rights places greater monetary rewards on the private practice of law than existed under Communism. Back then, the more prestigious service was as a judge or prosecutor in the government's judicial system. One result is that the well-intentioned judicial selection process is not bringing to the bench the best qualified persons. He also laments the constitutional provision granting judges life tenure. He thinks that instead of life tenure judges should have renewable five- or ten-year terms. He is uncertain whether professional competence should be demonstrable by professional record or examination. Nonetheless, he expressed the view that every magistrate should be able to defend their competence. He put it this way: "Otherwise we'll go to this lifetime sinecure for judges and not to making justice."

Thus, one way to interpret whether the system of selecting judges through the Supreme Judicial Council is functioning well is to affirm that council members are doing the best job possible under unfortunate circumstances. To the extent there are unqualified judges, blame the transition to democracy. Privatization of the economy makes the services of private lawyers more valuable than that of judges. Alternatively, one may identify the life tenure system as an extreme reaction to the patronage system under the old totalitarian regime. Eliminating life tenure would require a constitutional amendment, and no doubt any such proposal would raise serious questions about the motivations of those promoting the change. Supporters of life tenure might naturally appeal to the norm of judicial independence in a "law-governed state." As we have already seen, however, it is now theoretically possible to devalue life tenure by moving judicial personnel from one position to another and by reducing their salaries. Again, though some fear this might happen, thus far neither the National Assembly nor the Council of Ministers has tried it. Yet, other attacks on the judiciary have been mounted.

Attacks on the Judiciary

The first outward and visible warning sign that the judiciary may be subject to political maneuvers is that the National Assembly failed for several years to enact a judiciary law establishing the court system as outlined in the July 1991 Constitution. Members of Parliament had introduced legislation since the early days under the new Constitution. However, action was put off with the explanation that the National Assembly had to deal with more pressing problems. Therefore, although the Constitution provides for a Supreme Court of Cassation and a Supreme Administrative Court, the National Assembly failed to create either one; that is, until the enactment of the Law on the Judiciary in June 1994. At one point, the Constitutional Court ruled that the existing Supreme Court possessed the jurisdiction allocated to the constitutionally mandated Supreme Court of Cassation and Supreme Administrative Court.[8] Consequently, with some confusion and modification, including the creation of the Constitutional Court and the law on the Supreme Judicial Council, the organization of the judiciary continued in its pre-July 1991 form until June 1994.

A second indicator that the independence of the judiciary is at issue was the attempt by the Council of Ministers to clear the budget requests of the Supreme Judicial Council. Obviously, if the executive could directly control the budget request of the judiciary, the Council of Ministers could dictate how it performs its function. The Constitutional Court, however, came to the rescue of the Supreme Judicial Council. It declared the Constitution mandates that although the Council of Ministers will submit the budget of the judiciary to the National Assembly, the executive branch may not alter the original budget request of the Supreme Judicial Council without its permission.[9]

A more important decision favorable to SJC independence was rendered in 1995. Prosecutor General Ivan Tatarchev challenged a provision in the National Budget Act denying the SJC independent budgetary authority. Pursuant to this act, the Ministry of Finance had insisted that the SJC budgetary accounts be given to the Justice Ministry. This act also located the administrative servicing of the SJC in the Ministry of Justice.[10] The Constitutional Court held that the SJC is entitled to independent budgetary authority without executive branch control.[11]

As potentially damaging as the tardiness of installing the judicial system and the attempts to interfere with the budgetary process may seem, the event of June 17, 1994, is clearly the type of frontal attack on the judiciary that many persons I interviewed feared most. The National Assembly passed on its second reading the long-awaited Law on the Judiciary. The new law contains two features that affect judicial independence and a third section that impacts the participation of private client lawyers in the Supreme Judicial Council. President Zhelyu Zhelev returned the June law to Parliament with his objection that parts of the statute were unconstitutional.[12] The National Assembly, however, passed the law again and, as required by the Constitution, Zhelev signed the law. For each controversial statutory provision, the Constitutional Court was then asked to render judgments crucial to the role of jurists in the creation of a law-governed state.

A contentious element of this law is that every person occupying top positions in the judicial system must have at least five years of prior judicial experience, either as a judge or as a prosecutor. On its face, this provision requires high qualifications for office and, in the abstract, should not elicit opposition from those in favor of a professionally oriented independent judiciary. This is consistent with the idea that important judicial officials ought to be chosen on a merit basis. But the practical effect of this law is to purge the judiciary of anti-Communists. This is true because the only jurists meeting the five-year requirement must have necessarily come to their judicial posts during Communist Party rule, that is, before the November 1989 coup d'état. Only members of the Communist Party or individuals acceptable to the ruling oligarchy could become judges, magistrates, or prosecutors during the years of the old regime. It is widely thought that this qualifying provision was written into law so that two well-known figures who at the time lacked five years of previous experience could be ousted from office.[13]

The first is Ivan Grigorov, the chair of the Supreme Court. He is widely seen as the symbol of an independent judiciary and considered a staunch anti-Communist. This law also applied to Chief Prosecutor General Ivan Tatarchev. He is a highly visible opponent of illegal money-laundering operations and other white-collar criminal activity. Many Bulgarians believe that former and present leaders of the Communist Party, renamed the Bulgarian Socialist Party, are linked to these nefarious, self-serving activities. The most celebrated trial was that of Todor Zhivkov, the former president and Communist Party leader. But the net was cast wider to include contemporary politicians associated with the former Communist Party.[14] The chief prosecutor, appointed by the National Assembly before the anti-Communist bloc split and lost majority control of the National Assembly at the end of 1992, has also prosecuted three prominent BSP members of the Parliament for their activities in the years of the Communist rule. Andrey Lukanov, a leading member of the reform element of the Communist Party and a prime minister in the post-Communist era, and former interior minister Alexander Lilov have been subjected to criminal prosecutions. It is alleged that they used their official positions to provide weaponry and ammunition to countries with terrorist and totalitarian regimes.[15] Dimitar Velev was prosecuted for his connection with the regeneration process, the coercive change of ethnic Turk names during the 1980s.[16]

Members of the Bulgarian Socialist Party view these and other prosecutions as transparent attempts to exact revenge. They believe these actions represent a violation of earlier agreements for a peaceful transition to democracy; it was agreed that all sides would live together in a humane state without repeating the cycle of revenge and violence characteristic of Bulgaria's history. They assert the prosecutions are cynical attempts to cover up illegal activities in the years 1991–92 by the anti-Communist forces when the Union of Democratic Forces was in power. Lukanov contested his prosecution unsuccessfully in the Constitutional Court. He argued that it was a denial of his parliamentary immunity guaranteed under the July 1991 Constitution.[17] After Lukanov's death, the case was won, in November 1996, in the European Court of Human Rights at Strasbourg.[18]

Without specifying the targets of the legislation, the 1994 Judiciary Act, as fashioned by BSP members in cooperation with members of other parliamentary groups, required the immediate removal of both Supreme Court Chairman Grigorov and Chief Prosecutor Tatarchev. Neither person met the five-year prior experience requirement.

The Supreme Judicial Council (SJC) objected to the statutory provision requiring that its members have at least five years of professional experience as judges, prosecutors, investigating magistrates, or academics and that new elections for the SJC should be held within one month of the promulgation of the act. This statutory provision also provides that private lawyers shall not be eligible as SJC members. The latter provision is widely believed to be aimed at particular SJC members viewed as BSP enemies. The SJC complained about these provisions in the strongest possible terms, and the leader of the opposition UDF termed this situation a constitutional crisis. Days before the final vote on the 1994 Judiciary Act, Philip Dimitrov, then the leader of the opposition Union of Democratic Forces, said that the judiciary law represents a constitutional crisis because, under the Constitution, judges are permanent.[19]

The Council of Europe (CE) issued a memorandum criticizing the Judiciary Act as part of a larger assessment of Bulgaria's performance of its responsibilities under CE conventions and agreements.

Predictably, Bulgaria's CE representatives who were delegates of the Bulgarian Socialist Party and the Movement for Rights and Freedoms defended the new law. The UDF representatives walked out during the defense of the new law. Later, however, they issued a separate statement explicitly agreeing with the observations of the CE memorandum.[20]

President Zhelev petitioned the Constitutional Court for a ruling on the constitutionality of those sections of the act limiting the tenure of members of the judicial system and of the inclusion of private lawyers among the ranks of the Supreme Judicial Council. The Court ruled in favor of the proponents of judicial independence.[21] It found that paragraph 8 of the act requiring the dismissal of judges and prosecutors who lack five years of prior experience violates Article 129, section 3 of the Constitution, providing for life tenure of judges. Once appointed to the judiciary and having served the probationary period, the jurists' tenure cannot be violated but for the reasons specified in the article.

The Court also ruled that section 11 of the act, calling for new elections for members of the SJC, contravenes Article 130(4) of the Constitution requiring five-year terms of office. It is unconstitutional because section 11 of the Judiciary Act reduces the terms of office for SJC members by requiring elections within one month after promulgation of the act.

Finally, the Court addressed the issue of prohibiting private lawyers as SJC members. The decision refers to an earlier one decided on April 3, 1992.[22] The Court held that Article 130, section 2 of the Constitution determines in detail the requirements for SJC membership. It precludes the possibility of lawmakers narrowing the definition of the term *jurists* to exclude practicing lawyers other than judges, prosecutors, magistrates, or academics.

The election of the new Socialist government in late 1994, and the subsequent legislative enactments of the new Parliament in 1995, led to tensions between the Constitutional Court and the National Assembly. As I indicated in chapter 8, during the first nine months of the Socialist government, the Constitutional Court struck down six new laws.[23] During this period a disagreement of considerable constitutional importance involved the amendments to the Agricultural Land Tenure Act. President Zhelev, the petitioner, won the case. The Constitutional Court ruled unconstitutional that provision of the law

The Constitutional Court of the Republic of Bulgaria, 1994 term. From left to right: *Seated:* Tsanko Hadhystoyehev, Mladen Danailov, Assen Manov (president), Professor Milcho Kostov, Stanislav Dimitrov. *Standing:* Nikolay Pavlov, Alexander Arabadjiev, Georgi Markov, Ivan Grigorov, Professor Todor Todorov, Pencho Penev, Dimitar Gotchev

requiring landowners to first offer their property for sale to municipalities and the state before offering it to other buyers. The act violated the constitutional principle of the inviolability of property. The Court also struck down a provision of the new law that restricted the rights of former owners when their land had been improved by subsequent owners. Other provisions restricting the rights of property owners were similarly invalidated by the Constitutional Court.[24]

The press reported mass protests in the countryside against the decision of the Constitutional Court that invalidated nineteen amendments to the Land Act sponsored by the Socialist Party.[25] In a move viewed by the opposition Union of Democratic Forces as "a very dangerous signal," National Assembly chairman Blagovest Sendov met with the president of the Constitutional Court, Assen Manov.[26] Within weeks, President Zhelyu Zhelev and Prime Minister Zhan Videnov exchanged bitter remarks about the role of the Constitutional Court in the political life of the nation, and about the respective roles of Parliament and the presidency in the controversy.[27]

The interinstitutional conflict became less theoretical when, on August 3, 1995, the Council of Ministers evicted the Constitutional Court from its offices. This move was said to be temporary. The government explained that this was a necessary move to accommodate the space needs of the Central Electoral Commission in the building. However, commission members reportedly said that they did not need that much office space and that the decision was a "purely political act." The Court was told by the government to ask Parliament for new offices in the former Communist Party headquarters. But Justice Georgi Markov commented to the press that the government has "declared war on the Constitutional Court."[28]

Members of the Constitutional Court then unanimously decided to appeal the matter to its sister institution, the Supreme Court. But before the disposition of this matter was resolved, President Zhelev initiated an action before the Constitutional Court. He asked for an interpretation of an article in the Constitution that governs the authority of the Council of Ministers to manage state property.[29] On September 12 the Court rendered its predictable decision. It unanimously found that the Council of Ministers may not dispose of state property occupied by the president, the National Assembly, or judicial authorities without the consent of each.[30]

With the leasehold secure, the Constitutional Court survived the institutional attack. Nevertheless, Court members continue to find themselves entangled in the political thicket. Among other controversies coming before it in 1996, it adjudicated the respective authority of the president and Parliament in the appointment of judges. It also effectively disabled a popular BSP nominee to be placed on the presidential ballot.

The Supreme Judicial Council acted in anticipation of a parliamentary enactment that would finally resolve the processes and procedures of two constitutionally mandated courts. On June 26, 1996, this body, by majority vote, named chief judges of the Supreme Court of Cassation and the Supreme Administrative Court. Because these judicial institutions had not yet come into existence, the Socialist press dubbed them "phantom courts." Twenty-one of the twenty-five members of the

SJC took part in the vote by secret ballot. But the elections were held after its ex officio chairman, Justice Minister Mladen Chervenyakov, had left the room and declared the meeting adjourned. Chervenyakov and BSP parliamentarians declared that this action was a transparent attempt to pack the courts with antigovernment cadres.[31]

A day after the SJC action, President Zhelev signed the two judicial appointments, but Justice Minister Chervenyakov refused to countersign the decrees. Within twenty-four hours, the BSP-led Democratic Left parliamentary majority enacted a resolution declaring impermissible the actions taken by the SJC and President Zhelev. The National Assembly resolution obligated Zhan Videnov's BSP government to introduce by October 1996 a Supreme Administrative Court bill and other acts regulating a three-tier court system. A week later, Parliament enacted amendments to the Judiciary Act; the law mandates that the presidents of the courts in question may not be named before their creation and the passage of procedural laws regulating the three-instance judicial institutions.[32] President Zhelev issued a suspensory veto, which the National Assembly later overrode by a comfortable majority vote.

There was also an apparent attempt to foil by bureaucratic means President Zhelev's decree. The editor of the *State Gazette* caused the official announcement to appear in only some undistributed copies of the print run.[33] Zhelev publicly proclaimed that this action was a flagrant violation of the Constitution. He said: "Nobody can presume to halt the promulgation of an instrument issued by the head of state, even the chairman of the National Assembly, who is enjoined with the implementation of the 'Official Gazette' act. . . . Today's case sets a dangerous precedent which deals a blow to statehood and calls into question the functioning of the institutions of state."[34]

On July 25, 1996, the Constitutional Court rendered an opinion reminiscent of John Marshall's U.S. Supreme Court decision in *Marbury v. Madison* (1803). By a 11–1 vote, it held that after the president signed the decrees in question, the effect was immediate. The fact that the promulgation of the decrees in the official *State Gazette* was circumvented by a failure to circulate that document is of no consequence because the "Official Gazette" is only important as an announcement device; it does not concern the validity of any particular appointment.[35] The Court also ruled that the National Assembly exceeded its constitutional powers by attempting to limit the authority of the Supreme Judicial Council in naming the judges. Despite the obvious in-principle victory for the SJC and President Zhelev, the Constitutional Court did not rule on whether the two controversial persons named to the new courts could serve. That question awaited future adjudication.[36]

This controversy illustrates again the resolve of members of the Constitutional Court to use their authority to settle interinstitutional conflicts. It demonstrates how a Constitutional Court may employ its authority to settle conflicts among separate branches of government, and in the process contribute to the overall stability of the political system. Yet, at times, the exercise of constitutional authority may produce a negative response. To the extent that courts render controversial decisions that are difficult to explain, popular and elite support for the judiciary may erode and possibly undermine the level of legitimacy necessary for courts to function effectively.

The Constitutional Court's decision to interpret Bulgarian law in such a way as to invalidate the candidacy of a popular figure for president of the Republic presents such a problem. Foreign Minister Georgi Pirinski was the designated BSP candidate for president for the October 1996 elections. He was born in New York City in 1948 to an American mother and a Bulgarian father. The Constitutional Court interpreted Bulgarian law in force at the time of Pirinski's birth to mean that because U.S. law regards persons born in the U.S. as citizens, such a person is not a Bulgarian by birth. Therefore, under Article 93(2) of the 1991 Constitution, individuals born in such circumstances are ineligible *to be president,* although the Constitution contains no citizenship limitations on *who may be a candidate* for the presidency.[37]

From beginning to end, election politics engulfed the proceedings surrounding this case. Public opinion polls showed that Pirinski was either a likely winner or a serious contender in the elections to be held in late October 1996. It is therefore not surprising that fifty-four opposition members of Parliament filed the petition asking the Constitutional Court to rule on the citizenship question. In response, the BSP rushed through the National Assembly a bill stipulating that Bulgarian nationals by origin are persons who have one Bulgarian parent, no matter where they are born.[38]

The day after the Court's July 23, 1996, ruling, the BSP and the

UDF exchanged strident attacks on national television. The Socialist spokesperson charged that the UDF was trying to disqualify Pirinski and that they were "making a cat's paw of the Constitutional Court."[39] Later Pirinski and other BSP leaders denounced the decision as a politically motivated act. And they claimed that "the ruling heightens the tension and can destabilize the society."[40]

In the complaint the Constitutional Court was asked by the petitioners to rule on the abstract question of when citizenship obtains. In a rather awkward display of judicial self-restraint, the Court's rapporteur emphasized that the majority did not rule on the particular case of Georgi Pirinski. He indicated that if Pirinski should win the presidential election, then upon proper application the Court could rule on his eligibility to hold office. Few thought, however, that Pirinski's ability to obtain ballot access was anything but doubtful.

Nevertheless, Pirinski took the next formal step in advancing his candidacy: he petitioned the Central Election Commission (CEC) to have his name placed on the election ballot. Under law, this body is responsible for evaluating the credentials and documents of presidential contenders. On August 27, 1996, the CEC announced that it found inaccuracies in both the documents submitted by the UDF candidates and Pirinski. The defect in the documents submitted by the UDF candidates was minor: it was a technical failure to state clearly the status of the political forces supporting them.

The case against Pirinski, however, was more serious. The CEC voted eleven for and ten against his registration, three votes short of the two-thirds requirement necessary for ballot certification. The commission found that the documents submitted by Pirinski did not establish clearly how he acquired Bulgarian citizenship. With this negative result, the BSP again publicly registered its disapproval; the opposition forces displayed satisfaction with their opponents' predicament and revealed little apprehension for their own.[41]

Within days, the opposing forces, each for their own reasons, appealed the matter to a five-member panel of the Supreme Court. On September 2, 1996, this court unanimously rejected the BSP petition. It found that Pirinski did not hold Bulgarian citizenship at the time of his birth. The decision was final and unappealable. On September 4, 1996, the Supreme Court panel ruled on the UDF petition. This time, however, the Supreme Court found for the UDF, ordering the UDF candidates for president and vice president to be placed on the October ballot.[42] BSP officials bitterly denounced the Supreme Court's negative decision respecting Pirinski's candidacy. The candidate himself initially said he would appeal his case to the European Court of Human Rights.[43] But behaving as practical politicians and, in the process, avoiding a constitutional crisis of major proportions, the BSP leadership decided to name new candidates: Ivan Marazov, Pirinski's vice presidential running mate, as the presidential candidate and Deputy Foreign Minister Irina Bokova as the new vice presidential entry.[44]

In the end, the Socialist Party candidate lost to the UDF candidate in a November 3, 1996, runoff. Petar Stoyanov won 60 percent of the total vote. The voter turnout is comparable to the first presidential election in January 1992, with 62 percent of the eligible voters going to the polls.[45] Despite widespread dissatisfaction with the ability of the parliamentary majority to cope with the nation's problems, the result of this election reflects diffuse support for the democratic regime. This conclusion is especially warranted if one makes the invidious comparison to the presidential election held a few days later in the United States. With only 48 percent of the eligible voters going to the polls, President William Clinton defeated former senator Robert Dole while receiving only 49 percent of the total votes.

Clearly, constitutional politics played an important part in the struggle for power between rival forces in Bulgaria's 1996 presidential elections. Significantly, the willingness of BSP leaders to abide by the problematic decision of the Constitutional Court supports the conclusion that among ruling elements within Bulgarian society there is an adherence to the constitutional rules of the game, even when the rules are used in ways that disadvantage them politically. This speaks eloquently for a successful transition to democracy. Yet, members of the Constitutional Court cannot but realize that decisions such as this one will reinforce the resolve of their opponents in high places. Furthermore, it may make it difficult for them to elicit widespread public support for interinstitutional battles that are yet to come.

Expectation of Interinstitutional Conflict

The incidents of interinstitutional conflict may be interpreted as indicative of basic instability. Though it is true that the outcomes of the various clashes among government institutions may be detrimental to the maintenance of democracy, there is an alternative interpretation that is more favorable. Particularly where there is inexperience with institutions, reasonable persons may disagree about how each institution should function and relate to the other. The Constitutional Court is new to Bulgaria. How active it should be in the political life of the nation is a question that can be answered only within the context of events. The presidential institution is endowed with few independent powers, and yet, the officeholder is elected by all of the people on a separate ballot. This raises a serious issue: How and for what purpose should the president exercise leadership? With respect to the proper conduct of political parties in the National Assembly, it must be asked: Where there is a long-standing void of competing political parties, what is the responsibility of a loyal opposition in Parliament? Furthermore, constitutional issues are resolved within the context of practical politics. Political forces operate to shape constitutional structures. They bend these structures to the felt necessities of the time, or, in other words, interinstitutional conflicts reflect the struggle for policy domination. President Zhelev, for example, used the Constitutional Court to challenge the land reform, privatization, and other policies of the Socialist government. The Court rendered authoritative decisions that the National Assembly then employed to adjust its legislative judgments to conform with constitutional strictures.

Prime Minister Zhan Videnov commented that conflict among the various institutions of government is common in those societies in Eastern Europe undergoing a transition to democracy.[46] The evidence supports his conclusion. For example, scholarly articles have been written on the conflict between the Romanian Constitutional Court and Parliament, the struggle between the president and Parliament in Slovakia, and constitutional brinkmanship in Poland.[47] The *East European Constitutional Review* features country-by-country updates on constitutional politics in Eastern Europe and the former republics of the Soviet Union.

In the final analysis, the constitutional politics practiced in Bulgaria are not unusual or particularly abhorrent. In the process of *practicing* democracy, Bulgarians are giving meaning and shape to their new institutions. In the aftermath of the transition to democracy, the consolidation phase is progressing as might reasonably be expected.

10

Conclusions

The Bulgarian experience contributes to an understanding of what may be necessary for successful transitions from totalitarianism or authoritarianism to democracy. One important conclusion is that it is erroneous to suppose that certain oft-cited prerequisites are necessary for democracy to succeed. Democracy may come into existence when opposing sides negotiate an agreement that is in their mutual self-interest. Giuseppe Di Palma's analysis fits the Bulgarian experience. Democracies may be created even when the supposed macro political, economic, and social preconditions for their creation and survival are absent. There is no doubt that the principal cause for elite support from within the BCP for the creation of democratic institutions was a desire to share political power rather than lose it completely. The result of accommodating the old and new forces in Bulgaria was the creation of institutions that have had an autonomous influence on subsequent political relations. Parliamentary government is a fact of Bulgarian political life. The new institutions created by the Roundtable and the Grand National Assembly have taken on a life of their own. Although fragile, these institutions are shaping the manner and nature of political discourse and coaxing civil society into what may become a stable and vigorous existence.

No one denies that a survey of the world will confirm the observation that, historically speaking, democracy as a working system of government is the exception and not the rule. To be sure, authoritarian and totalitarian regimes are easier to create and maintain than democratic ones. But the prior successful transitions in Western Europe and Latin America and now the successful transitions in Eastern Europe suggest that something is wrong with the conventional wisdom. In

Bulgaria, like the rest of Eastern Europe, there was no meaningful competition among political parties. There was little in terms of a middle class. During the last years under Communism, Bulgaria's economy suffered from stagnation and insufficient growth to satisfy both mass and elite expectations.[1] Though many Bulgarians owned their own homes and even country cottages, they were not free to own property in the Western sense of an entitlement to do with it whatever they wanted; they needed permission of one government body or another to use or dispose of their possession. There was no entrepreneurial class that might serve as the rudiments of interest group pluralism. Other than the Communist Party, and unlike the Polish case, for example, there were few power-wielding groups to which one might belong.[2] Consequently, it was difficult for most people to acquire the skills necessary for creating a civil society. Indeed, most observers viewed Bulgaria as a repressive regime. Yet, the history of post-Communist Bulgaria tells another story and beckons us to search for new explanations.

Pacts, Will, and Results

The objective facts militating against transitions to democracy are significant. But as the Bulgarian case illustrates, the reduction of these probabilistic findings to individual cases is quite another matter. In brief, there is no iron law of preconditions necessary for democracy. Giuseppe Di Palma is correct: it is possible to *will* a democratic system into existence. It can happen if the participants in the struggle for power understand it is in their mutual interest to reach an accommodation that guarantees the principal competing forces a place at the table. In Bulgaria, the forces of the opposing sides came together to negotiate what Di Palma calls in another context *reforma pactada:* taking their chances in an uncertain democratic order, this is an agreement to live by new rules that sanction the *legitimacy* of reform elements of the old regime and opposition groups. If the negotiators carefully craft such an agreement, as was true for Bulgaria, democratization can be more than a pipe dream. In short, as Di Palma maintains, transferring loyalties from authoritarian or totalitarian regimes to democratic ones is less difficult than most scholars think.[3]

In Bulgaria, the principals agreed on particular democratic rules, including a parliamentary system and a Constitutional Court with the authority to protect human rights. Rather than attempting to forge a new regime by itself, reform elements within the then existing Communist Party actively sought to create agreements with their opponents that were organized under the auspices of the Union of Democratic Forces. Furthermore, though not a perfect umbrella organization, the UDF spoke for most oppositionist groups; it forcefully placed demands upon the reform leaders of the Communist Party to yield concessions in return for a place in Bulgaria's uncertain democratic future. Finally, the conscious timing of the accommodation for political change was superb. The day after the Berlin Wall fell, reformers within the Communist Party executed a coup d'état against their aging leader, Todor Zhivkov. The preexisting Ecoglasnost movement served to bring together regime opponents to negotiate with the new leaders of the Party and government. Together, they agreed within months upon the basic rules for the prospective democracy, including free elections for a Grand National Assembly. And while the politics of the Grand National Assembly were occasionally tumultuous, the deputies were able to forge a new Constitution. This document serves as the operating guide for how to conduct the governmental process in a democratic Bulgaria.

But beware of those who scheme to use democratic processes to defeat and subjugate their enemies. Distrust of the motives of the reform remnants of the discredited Communist regime renders the democratic pact suspect and those who created it as potential enemies of the peoples' true aspirations. While recognizing the basis for such trepidation, it is nonetheless unnecessary for functionaries of the past undemocratic regime to undergo a profound conversion at the altar of democracy to conjure up a new order. The enlightened self-interest of the leaders of the renamed Communist Party, now the Bulgarian Socialist Party, operated to convince party functionaries that their future survival depended upon the formation of a new democratic form of government. They understood that if they were to survive they would have to compete with opposing forces for the votes of the people.

Given the alternative, there is little wonder that the leaders of the BSP participated in the creation of the July 1991 Constitution. At the same time, opponents of the former Communist Party sought to avoid civil war while also guaranteeing a democratic future. They agreed to accept the possibility that their former oppressors might retain power by winning elections. In fact, after the BSP won a majority of the seats in the Grand National Assembly at the June 1990 elections, their democratic opponents resolved to continue the process of democratization. Despite suffering disunity from within their own ranks, they struggled to draft a new constitution. This was done with the faith that by participating in democratic politics now, they would get their chance later to dislodge the BSP from control of the government. The combined anti-BSP forces did just that at the next general election in October 1991. But one year later, the UDF lost control of the government. Many opposition leaders who participated as GNA deputies suffered defeat at the polls. Parties led by such luminaries as Dertliev, Ganev, and Simeonov were unable to garner the requisite 4 percent of the votes necessary for seats in the National Assembly. Ironically, therefore, some important architects of Bulgaria's democratic Constitution have been relegated to the sidelines of a political system they were responsible for helping to create.

It is problematic whether political parties played a positive role in creating parliamentary government in Bulgaria. As the Bulgarian political scientist Georgi Karasimeonov points out, the highly confrontational relationship between the major parties makes it difficult to institute needed reforms, particularly economic changes. Indeed, the promise of the Bulgarian transition to democracy is one of accommodation, compromise, tolerance, and political dialogue. To the extent that the parties have behaved in ways that are contrary to the institutionalization of political pluralism, progress toward democratic consolidation is retarded.[4] Yet, there is sufficient evidence to support the conclusion that Bulgaria's existing parties are fulfilling the major tasks thought desirable for the functioning of democratic institutions. They nominate candidates for the principal elective and appointive offices. They conduct election campaigns. They educate the voters through the comparison of the alternative candidates and treatment of issues. And they are integrating the various societal groups into the political system. In essence, political parties are providing citizens with genuine choices, and this is the central feature of a working democracy.

Roundtable and New Constitution Linkage

In medieval Europe legislative assemblies arose because monarchs sought consultation and consent from powerful forces in society. This sometimes difficult process was important for knitting society together in the pursuit of both specific and diffuse policy goals.[5] As a representative assembly of divergent sources of opinion and power, Bulgaria's National Roundtable Talks fulfilled a similar function. The event of the National Roundtable Talks was an important step in the creation of a democratic constitution on the way to regime change. It is the foundation for creating a civil society and was an important and effective step in the de-Stalinization of Bulgarian society.

Yet, some criticize the Roundtable because it failed to eliminate completely the power and influence of the Communist Party, which became the Bulgarian Socialist Party. Indeed, following the June 1990 elections held after the Roundtable Talks, Bulgaria had a Socialist president, a Socialist government, and a Socialist majority in its parliament. The old Communist Party was still in business, albeit under a different name. Moreover, the Roundtable had conferred legitimacy on what some might term wolves in sheep's clothing.[6] This analysis, however, overlooks the broader systemic results. With a minimum of violence and bloodshed, it is no longer appropriate to classify Bulgaria as a totalitarian or authoritarian state. The Constitution adopted in July 1991 reflects the fundamental agreements negotiated at the Roundtable. It contains most of the institutional features of what are universally understood as embodying democratic values. A deep commitment to human rights is clear, and there is a mechanism for defending those rights through an independent judicial system, including a Constitutional Court whose essential role is to do just that.

On the other hand, a fundamental difficulty with the July 1991 Constitution may be traced to an early Roundtable decision. Representatives of the Turkish ethnic minority were never part of the Roundtable deliberations, although both sides publicly invited them to participate. The Roundtable subsequently failed to come to terms with representation of the Turkish minority. In so doing, it missed an important opportunity to deal with an underlying tension in Bulgarian society. The 1991 Constitution denies the right of political parties to be based on ethnic, racial, or religious lines. The Bulgarian Constitutional Court successfully turned back this threat to democratic representation in the political process when it ruled in favor of the right of the Turkish movement, MRF, to participate in elections.[7] Moreover, between August 1990 and the end of 1997, Bulgaria has had six different governments, and the MRF has been a pivotal force in the creation and maintenance of several of those shaky governments. But do not jump to the hasty conclusion that evidence of failed governments proves that democracy is faltering. When governments fail, it is as much a sign that democracy is working as it is an indication of system disequilibrium and instability.

Participants in the Grand National Assembly disagree whether the time spent in crafting a new constitution was worth the result. Some well-meaning and informed persons believe the energy and political capital expended on this secondary task detracted unnecessarily from the primary duty of truly reforming Bulgarian society. The more pressing problem, they argue, was how to purge Bulgaria from its Communist Party–driven bureaucratic structures and its commitment to socialist solutions for economic problems. What was needed in its place, the critics say, is a government completely free of its past organizing principle and an economy amenable to strong capitalist influences. The Hungarian example, they argue, may have been a better model. The lesson is to amend the constitution as needed in a piecemeal fashion. Meanwhile, get on with the pressing problems of substantive reform. I am hard-pressed to argue that a new constitution was a condition precedent for Bulgaria to become a democracy. After all, most other former totalitarian states have not had constitutional conventions. Nonetheless, they have amended as needed their basic constitutions, reflecting an understanding of what new political rules of the game might be required given the changing political order.

Thus, looking at it from an American historical viewpoint, one plausible lesson of the Bulgarian experience may be just the opposite of what one might suppose. In one sense, the critics may have been right: it was a waste of time, energy, and political capital to hold a constitutional convention. What is essential is reaching an accommodation for a peaceful transition to democracy. This can be done with or without holding a constitutional convention. On the other hand, the symbolism of writing new constitutional rules is important evidence that the political system is undergoing fundamental change. Bulgaria's July 1991 Constitution is a progressive one, and the notion of a law-governed state is central to its design. In this sense, the new Constitution is an outward and visible sign of the rejection of the past forty-five years. Additionally, beginning with the first one held in 1879, Bulgarians redefine their political identity by holding Grand National Assemblies. In this sense, the GNA is a historical device linking Bulgarians to their past. For the anti-Communist forces, the July 1991 Constitution is concrete evidence of basic change. And for their part, the reform Communists can lay claim to a legitimacy that otherwise would be denied to them.

But there is more to the argument in favor of constitution writing when the goal is to create a successful transition to democracy. In the Bulgarian context, crafting a new constitution made good sense and may very well have important applications elsewhere.

The idea for rewriting the entire Constitution was one insisted upon by the anti-Communist forces within the UDF. The democratic opposition expended considerable energy in the constitution-making process, while the leaders of the former Communist Party acquiesced willingly and contributed considerably to that process. Ironically, in the end the renamed Bulgarian Communist Party strongly endorsed the new Constitution, leaving in its wake a severely split democratic opposition. The source of the disunity is not so much criticism of particular constitutional provisions as it is the failure of the opposition to exact revenge against the ruling elite of the ancien regime. That is, some democratic opponents to the Bulgarian Socialist Party would have preferred something akin to a de-Nazification program. A large net would be cast that in the end would punish a large number of Party functionaries for their past misdeeds. To have yielded to such demands, however, would mean the nullification of the *reforma pactada,* and the unraveling of the agreement to live together with all the uncertainties implicit in democracy.

A fortiori, by committing to paper basic understandings in the form of constitutional rules and principles, the opposition leaders insured for themselves an opportunity to compete in the new order. They were outlining in advance the rules of the game, including the norms for how institutions are to function. These perceptive democrats understood that inevitably there would be conflict over substantive policy goals, but they resolved to minimize conflict over the rules. For them, an *implicit* rather than an *explicit* acceptance of democracy by consent is as unacceptable as totalitarianism by consent. Like the couple who tie the wedding knot in a civil ceremony but then renew their vows before God in a church, the democratic opponents who insisted upon a new constitution sought to insure that the vows that tie the nation together are indeed secure.

It is not surprising that opposition leaders were not united during and after the Grand National Assembly proceedings. Although they could all agree on the desirability of displacing forever the former party state with a law-governed one, they came to the bargaining table with differing personal and group agendas. It was not unexpected that some movements and parties would, as they did, fall by the wayside along the route to a civil and political society. Parties have been reconstituted and different segments of the changing society are now represented in politics. These organizations were not present at the time of either the National Roundtable Talks or the Grand National Assembly. Some of these change agents preferred a different kind of political order than the one contemplated by the reformed Communists and most of their so-called democratic opponents. For example, monarchists sought a return of a bygone era with the restoration of the dead king's son to the throne. I do not think, however, that monarchy was an alternative that ever had a realistic chance to win constitutional sanction. Instead, the monarchist movement represents an example of the wide range of views within the opposition circle. The extent of internal disunity experienced within the ranks of the democratic opposition was not experienced by the post-Communist Bulgarian Socialist Party, although hard-line advocates were present. Those closet Communists longing for the past regime wisely muted their feelings; and in the process they allowed their reform-minded comrades to negotiate the tricky path toward survival.

At bottom, what is most important is not a few specific criticisms of the new Constitution offered up by a variety of malcontents. Rather, the opponents of the new Constitution object fundamentally to the willingness to work with the members of the former Communist Party in creating a new constitutional system. And this view extends to working with them on the everyday issues facing the nation.

Those who oppose cooperation with the functionaries of the former Communist Party have good reasons to resist the task. But these otherwise well-intentioned persons commit a fundamental error that is detrimental to the future of democracy in their homeland. They make support for reform of the everyday workings of the system the test of legitimacy, when, instead, coexistence should be the test of whether the system is the expression of the national will. In the extreme, some opposition leaders make the test for support of the new system whether the former leaders and their political progeny have suffered sufficiently. They want assurances that the power and privilege that accompany it are forever gone. Concomitantly, they seek the liberal democratic antidotes of capitalism and tend to damn social democratic programs associated with the welfare state as residual vestiges of the previous totalitarian regime.

But, as Di Palma teaches, democracy is about process and procedures, not substantive ends. Democracy is a way to organize political discourse and competition among societal forces. In other words, democracy has proven an unreliable guarantor of social progress.[8] No doubt many Bulgarians assume that with democracy comes capitalism and with capitalism they will experience prosperity. Yet, in the aftermath of the downfall of the old regime and the creation of democratic institutions, Bulgarians have experienced an unfortunate deterioration in the quality of their lives. A report of the United Nations indicates that in 1995, five years after the coup d'état, unemployment in Bulgaria is conservatively estimated at 12 percent, there is outrageous inflation, the quality of medical care is said to be deteriorating, and the crime rate is fantastically high.[9] In 1996, the Bulgarian lev depreciated by 600 percent against the U.S. dollar.[10] Along with this inflation, there was a serious bread shortage, rendering Bulgaria even poorer than in the last days of the Communist regime. Nonetheless, despite the failure to achieve the good life and regardless of who might be to blame for its nonrealization, democracy as a set of procedures is desirable.

Di Palma's argument is persuasive. Democracy curbs government oppression of groups and individuals. The guarantee to the ethnic Turkish minority is a major example of how democracy as a set of procedures has allowed this minority to protect themselves from a potentially abusive majority. Further, democracy as a set of procedures not only guarantees the mutual coexistence of the reform Communists and their democratic opponents but also has reconstituted the community in a way that establishes the personal self-worth of individuals.[11]

The Bulgarian experience also reaffirms the common but little expressed observation that if citizens are to become rulers they must learn how to manage democratic institutions. It was not enough for opposition leaders to engage in vigorous protest against the Communist leadership. There is evidence of a self-consciousness among the proponents of Bulgaria's new Constitution. They knew it is not enough to go from the streets to Parliament armed only with good intentions. Instead, it is necessary to comprehend the importance of legislative deliberation and to fully discuss matters that would come before the Grand National Assembly.

In this respect, it is instructive to recall the role of particular individuals in persevering to the end. The institutional norm that voting be not automatic but something resembling reasoned analysis among colleagues did not just happen. Certain individuals at the Grand National Assembly insisted upon it. It is also noteworthy, but hardly a new revelation, that persons who stick their political necks out to make accommodation work will be blamed for whatever goes wrong. That happened to many talented and dedicated opposition leaders. They have been consigned to the political wilderness. Perhaps, however, history will be kind to them. Finally, there were sufficient opportunities for the Grand National Assembly to fold its tent and for the deputies to return home. But certain individuals insisted that the peoples' deputies persevere. The result of this individual effort by a relative few was the promulgation of a fundamentally democratic and modern constitution. Today, that same basic document functions as a set of principles and rules. It points Bulgaria to the goal of a law-governed state and is a break against backsliding into a totalitarian abyss.

Herein lies an important residual consequence of crafting a new constitution. When ascertaining the relative advantage each group may have over the others, all sides are compelled to calculate the short- and long-term implications of their collective decisions. And in the process of negotiation they must work with opponents no matter how respected or despised. Crafting a new constitution for Bulgaria was a lesson in democracy that participants can draw upon to meet future challenges. They may apply these lessons, even the negative ones, to understand how to craft agreements in an emerging democratic political culture.

A Successful Transition?

Bulgaria's leaders of all ideological stripes know it is necessary to work at the democratic process by institutionalizing procedures and inculcating democratic attitudes. It is a delicate matter. Ginio Ganev's insistence that "automatic voting" must be eschewed in favor of full debate manifests the importance of creating democratic habits that in turn contribute to the legitimacy of the system as a whole. Then, too, in October 1993, the father of the Constitution, Petar Dertliev, was encouraging the type of dialogue necessary to create and sustain democratic habits. Long after the GNA had finished its business, and governments had come and gone, he convened a meeting of a variety of political parties and movements to discuss how the nation should in the future treat ethnic minorities. Moreover, as the parliamentary system is institutionalized and the roles of the president, the Council of Ministers, and the judiciary are better understood, the concept of constitutionalism will become more deeply embedded within the psyche of the body politic. Though this process is fraught with peril, the prospects are encouraging.

Admittedly, the path toward democracy is not a straight one. Despite the guarantees of the National Roundtable Talks and the explicit agreements found in the July 1991 Constitution, political actors of all stripes find it difficult to work in harmony with their opponents. There is evidence of interinstitutional conflict among the separate constitutional authorities. But this occurs in most every democracy because boundaries of authority tend to be unclear or ambiguous. These kinds of disputes are exacerbated by the tradition of vendetta endemic to Bulgaria and the Balkans generally. Mistrust and hatred can operate as sturdy impediments to the task of institutionalizing democratic norms. Furthermore, the misunderstood promise of democracy as a way to achieve economic prosperity is bound to breed cynicism and despair. Yet, everyone I interviewed insists that Bulgaria will not return to its totalitarian past. In the years since the 1989 coup d'état ending Communist rule, Bulgarians have been practicing the democratic arts.

Parliamentary elections have been held. As of September 1997, there have been only a few notable incidents involving violence. In the meantime, governments with different agendas have come and gone. The courts are functioning, and they have defended the Constitution from attack. With a few notable exceptions, there is healthy debate about policy choices conducted in an environment relatively free from oppression and intimidation. Significantly, Bulgarians achieved these huge accomplishments without the existence of the so-called prerequisites for democracy.

But is it true that Bulgaria has successfully made the transition to democracy? This query is particularly pertinent because I have not presented new empirical evidence of my own that the masses in Bulgaria support the new democratic order. Where, one might ask, is the original research demonstrating a deep reservoir of diffuse support for the democratic regime and where is the analysis of how specific support may or may not impact diffuse support?

My answer is twofold. First, survey opinion research conducted by researchers in Bulgaria indicates that while there may be disappointment in political personalities, parties, and the slow pace of economic progress, there exists mass support for the democratic regime. Moreover, there is widespread participation in elections far beyond voter turnout found in the United States.[12] However, the second part of my response is more important. We do not need public opinion surveys to demonstrate that consent, compliance, and support are present within a transitional political system. Di Palma is correct: if the pact agreement with its protection for the participation of all relevant parties in the new political order is carefully crafted, then, by definition, legitimacy is an accomplished fact. The threat of breakdown games is removed when the choices are made for democratization.[13]

Although there are noteworthy differences between the transitions in Spain and in Bulgaria,[14] in both places the transition to democracy was a movement from the top. Leading reform elements of the old regime came together with regime opponents who were mostly members of Bulgaria's intellectual elite. Though there were mass protests, they were often organized by intellectuals who succeeded in keeping demonstrations from deteriorating into mob rule. Further, to the extent that the Communist regime of Todor Zhivkov may have enjoyed some public support (albeit support of the quiescent variety borne of resignation), and because the proximate origin of the transition to democracy came from within the existing regime itself, it is fair to conclude there must have been widespread support for change. This conclusion is buttressed by the fact that the November 10, 1989, coup d'état was bloodless and there is no evidence that the people rose up to restore Zhivkov and his confidants to power. There were no strikes, no mass demonstrations, and no opposition from below remonstrating in favor of the old government. Soon after the time of regime change and the events surrounding the National Roundtable Talks, there were free and competitive elections: citizens formed political parties and movements; Bulgarians participated in the political process by voting in large numbers, with 91 percent of the eligible voters casting votes in the first ballot and 84 percent in the second round of the June 1990 elections for the Grand National Assembly.[15]

Though there is considerable debate among Bulgarians about which political parties are best suited to lead the nation, no one seriously believes that totalitarian communism will return. Democratic institutions and processes will survive. Yet, at the same time, there is doubt about the wisdom and ability to achieve the substantive ends sought by many arch-opponents of communism.

Former President Zhelyu Zhelev, onetime academic philosopher and a leading figure in Bulgaria's transition to democracy, expresses the anxiety of many opponents of the failed Socialist government of Zhan Videnov and others who would presume to lead under the BSP banner. In Berlin on September 22, 1995, Zhelev presented a lecture at an international conference. He said in part: "Communism cannot return in its classical form."[16] This is the case, as he explains, because the dominant elite cannot abolish the multiparty system, eliminate the opposition, prohibit freedom of speech and of the press, or resurrect the concentration camps. It is no longer possible to close off the boundaries of a country and revive the Warsaw treaty.[17] In other words, Zhelev affirms the proposition that from a procedural viewpoint there is no dispute that Bulgaria has achieved a successful transition to democracy.

But there is an important difference between process and substantive meanings of democracy. There are no guarantees that because a nation-state adopts democratic ways of conducting public affairs that policy goals aimed at elevating individual freedom over various forms of collectivism will finally triumph. In fact, the exercise of procedural democracy may, depending upon the fashion of the day, result in viewing the state as the guarantor of human happiness. For this very reason, Zhelev is critical of the Socialists. He exclaims: "What we are faced with now is a substitution of the democratic idea for multiparty authoritarian chaos, breeding crime, organized crime, mafia structures, corruption and political partisanship, and a substitution of the idea of a free market for non-market capitalism." Bulgaria is facing, according to Zhelev, the threat of "communism dragging fledgling democracy into its grave."[18]

Though Zhelev's hyperbole ought to be placed in perspective as political rhetoric, the concern is a genuine one. What worries Zhelev, and other thoughtful persons, are the residual effects of the past political culture. The Bulgarian Socialist Party promotes the state as the salvation of society. According to Zhelev, the Socialists are the authors of the view that public ownership is good and private property is bad. He believes the Socialists are trying to use the state to dominate the nongovernmental sector of society.[19]

Though Zhelev's concern should be taken seriously, opponents of socialism must recognize the probability that Bulgarians will reject the most extreme classical liberal vision of democracy: one that exalts individual liberty with its emphasis on private property over a social democratic perspective that focuses on equality, especially in the economic realm. In this sense, there is little reason to expect Bulgarians to differ significantly from their Western European cousins. There will be continuing conflicts between those who place a value on limited government, on one hand, and those who view government as a positive force for achieving equality, on the other. Surely, the two views will collide and various political parties will exist to champion variations on each theme. The point worth recalling is that a central precept of democracy is the acceptance of the unpredictability of the result. The only certainty is that all sides must behave according to the rules of the game.

Under tragic circumstances, various institutions and factions within Bulgaria's parliamentary government had the occasion to reaffirm their commitment to the democratic transition. On October 2, 1996, Andrey Lukanov, the former prime minister and articulate leader of the BSP, was assassinated. As of December 1997, it is not known who fatally shot Lukanov twice outside his apartment in downtown Sofia and for what reason. All agree, however, that it was a professional murder reminiscent of the assassinations that characterized Bulgarian political life between 1878 and the mid-1930s. In the months preceding his murder, there had been a few minor incidents involving pipe bombs exploded in the typical terrorist fashion. As my interview with him reported in earlier chapters indicates, Lukanov was a chief architect and engineer in the peaceful coup that brought down the regime of Todor Zhivkov. He was also an active BSP leader at the National Roundtable Talks, a deputy at the Grand National Assembly, twice prime minister, and an active parliamentarian. Ironically, Andrey Lukanov became the victim of the same type of violence that had touched his grandfather and other notable Bulgarian families.

At the time of his death, Lukanov had become a very controversial figure. In 1992 he was stripped of his parliamentary immunity and charged with misappropriation and misuse of power and jailed for several months. He took his case to the European Court of Human Rights in Strasbourg. Eight weeks after his death the court vindicated him; it found that the UDF government of Philip Dimitrov had violated his rights and should award him FFr 1,000 for each day of his arrest.[20] By mid-1996, Lukanov had become a vocal critic of the BSP government of Zhan Videnov; he accused the government of trying to revive Stalinist structures and attempting to reestablish links between the secret service and the party. Moreover, Lukanov became a successful businessman and was accused by his opponents of using his political position to make himself and his friends rich.

There is some speculation that Lukanov's assassination was not for political reasons but might be related instead to his business dealings. But the political establishment reacted to the assassination as an attack on democracy itself. Parliament issued a declaration on the same day as the assassination. It said it part:[21]

> The National Assembly of the Republic of Bulgaria categorically denounces this flagrant terrorist act targeted at a political figure. We insist that its perpetrators and instigators be apprehended and punished with all the stringency of the law. In these times of difficulties and crisis the Bulgarian parliament declares its firm will to uphold the democratic processes in the country. We decisively oppose all attempts to destabilize Bulgaria's political and social life through

> such provocations. We shall not permit this act of terrorism to lead to the introduction of a state of emergency in the country. The presidential elections will be held on October 27, as previously scheduled by the National Assembly. We summon all Bulgarian citizens to keep their calm and, together with us, stand for the constitutional order and the irreversible democratic development of Bulgaria.

Other political bodies, including the president, the Constitutional Court, and political parties issued similarly worded declarations in support of democratic institutions.[22] Thus, Bulgarian leaders used the tragic occasion of Lukanov's murder to reaffirm their commitment to hold to the democratic course. They stay the course although democracy has not delivered the substantive ends that many thought would accrue with the rejection of Communism. And, of course, the urge to insure order at the expense of liberty is an option that authoritarian personality types eagerly pursue when the moment is ripe. Responsible officials understand that resorting to violence is an option that some may be preparing to pursue. The murder of Lukanov is the type of event that could trigger the cycle of violence that so many leaders, including the slain leader himself, had hoped the transition to democracy might avoid. To their credit, the nation's leaders unanimously and publicly rejected any suggestion that it is time to give up on democracy. Instead, democracy as a way to conduct government affairs remains the only option they are willing to consider, or so it would seem.

Qualifying language is necessary because in January 1997 political leaders violated if not the letter then the spirit of the constitutional rules. By using street demonstrations and labor strikes, opponents demanded that the Socialist government forego its mandate to form a new government and instead to call early elections. From a constitutional perspective, the BSP had every right to form a new cabinet and to continue to rule until the end of their election mandate in 1998. That is, unless at some point a majority of members of the National Assembly were to vote no-confidence. Instead, the BSP leadership capitulated to the demands of their opponents both in and outside the National Assembly. Though properly speaking the BSP agreed to new elections, there can be no mistake: they were forced from office by opponents employing extraconstitutional means to achieve what passes for a democratic end. While this episode is troubling from the viewpoint of a law-governed state, the willingness to give up power without resorting to the use of force reaffirms the basic commitment made at the National Roundtable Talks. The incumbent rulers agreed to take their chances with the competition at the ballot box. In this sense, Bulgarians renewed their commitment to political competition as a way of choosing leaders. Under the circumstances, the expression of three cheers for democracy may be excessive, but two cheers are in order.

Policy Implications

There are additional implications for scholars and policymakers in the so-called developed Western democracies. The first has to do with the general theory of politics, and the second with the practical implications of economic, political, military, and moral aid to authoritarian or totalitarian governments that are not yet democratic. As one might expect, there is an interrelationship between the theoretical and practical questions.

No doubt if a number of favorable environmental conditions are present, the chances for democracy taking root are greater than if such conditions are not present. Thus, if a state is blessed with a strong economy, a middle class, competitive political parties, and a civic culture, for example, then democracy is more likely to take root and to flourish than if they are not present. Variations on this theme may be gleaned from the works of the world's best minds, beginning with the Greeks, including Plato and Aristotle.[23]

With the addition of key concepts and variables, the careful and thoughtful scholars of the post-World War II era reinforced and modified the earlier conclusions, applying them to the problems of the Cold War era. Because certain anomalies appeared in such places as Spain, Turkey, Portugal, and Greece in the 1970s and early 1980s, scholars, had, however, sufficient reason to question the accepted wisdom. But the events in the former Soviet Union and in the Eastern bloc countries of the Warsaw Pact shook our confidence even more profoundly. Extant theories could not explain the demise of the Soviet Union and her empire. The failure to anticipate these events is a significant reason for the lack of a coherent foreign policy to deal with the new realities in Eastern Europe and the republics of the former Soviet Union. At bottom, this failure is due to a theoretical approach that fails to consider the role of individuals in bringing about change.

One cannot understand the demise of the Soviet Union without considering the pivotal roles of Gorbachev with his perestroika and glasnost. At the same time, the impact of the ideological determination of Gorbachev's American counterpart was pivotal. Ronald Reagan's relentless anticommunism manifested by an enormous defense buildup that forced the Soviets to respond in kind helped to bankrupt that country, to say nothing of the United States. By exercising their will and knowing how to translate their individual judgments into collective government action, both Gorbachev and Reagan changed the world. Yet, our theories failed to anticipate such an eventuality.

Giuseppe Di Palma's *To Craft Democracies* is a welcomed antidote to the sociological and economic determinism of modern social science. No doubt, *interests, ideas,* and *institutions* play significant roles in shaping events. But so do *individuals.* Individuals often behave in predictable ways. Without such an understanding a science of man would be impossible. But while it is important to understand the centrality of that behavior, we must remember that such predictions are based upon probabilities and that deviations from the central tendency also need explanation. Indeed, quite often the most interesting problems begging explanation are why and how events deviate from the norm. The anomalies, in other words, are often the most engaging and scientifically important questions worth pursuing. Yet, they are also the most difficult to explain. For some important cases, such as transitions to democracy, explanation may lie in the exercise of individual will. Even one of the most extreme forms of determinism, the historical materialism of Karl Marx, is often misunderstood. He did not argue that revolution was simply the function of our sociology borne of economic conditions wherein individual decisions and psychology have no role to play. Rather, properly understood, Marx argued that we will *will* a revolution.[24]

Bulgaria's transition to democracy illustrates one scenario of how to overcome the odds against democracy. It is similar to the Spanish experience, but as Di Palma argues, there may be other ways to accomplish the same end. What is important to note is that political science investigations should seriously focus at the micro level, that is, upon the actions of individuals, while not ignoring macro-level phenomena.

By employing *micro* and *macro* level analysis together, it will be possible to create conditional universal propositions that establish sounder explanations capable of more accurate prediction. Though this result should be reward enough, the Bulgarian case also suggests important policy implications for the United States and the so-called free world.

The United States and other Western powers have for some time provided economic and other aid to dictators of one type or another. Justifications vary from the most blatant linkage of national self-interest and stability in the underdeveloped world to the argument that aid will lead to democracy. The most short-sighted approach is one attributed to President Harry Truman when justifying support for the dictator of the Dominican Republic, Rafael Trujillo. Truman allegedly said: "Trujillo may be an SOB but he is our SOB." A sophisticated and more defensible position is presented by the development theorists of the 1950s, 1960s, and 1970s. Though there are differences among them, they commonly argue that providing aid to nondemocratic societies is justifiable not as an instrument of immediate national self-interest but as a way to promote democracy as an alternative to communism.

Scholars in the tradition of Deutsch, Lerner, Lipset, and Rostow believed that a strong economy implies the development of a middle class that also creates the necessary conditions for plural groups in society. And this will result in competitive political parties that will in turn help to create democratic habits in the body politic, resulting in a civil society supportive of democratic institutions.[25] Huntington warned, however, that a preoccupation with rapid economic development could lead to increased expectations for a better life than the political institutions may be prepared to deliver. Therefore, he cautions that development theorists should focus more attention on stability and the institutions that insure orderly change.[26]

Significantly, then, the prerequisites-to-democracy perspective of the Cold War past carries with it important policy implications. Though there were variations in outlook and purpose, this approach to political development was used to justify propping up antidemocratic regimes that practiced repression and tyranny. But if it is possible to create a democracy without the so-called prerequisites, then it is unnecessary to invest in dictators and tyrants of all sorts. As a precondition for any aid at all, democrats everywhere might insist upon clear agreements with ruling elites and opposition forces to form new constitutional orders. Aid should come only after the creation of institutional frameworks accompanied by pacts guaranteeing a peaceful transition to democracy.

An additional question remains, however. Besides the creation of pacts and agreements to create democratic institutions and procedures, should the powers of the new world order insist upon particular policy prescriptions as a quid pro quo for aid? The answer is no. To insist, for example, that Bulgaria must privatize a certain percentage of its public economic institutions within a particular time span is to ask too much of sovereign people. A nation should be free to choose the nature and timing of substantive policy reforms without interference from outside powers. It is accomplishment enough to create democratic institutions. The faith of democracy is that people will know and follow their own best interests when they are free to make their own choices. To be sure, the Bulgarian experience provides ample evidence in support of the proposition that political leaders will not necessarily make the correct choices. In this sense, democracy insures the unpredictability of results. What it guarantees, however, is the right to make choices without fear and intimation while respecting human rights.

Notes

Chapter 1

1. Guillermo O'Donnell, Philippe C. Schmitter, and Laurence Whitehead, eds., *Transitions from Authoritarian Rule: Prospects for Democracy* (Baltimore: Johns Hopkins University Press, 1986); Adam Przeworski, *Democracy and the Market: Political and Economic Reforms in Eastern Europe and Latin America* (Cambridge: Cambridge University Press, 1991), 1.

2. Russell Bova, "Political Dynamics of the Post-Communist Transition: A Comparative Perspective," *World Politics* 44 (Oct. 1991): 113–38.

3. Samuel P. Huntington, "Will More Countries Become Democratic?" *Political Science Quarterly* 99 (Summer 1984): 217.

4. Przeworski, *Democracy and the Market,* 1.

5. Giuseppe Di Palma, *To Craft Democracies: An Essay on Democratic Transitions* (Berkeley: University of California Press, 1990).

6. Samuel P. Huntington, *Political Order in Changing Societies* (New Haven: Yale University Press, 1968); Robert A. Dahl, *Polyarchy: Participation and Opposition* (New Haven: Yale University Press, 1971).

7. For a fine summary of the political development literature see, Howard J. Wiarda, *Introduction to Comparative Politics: Concepts and Processes* (Belmont, Calif.: Wadsworth, 1993), 52–53, 60, 58–64. See also for original sources: Karl Deutsch, "Social Mobilization and Political Development," *American Political Science Review* 55 (Sept. 1961): 493–514; Huntington, *Political Order;* Daniel Lerner, *The Passing of Traditional Society* (New York: Free Press, 1958); Seymour Martin Lipset, "Some Social Prerequisites of Democracy: Economic Development and Political Legitimacy," *American Political Science Review* 53 (Mar. 1959): 69–105; Robert Packenham, *Liberal America and the Third World: Political Development Ideas in Foreign Aid and Social Science* (Princeton, N.J.: Princeton University Press, 1973); W. W. Rostow, *The Stages of Economic Growth* (New York: Cambridge University Press, 1960). Also see for modern views, Ronald H. Chilcote, *Theories of Comparative Politics: The Search for a Paradigm Reconsidered* (Boulder: Westview Press, 1994), 217–84; Louis J. Cantori and Andrew H. Ziegler Jr., eds.,

Comparative Politics in the Post-Behavioral Era (Boulder: Lynne Rienner, 1988), 353–415.

8. Geoffrey Pridham, ed., *Securing Democracy: Political Parties and Democratic Consolidation in Southern Europe* (London and New York: Routledge, 1990), 7.

9. Di Palma, *To Craft Democracies,* 9.

10. Ian Shapiro, "Democratic Innovation: South Africa in Comparative Context," *World Politics* 46 (Oct. 1993): 122–24.

11. Di Palma, *To Craft Democracies,* 16–23.

12. United Nations Development Programme, *Bulgaria: Human Development Report 1995* (Sofia: National and Global Development UNDP, 1995).

13. Elizabeth Han Hastings and Philip K. Hastings, eds., *Index to International Public Opinion, 1993–1994* (Westport, Conn.: Greenwood Press, 1995), 612–19.

14. Di Palma, *To Craft Democracies,* 54–57.

15. Georgi Karasimeonov, "Bulgaria's New Party System," in *Stabilising Fragile Democracies: Comparing New Party Systems in Southern and Eastern Europe,* edited by Geoffrey Pridham and Paul G. Lewis (London and New York: Routledge, 1996), 293.

16. William Mishler and Richard Rose, "Support for Parliaments and Regimes in the Transition Toward Democracy in Eastern Europe," *Legislative Studies Quarterly* 19 (February 1994): 6.

17. Ibid., 25.

18. Ibid., 6; see also, Gerhard Loewenberg and Samuel C. Patterson, *Comparing Legislatures* (Boston: Little, Brown, 1979), 280–304.

19. Mishler and Rose, "Support for Parliaments," 27.

20. Jon Elster, "Constitution-Making in Eastern Europe: Rebuilding the Boat in the Open Sea," *Public Administration* 71 (Spring/Summer 1993): 188.

21. Krzysztof Jasiewicz, "Structures of Representation," in *Developments in East European Politics,* edited by Stephen White, Judy Batt, and Paul G. Lewis (Durham, N.C.: Duke University Press, 1993), 124–33.

22. David S. Mason, "Poland," in *Developments in East European Politics,* edited by Stephen White, Judy Batt, and Paul G. Lewis (Durham, N.C.: Duke University Press, 1993), 40–42.

23. Nigel Swain, "Hungary," in *Developments in East European Politics,* edited by Stephen White, Judy Batt, and Paul G. Lewis (Durham, N.C.: Duke University Press, 1993), 70–74.

24. Jasiewicz, "Structures of Representation," 137, table 8.1.

25. Gordon Wightman, "The Czech and Slovak Republics," in *Developments in East European Politics,* edited by Stephen White, Judy Batt, and Paul G. Lewis (Durham, N.C.: Duke University Press, 1993), 53.

26. Jasiewicz, "Structures of Representation," 133.

27. Robert K. Yin, *Case Study Research: Design and Methods* (Beverly Hills: Sage Publications, 1984), 39–40.

28. Gary King, Robert O. Keohane, and Sidney Verba, *Designing Social Inquiry: Scientific Inference in Qualitative Research* (Princeton: Princeton University Press, 1994), 4–5.

Chapter 2

1. John D. Bell, "'Post Communist' Bulgaria," *Current History* 89 (December 1990): 417; R. J. Crampton, *A Short History of Modern Bulgaria* (Cambridge: Cambridge University Press, 1987).

2. Bell, "'Post-Communist' Bulgaria," 417.

3. Ibid.

4. Andrey Lukanov, Member of Parliament, interview by author, Sofia, Bulgaria, October 14, 1993.

5. Robert J. McIntyre, *Bulgaria: Politics, Economics, and Society* (London and New York: Pinter, 1988), 17.

6. Ibid., 18.

7. Richard J. Crampton, *Bulgaria, 1878–1918: A History* (New York: Columbia University Press, 1983), 81.

8. McIntyre, *Bulgaria,* 19.

9. Marin V. Pundeff, *Bulgaria in American Perspective: Political and Cultural Issues* (Sofia, Bulgaria: St. Kliment Ohridski University Press, 1993), 164.

10. R. J. Crampton, *A Short History of Modern Bulgaria* (London: Cambridge University Press, 1987), 18–31.

11. McIntyre, *Bulgaria,* 19.

12. Pundeff, *Bulgaria in American Perspective,* 166.

13. McIntyre, *Bulgaria,* 19–20.

14. The Bulgarian Communist Party evolved from the Social Democratic Party, created in 1890. The difference between the Narrow and Broad Socialists is a factional one involving ideological cleavages. The Narrows, led by Dimitur Blagoev, became the Bulgarian Communist Party; see Nissan Oren, *Bulgarian Communism: The Road to Power, 1934–1944* (New York: Columbia University Press, 1971), 3.

15. Pundeff, *Bulgaria in American Perspective,* 172.

16. McIntyre, *Bulgaria,* 30.

17. Ibid., 30–31.

18. Ibid., 32–33.

19. Pundeff, *Bulgaria in American Perspective,* 175.

20. Ibid., 176.

21. John D. Bell, *Peasants in Power: Alexander Stamboliski and the Bulgarian Agrarian National Union, 1988–1923* (Princeton: Princeton University Press, 1977), 222–24.

22. McIntyre, *Bulgaria,* 34–37.

23. Pundeff, *Bulgaria in American Perspective,* 177.

24. McIntyre, *Bulgaria,* 39.

25. Pundeff, *Bulgaria in American Perspective,* 180–81; McIntyre, *Bulgaria,* 40–41.

26. McIntyre, *Bulgaria,* 42.

27. Ibid., 44.

28. Ibid., 49.

29. Ibid., 49–51.

30. Crampton, *Short History,* 145, 166, 170–72.

31. Ibid., 186.

32. Pundeff, *Bulgaria in American Perspective,* 193–95.

33. G. T. Kurian, *The New Book of World Rankings,* 3rd ed. (New York: Facts on File, 1991), 50, 51, 69.

34. Bell, "'Post-Communist' Bulgaria," 419–20.

35. C. Charles Bertschi, "Lustration and the Transition to Democracy: The Cases of Poland and Bulgaria," *East European Quarterly* 28 (January 1995): 441–43, 436.

36. Vladimir Boyadjiev, "Socio-Economic Platform of the Bulgarian Opposition," *Peace Research* 22 (August 1990): 45–46.

37. George J. Szablowski and Hans-Ulrich Derlien, "East European Transitions, Elites, Bureaucracies, and the European Community," *Governance* 6 (July 1993): 309.

38. Daily Report, East Europe, "Preparations Under Way for Roundtable Talks," FBIS-EEU-90-003, January 4, 1990, p. 15.

39. Bulgarians holding this view include Rumyana Kolarova and Dimitar Dimitrov, "Round Table Talks in Bulgaria" (Center for Constitutionalism in Eastern Europe, University of Chicago Law School, 1991), 6.

40. Di Palma, *To Craft Democracies,* 175–76.

41. Ibid., 31.

42. Georgi Karasimeonov, "The Legislature in Post-Communist Bulgaria," in *The New Parliaments of Central and Eastern Europe,* edited by David M. Olson and Philip Norton (London and Portland: Frank Cass, 1996), 41–42. This author makes the argument that the Roundtable's use of the existing parliament is the first of three phases of legislative development in post-Communist Bulgaria. Although this is a plausible argument, it is not mine.

43. Daily Report, "Relay of Sofia Roundtable Talks," FBIS-EEU-90-019, January 29, 1990, p. 3. The timeline information found in this chapter is based

on a report provided to me by the Bulgarian news agency, the BTA. BTA Reference Service/NM, "The National Roundtable," October 1993.

44. C. Charles Bertschi, "Lustration and the Transition to Democracy: The Cases of Poland and Bulgaria," *East European Quarterly* 28 (January 1995): 439.

45. Charles Moser, *Theory and History of the Bulgarian Transition* (Sofia: Free Initiative Foundation, 1994), 100.

46. Ibid., 48.

47. Ibid., 100.

Chapter 3

1. John D. Bell, "'Post Communist' Bulgaria," *Current History* 89 (December 1990): 420.

2. Daily Report, East Europe, "Democratic Union Delegation," FBIS-EEU-90-003, January 4, 1990, p. 15.

3. Interview with Alexander Karakachanov, president of the Green Party, Party Headquarters, 3 Alabin Street, Sofia, Bulgaria, October 4, 1993. Karakachanov was born on September 11, 1960, in Sofia. He attended high school in Moscow where his father, Panayot Karakachanov, was working as a military attaché at the Bulgarian Embassy. Alexander took his university degree in philosophy at Sofia's St. Kliment Ohridski University in 1983. He speaks Russian and English. In 1988, he started work as an assistant at the Medical Academy in Sofia. In 1988, he was elected as a city council member of the capital Sofia. Karakachanov was among the founders of the Environmental Protection Committee in the city of Ruse, and of the Glasnost and Democracy Club. He was one of ten coordinators of the Ecoglasnost Movement that was founded in his apartment. He served as the movement's secretary until November 25, 1989. He is also known as "the first beaten city council member" because of his involvement in the unrest during the 1989 International Ecoforum held in Sofia. He initiated the founding of the Green Party in Bulgaria and became its leader. As a UDF candidate from Sofia, he was elected a deputy to the Seventh Grand National Assembly. On October 17, 1990, he was elected mayor of the city of Sofia. From July 1 to September 5, 1995, he was the leader of the political movement called the Democratic Alternative for the Republic. Both his sympathizers and opponents refer to Alexander Karakachanov as a modern political leader: well-read, highly intelligent, persevering, and impressively broad-minded. Some people call him "a child of the revolution" or "the young symbol of change."

4. Interview with Petar Beron, former leader of the Union of Democratic Forces, Natural History Museum, 1 Tsar Osvoboditel Blvd., Sofia, Bulgaria, October 7, 1993. Born in Sofia on March 14, 1940, Petar Beron graduated in

1963 from the St. Kliment Ohridski University with a biology degree. In 1975, he obtained the rank of associate professor of biology at his alma mater. In the period 1976–79, Beron worked as a manager of wild reserve areas and as an organizer of the struggle against poachers in the state of Plato, Nigeria. Dr. Beron has studied and done research in France and Czechoslovakia. He also participated in the British speleological expedition in New Guinea. Besides biology, his interests include biospeleology, literature, languages, geography, and ancient art. He speaks Russian, French, English, and German.

On December 7, 1989, Dr. Beron was elected secretary of UDF's Coordination Council and occupied this position until July 6, 1990. From August 3 to December 6, 1990, he was the council's chairperson. He also worked as the chair of Ecoglasnost's Controlling Council from November 1989 to March 31, 1990, when he was elected secretary of the association.

In the Seventh Grand National Assembly he was a UDF representative. From August 9 to December 6, 1990, Beron was the chair of UDF's Parliamentary Union. Within the Grand National Assembly he was a member of the Commission for Foreign Policy and the Commission for Environmental Protection. On April 15, 1991, he became the chair of the board of directors of the Kurdish Children Fund. He is the vice chairperson of the Unification for Bulgaria Party and a member of the Managing Board of the Regional Center for Environmental Protection in Central and Eastern Europe.

5. See, for example, Crane Brinton, *The Anatomy of Revolution: Revised and Expanded Edition* (New York: Vintage Books, 1965).

6. Interview with Dr. Konstantin Trenchev, leader of the Podkrepa Syndicate, at the Syndicate headquarters, 1 Garibaldi Square, Sofia, Bulgaria, October 19, 1993. Trenchev was born to a family of physicians on February 8, 1955, in the city of Stara Zagora. Konstantin Trenchev finished the Romen Rolan French Language High School with excellent grades. He then graduated from the Higher Medical Institute in Sofia, again with high marks. Beginning in April 1987, he served as an assistant professor at the General and Clinical Pathology Department in Stara Zagora. In 1988, he joined the Independent Association for Human Rights Protection. In February of the following year, he performed a physical examination on the purposefully starving poet and dissident Petar Manolov. With other intellectuals, Trenchev and Manolov formed a syndicate for protecting intellectual labor. The Podkrepa Labor Confederation was formed on Dr. Trenchev's birthday. In May 1989, Trenchev was arrested with other dissidents on charges of violating Article 273 of the Punitive Code. They helped a group of ethnic Turks with the drafting of a declaration intended to precede a hunger strike. Trenchev was detained for three months at the headquarters of the Main Bureau for Investigations in Sofia. In March 1990, at the First Congress of the Podkrepa Labor Confedera-

tion, Dr. Trenchev was elected president of the syndicate. Podkrepa's syndicate activities in the fall of 1990 precipitated the collapse of Andrey Lukanov's Socialist government. Trenchev was never a member of any party or political organization other than Podkrepa. He has a second wife, Koyana Zheleva Ivanova-Trencheva, who has studied medicine in the United States. In March 1992, Dr. Trenchev was elected vice president of the International Confederation of Free Labor Unions.

7. The interview with Petko Simeonov took place on October 4, 1993, at the headquarters of the Bulgarian Liberal Party, 3 Alabin St., Sofia, Bulgaria. Petko Simeonov, also known as Petko Simeonov Petkov, was born on May 11, 1942, in the city of Montana. Simeonov's parents were active fighters against what is perceived by many as the pre–World War II Fascist regime. He graduated from the St. Kliment Ohridski University in Sofia with a degree in philosophy and is an associate professor of philosophy. Until January 1, 1990, Petko Simeonov was a member of the BCP. He was an active participant in the National Roundtable Talks.

Simeonov was the president of the Democratic Clubs Foundation when it began in 1990. Until September 3, 1990, he worked as the director of the *Demokratsiya* (Democracy) newspaper. On November 1, 1990, he became the president of a foundation called "A World for Everyone"; on November 3, 1991, he became the leader of the Liberal Party. On May 26, 1992, he became the leader of the Bulgarian Democratic Center. In the Seventh Grand National Assembly, he was a UDF deputy. Within the assembly, he was a member of the Commission for Inspecting Elections, a member of the Research Commission for Determining the Reasons for the Economic and Political Crisis, and the chair of the Commission for Demographic Problems. From August 3, 1990, to May 23, 1991, he was vice chairperson of the UDF's Coordination Council. His signing of the July Constitution with other UDF deputies caused the splintering of the Democratic Clubs Federation into two wings: one led by Jordan Vasilev that remained within the UDF, and the other led by Simeonov. The Simeonov wing became the legally registered organization known as the Bulgarian Party of Liberals on November 3, 1991. From January 1991 to July 1992, Simeonov was the director of the Foreign Aid Agency. On May 26, 1992, he was elected the leader of the Bulgarian Democratic Center Coalition.

Petko Simeonov is married and has four children.

8. The interview with member of parliament Georgi Bliznashki took place on October 8, 1993, at the National Assembly Building, 1 Narodno Sabranie Square, Sofia, Bulgaria. Bliznashki was born on October 1, 1956. He is a graduate of the St. Kliment Ohridski University law school where he is associate professor of law specializing in comparative constitutional law. At

the Thirty-ninth Congress of the BSP, on September 25, 1990, Bliznashki was elected to the executive board of the party's Supreme Council. In the Thirty-sixth National Assembly, he was a deputy from the Parliamentary Union for Social Democracy. In 1994, he was awarded a NATO scholarship to write a research paper on the topic of parliamentary government, its principles, models, and prospects. In 1997 he was associated with the Centre for European Studies in Sofia.

9. Todor Lukanov opposed the Comintern plan to change the Bulgarian Communist Party position of neutrality in the struggle between the Agrarians and their enemies. The Comintern wanted the Bulgarian Party to launch an uprising based on an alliance of workers and peasants for the purpose of establishing a Bolshevik regime. Todor Lukanov, Andrey Lukanov's grandfather, opposed the move, arguing that it promised only disaster for the Party. See Marin V. Pundeff, *Bulgaria in American Perspective: Political and Cultural Issues* (Sofia: St. Kliment Ohridski University Press, 1993), 177.

10. Interview with Andrey Lukanov, leader of the reform wing of the Bulgarian Communist Party and former prime minister of Bulgaria took place on October 14, 1993, at the National Assembly, 1 Narodno Sabranie Square, Sofia, Bulgaria. Andrey Lukanov was born on September 26, 1938, in Moscow, Russia. Majoring in political science and international relations, he completed his higher education at the Moscow State Institute for International Relations. He spoke English, Russian, French, and Spanish. Lukanov was married and had two children. He became the victim of an assassin's bullet on October 2, 1996.

Lukanov was a member of the BCP since 1965. Throughout his political career under Communism he occupied leadership positions in the Foreign Ministry and the Ministry of Foreign Trade. From 1968 to 1972, he worked as the first secretary of Bulgaria's permanent representation at the UN General Assembly in Geneva. In 1972, Lukanov became the deputy minister, and from November 1973, he served as the first deputy minister of foreign trade. On June 16, 1976, he was appointed vice chairman of the Ministerial Council. From August 1987 to November 1989, he was the minister of foreign trade.

From September 1976 to January 1990, Lukanov sat in the Council for Mutual Economic Assistance (CMEA) as Bulgaria's permanent representative. From July 1988 until January 1990, he was chairperson of the CMEA's executive committee. He was also a member of the state council of the People's Republic of Bulgaria from November 1989 to February 1990.

Lukanov was the head of two Socialist Party governments after the November 1989 coup: from February 3 to August 22, 1990, and from September 19 to November 30, 1990. At the BCP's Eleventh Congress (April 1976), he was elected an associate member of the BCP's Central Committee (CC), and at the committee's December 1977 plenary meeting, he was approved as a full member of the committee (his membership was reconfirmed at the BCP's Twelfth and Thirteenth Congresses in 1981 and 1986 respectively). In July 1979, he became an associate member of the Politburo and was reconfirmed on April 4, 1981, and April 5, 1986. From November 16, 1989, to February 2, 1990, Lukanov became a full member of the Politburo and the secretariat of BCP's Central Committee. During the period 1976–86, Lukanov was consecutively elected a people's representative to the Seventh, Eighth, and Ninth National Assemblies. From December 15, 1989, to February 8, 1990, he was the chair of the Parliamentary Commission for Reviewing and Resolving Some Critical Issues Related to the Deformities and Violations of Laws in the Governmental Economic and Social Spheres. In the period 1989–90, as a member of a parliamentary commission, he worked on drafting an amendment to the Constitution of Bulgaria. He was a leading figure in the National Roundtable Talks that took place in 1990.

In the Seventh Grand National Assembly, Andrey Lukanov was a representative from the BSP. From January 24 to July 19, 1991, he worked as the chairperson of the Foreign Policy Commission. In the Thirty-sixth and Thirty-seventh National Assemblies, he was a deputy from the BSP list.

During the term of UDF Prime Minister Philip Dimitrov, Lukanov was charged with misuse of power and misappropriation of funds. He was jailed for seven months but was never tried. After his death he was vindicated by an international tribunal.

Lukanov was a successful businessman and was chairman of the board of the Russian-Topenergy Company. At the time of his death, Lukanov was highly critical of the BSP government headed by Zhan Videnov.

11. Lukanov served as a Politburo member and was responsible for the economic reform under Zhivkov from 1984 to November 10, 1989, when he helped to organize the coup that toppled Todor Zhivkov.

12. Pundeff, *Bulgaria in American Perspective,* 192.

Chapter 4

1. Daily Report, East Europe, "Preliminary Talks Begin," FBIS-EEU-90-003, January 4, 1990, p. 16.

2. Ibid.

3. Daily Report, East Europe, "Opposition Spokesman Discusses Roundtable," FBIS-EEU-90-010, January 16, 1990, p. 21.

4. Rumyana Kolarova and Dimitr Dimitrov, "Round Table Talks in Bulgaria" (Center for Constitutionalism in Eastern Europe, University of Chicago Law School, 1991), 17–18.

5. Ibid., 7–8, 34–35.

6. Ibid., 22–23, 26–27.

7. I interviewed Stefan Gaitanjiev on October 13, 1993, at the headquarters of the Bulgarian Democratic Center Party, 12A Narodno Sabranie Square, Sofia, Bulgaria. Several party members were also in attendance during this interview. Gaitanjiev was born on January 9, 1947, in the city of Pleven. He completed his higher education degree in philosophy at the St. Kliment Ohridski University in Sofia. He is a first degree research associate and an associate professor of philosophy. He speaks Russian and German. Gaitanjiev is married with one child. He worked at the Laboratory for Legal and Sociological Studies at the Institute for State and Law. He was among the founders of the Social Committee for Environmental Protection that emerged in the city of Ruse and of the UDF. Gaitanjiev was a UDF-affiliated people's representative in the Seventh Grand National Assembly. He was secretary of the UDF's parliamentary group in the National Assembly. He also served as secretary of the Parliamentary Commission for Local Governments and Territorial Administration. He was secretary of the Ecoglasnost Political Club and on July 1, 1995, became the club's president. In the Thirty-seventh National Assembly, he was a deputy from the Democratic Left coalition that included BSP, the Alexander Stamboliiski Agrarian Party, and the Ecoglasnost Political Club. On December 28, 1994, Gaitanjiev became the vice chair of the parliamentary group of the Democratic Left. In February 1995, he became a member of the Commission for National Security, and the Commission for Controlling the Revenues, Expenses, and Property of the Political Parties in the Thirty-seventh National Assembly. On February 27, 1995, Gaitanjiev became vice chairperson of the Human Rights Committee in Bulgaria.

8. Daily Report, Soviet Union, "Bulgarian Roundtable Discussion Moving Ahead," FBIS-SOV-90-004, January 5, 1990, p. 19.

9. Daily Report, East Europe, "Procedures Discussed," FBIS-EEU-90-003, January 4, 1990, p. 17.

10. Daily Report, East Europe, "Roundtable Talks Scheduled for 16 Jan" and "Further on Talks," FBIS-EEU-90-004, January 5, 1990, p. 11.

11. Daily Report, East Europe, "Roundtable Expresses Views on Ethnic Issue," FBIS-EEU-90-004, January 5, 1990, pp. 7–8.

12. Daily Report, East Europe, "Thousands Attend Rally on Nationality Issue," FBIS-EEU-90-010, January 16, 1990, pp. 22, 29.

13. Daily Report, East Europe, "UDF Presents Demands at Roundtable 13 Jan," FBIS-EEU-90-011, January 17, 1990, p. 4.

14. Daily Report, East Europe, "Union Demands Listed," FBIS-EEU-90-011, January 17, 1990, p. 4.

15. Daily Report, East Europe, "BTA Reports Results," FBIS-EEU-90-011, January 17, 1990, p. 5.

16. Daily Report, East Europe, "Bokov Statement on Reports," FBIS-EEU-90-015, January 23, 1990, p. 7.

17. Daily Report, East Europe, "Zhelev on Beginning of Roundtable Talks," FBIS-EEU-90-015, January 23, 1990, p. 6.

18. Daily Report, East Europe, "Walkout Threatened," FBIS-EEU-90-012, January 18, 1990, p. 6.

19. Daily Report, East Europe, "BCP, Opposition Hold Roundtable Talks," FBIS-EEU-90-016, January 24, 1990, p. 5.

20. Ibid., 5–6.

21. Ibid., 6.

22. Ibid.

23. Ibid.

24. Ibid.

25. John D. Bell, "'Post Communist' Bulgaria," *Current History* 89 (December 1990): 427–28.

26. Georgi Karasimeonov, "Differentiation Postponed: Party Pluralism in Bulgaria," in *Party Formation in East Central Europe,* edited by Gordon Wightman (England: Edward Elgar, 1995), 161.

27. Daily Report, East Europe, "Democrats State Views on Elections, Roundtable," FBIS-EEU 90-044, March 6, 1990, p. 7.

28. Several persons I interviewed in October 1993 indicated that U.S. secretary of state James Baker urged UDF leaders to accept early elections.

29. Kolarova and Dimitrov, "Round Table Talks in Bulgaria," 21.

30. Ibid., 16–17.

31. Daily Report, "Sofia Lawyers Seek End to Party's Leading Role," FBIS-EEU-89-241, December 18, 1989, pp. 18–19.

32. Daily Report, "Lukanov Speech at National Assembly Session," FBIS-EEU-90-012, January 18, 1990, p. 11.

33. Daily Report, East Europe, "Amendments Considered," FBIS-EEU-90-010, January 16, 1990, pp. 15–16.

34. Daily Report, East Europe, "Commissions on Constitution," FBIS-EEU-90-040, February 28, 1990, p. 10.

35. Daily Report, East Europe, "Lukanov Speech at National Assembly Session," FBIS-EEU-90-012, January 18, 1990, p. 11.

36. Daily Report, East Europe, "Politburo Orders Dissolution of Army BCP Bodies," FBIS-EEU-90-019, January 29, 1990, p. 4.

37. Daily Report, East Europe, "Further on Discussions at Roundtable Talks: Comments by Zhelev," FBIS-EEU-90-026, February 7, 1990, p. 11.

38. Ibid.

39. Daily Report, East Europe, "Semerdjiev [Semerjiev] Speaks," FBIS-EEU-90-026, February 7, 1990, pp. 12–15.

40. Interview with General Attanas Semerjiev, chief of staff of the Bulgarian Armed Forces, minister of the interior, and vice president of the Republic, October 11, 1995, at his apartment in Sofia, Bulgaria. Attanas Semerjiev was born on May 21, 1924, in the city of Velingrad. In 1939, he became involved in revolutionary activities. In 1941, he was arrested on charges of revolutionary activity. He then joined the underground movement. In 1942, he fought as a partisan in the Anton Ivanov Guerrilla Squad. In 1943, Semerjiev joined the BCP. In August 1944, he became the commander-in-chief of the Chepinetz Guerrilla Brigade. He took part in the Great Patriotic War as a commander of an infantry division.

In 1944, he specialized in military preparation skills at the Military School in Sofia, and later studied at the K. E. Voroshilov and the M. V. Frunze Military Academies in the Soviet Union. From 1962 to 1989, he was the director of the Bulgarian National Army's headquarters. From 1966 to 1989, he was the first deputy minister of defense. On December 27, 1989, Semerjiev became minister of the interior. After retiring from military service, he became an associate professor of military science and received the rank of colonel-general. He was a member of BCP's Central Committee from 1966 to 1990. At the Party's Fourteenth Extraordinary Congress in 1990, he was elected a member of the BSP's Supreme Council. Semerjiev is the author of several books on operational and tactical military matters and has also published his memoirs of the guerrilla warfare years. He has won Bulgarian and international medals for military service. As minister of the interior, he participated in the Roundtable negotiations. From June to August 1990, he was a deputy from the BSP list in the Seventh Grand National Assembly. On August 1, 1990, Semerjiev became vice president of the Republic of Bulgaria.

41. By "nontypical functions" the general means the UBO was converted into a household service. It supplied top people with food and luxurious goods, cleaned their homes, provided twenty-four-hour transportation for their families, helped them organize their leisure time, and in general took care of all their needs.

42. Lenin is the author of the principle of democratic centralism. It means as a practical matter that all members of the Party must adhere to the policy articulated by the central Party.

43. Alvin Toffler is the author of *Future Shock*.

44. In early August 1990, a protester threatened to burn himself if the red star on top of a prominent building in Sofia was not removed. The BSP agreed to remove the star, but it was not taken down. The protester then renewed his threat and a demonstration in front of the building took place. Throughout August 26, 1990, the number of demonstrators increased and the building was stormed by mob. They looted and burned the building. It is reported that

despite the fire the red star remained on top of the building. Finally, on October 3, 1990, the offending star was removed. See C. Charles Bertschi, "Lustration and the Transition to Democracy: The Cases of Poland and Bulgaria," *East European Quarterly* 28 (January 1995): 440.

45. Daily Report, East Europe, "Further on Discussion at Roundtable Talks: Comments by Zhelev," FBIS-EEU-90-026, February 7, 1990, p. 11.

Chapter 5

1. Daily Report, East Europe, "Roundtable Negotiations 'Going Slowly,'" FBIS-EEU-90-027, February 8, 1990, p. 7.

2. Daily Report, East Europe, "Roundtable Contact Group Holds Session," FBIS-EEU-90-032, February 15, 1990, p. 3; Daily Report, East Europe, "Roundtable Draft Documents Published," FBIS-EEU-90-044, March 6, 1990, pp. 6–7.

3. Daily Report, East Europe, "List of Roundtable Agreements' Signatories," FBIS-EEU-90-052, March 16, 1990, pp. 11–12. Alexander Lilov, for the BCP; Zhelyu Zhelev, for the UDF; and the following delegation leaders participating in the National Roundtable Talks signed the three agreements: Alexander Karakachanov, the Green Party; Blagovest Sendov, National Assembly Deputy; Boris Kyurkchiev, the Democratic Party; Branko Davidov, the "Rodolyubie" Rhodope Union; Viktor Vulkov, the BZNS; Ginio Ganev, the Fatherland Front; Dimitur Batalov, the Club of People Repressed Since 1945; Dimitur Arnaudov, the All-People's Committee for the Defense of National Interests; Elka Konstantinova, the Radical Democratic Party; Emil Koshlukov, the Federation of Independent Students Association; Ivan Velinov, the Union of Lawyers in Bulgaria; Konstantin Tellalov, the Human Rights Committee; Konstantin Trenchev, the Podkrepa Independent Labor Federation; Krustyu Petkov, the Confederation of Independent Trade Unions in Bulgaria; Luben Kulishev, National Assembly Deputy; Lyubomir Sobadjiev, the Civic Initiative Movement; Milan Drenchev, the Nikola Petkov BZNS; Mihail Ivanov, the National Reconciliation Committee; Nora Ananieva, the Democratic Women's Union; Petar Beron, the Ecoglasnost Independent Association; Petko Simeonov, the Federation of Glasnost and Democracy Clubs; Petar Dertliev, the Bulgarian Social Democratic Party; Rossen Karadimov, the Bulgarian Democratic Youth; Rumen Vodenicharov, the Independent Association for Defense of Human Rights; Tanio Tanev, the Union of Fighters Against Fascism and Capitalism; Christofor Sabev, ordained monk, the Committee For Defense of Religious Rights, Freedom of Conscience, and Spiritual Values.

4. Daily Report, East Europe, "BCP Daily Denounces UDF Declaration," FBIS-EEU-90-044, March 6, 1990, p. 6.

5. Daily Report, East Europe, "Declaration on Roundtable Role, Status," FBIS-EEU-90-051, March 15, 1990, p. 6.

6. Daily Report, East Europe, "On Transition to Democracy," FBIS-EEU-90-051, March 15, 1990, pp. 6–7.

7. Giuseppe Di Palma, *To Craft Democracies: An Essay on Democratic Transitions* (Berkeley and Los Angeles: University of California Press, 1990), 31.

8. Daily Report, East Europe, "Further on Agreements," FBIS-EEU-90-049, March 13, 1990, pp. 2–4.

9. Daily Report, East Europe, "Roundtable Ethics Code for Elections," FBIS-EEU-90-101, May 24, 1990, pp. 8–9.

10. Daily Report, East Europe, "Lukanov Speaks at Roundtable," FBIS-EEU-90-052, March 16, 1990, pp. 7–10.

11. Daily Report, East Europe, "Roundtable Discusses Market Reform," FBIS-EEU-90-049, March 16, 1990, p. 11.

12. Di Palma, *To Craft Democracies,* 19.

13. Articles 17–22 of the Constitution of the Republic of Bulgaria.

14. Emilia Droumeva, "A New and Original Election System in Bulgaria," in *Law in a Fast-Changing Society,* translated and edited by Silvy Chernev (Sofia, Bulgaria: St. Kliment Ohridski University Press, 1994); Rumyana Kolarova and Dimitr Dimitrov, "Electoral Laws in Eastern Europe: Bulgaria," *East European Constitutional Review* 3 (Spring 1994): 50–55.

15. Daily Report, East Europe, "Elections 10, 17 June," FBIS-EEU-90-063, April 2, 1990, pp. 5–6.

16. Rumyana Kolarova and Dimitr Dimitrov, "Round Table Talks in Bulgaria," (Center for Constitutionalism in Eastern Europe, University of Chicago Law School), 24.

17. Daily Report, East Europe, "Roundtable's Agreement on Amendments," FBIS-EEU-90-064, April 3, 1990, p. 16.

18. Daily Report, East Europe, "BTA on Continuation of Roundtable," FBIS-EEU-90-061, March 29, 1990, pp. 3–4.

19. Kolarova and Dimitrov, "Round Table Talks in Bulgaria," 25–26.

20. Daily Report, East Europe, "BTA on Continuation of Roundtable," FBIS-EEU-90-061, March 29, 1990, pp. 3–4.

21. Daily Report, East Europe, "Roundtable Agrees on Mladenov as President," FBIS-EEU-90-063, April 2, 1990, p. 5.

22. For more on the politics of this incident, see the interview with Konstantin Trenchev in chapter 3 of this volume.

23. John D. Bell, "'Post-Communist' Bulgaria," *Current History* 89 (December 1990): 429.

24. Daily Report, East Europe, "Roundtable's Agreement on Amendments," FBIS-EEU-90-064, April 3, 1990, pp. 16–17.

25. Daily Report, East Europe, "UDF: Contradictory Assembly, Roundtable Rulings," FBIS-EEU-90-066, April 5, 1990, p. 4.

26. BTA Reference Service/VM, *The Seventh Grand National Assembly* (Sofia, Bulgaria: Bulgarian Telegraph Agency, 1993), 2.

27. Interview with Andrey Lukanov, member of Parliament, leader of the reform wing of the Bulgarian Communist Party, and former prime minister of Bulgaria, at the National Assembly, 1 Narodno Sabranie Square, Sofia, Bulgaria, October 14, 1994.

28. Lukanov is referring to the proposal that persons deprived of their property by the Communists in the 1940s should have their property returned or that payment should be made to them. The UDF was generally associated with this plan while the BSP was more reluctant to accept it.

29. This term is a contraction for the word *lumpenproletariat.* Marx wrote of the problem of the peasant class migrating to the cities. There they become urban dwellers who tend to be illiterate and unskilled. They are often unemployed or underemployed, and they are unorganized in trade unions. They are potentially a disruptive force that may be used by others as rioters, demonstrators, and looters. For a view of the role of the lumpenproletariat in a different context see: Howard J. Wiarda, *Latin American Politics: A New World of Possibility* (Belmont, Calif.: Wadsworth, 1995), 125–26.

30. Interview with Stefan Gaitanjiev, secretary of the Bulgarian Democratic Center, Roundtable participant, and former deputy in the Grand National Assembly, at the BDC Headquarters, 12 A Narodno Sabranie Square, Sofia, Bulgaria, October 13, 1993.

31. The Sheraton Hotel, located in downtown Sofia, was widely regarded at the time as the best hotel in the city. Many Western foreign diplomats, politicians, and businessmen met there with their Bulgarian contacts.

32. Recall that General Semerjiev of the Interior Ministry said that his officers aided the UDF during the elections. See chapter 4.

33. Georgi Avramov a.k.a. Georgi Avramov Dimov was born on July 8, 1953, in Sofia. He received his high school education in photography. He speaks Russian and English. He has worked in the cinematographic field of documentaries and has directed and written the scripts for such movies as *A Woman in the Elevator, Just a Comedian,* and *Breathe.*

Avramov was the secretary of the Environmental Committee of the city of Ruse, established in 1988. He was among the founders of Ecoglasnost and the UDF coalition. He took part in the Roundtable negotiations and was a member of UDF's Coordination Council until June 1991. In the Seventh Grand

National Assembly, he was a UDF deputy and the chairperson of the Ecoglasnost parliamentary group. Avramov has argued in favor of Bulgaria's membership in the International Monetary Fund and the World Bank, and supported abolishing the state monopoly on foreign trade.

In the Thirty-Seventh National Assembly, Avramov was a deputy from the parliamentary group of the Democratic Left. He proposed his own version of the Radio and Television Law to the National Assembly. Since March 12, 1996, Avramov has served on the board of directors of the Constitutionalism and Democracy Association.

34. Interview with Dr. Konstantin Trenchev, leader of the Podkrepa Syndicate, at Podkrepa headquarters, 1 Garibaldi Square, Sofia, Bulgaria, October 19, 1993.

35. More research is needed to confirm the date of the Sheraton meeting. It may be that Trenchev is mistaken about the date, casting doubt on whether his recollections are correct about this matter.

36. Di Palma, *To Craft Democracies,* 80.

Chapter 6

1. BTA Reference Service/VM, *The Seventh Grand National Assembly* (Sofia, Bulgaria: Bulgarian Telegraph Agency, 1993), 1.

2. Daily Report, East Europe, "National Assembly Adopts New Constitution," FBIS-EEU 91-135, July 15, 1991, p. 3.

3. Daily Report, East Europe, "Constitution Passed, 'Virtual Split of SDS'," FBIS-EEU-91-132, July 10, 1991, p. 9.

4. Daily Report, East Europe, "SDS Council Issues Declaration," FBIS-EEU 91-133, July 11, 1991, p. 4; Daily Report, East Europe, "Reaction to Zhelev Meeting with Hunger Strikers," FBIS-EEU 91-136, July 16, 1991, p. 4.

5. Daily Report, East Europe, "Poll on Constitution, Elections Reported," FBIS-EEU-91-135, July 15, 1991, p. 6.

6. Daily Report, East Europe, "Assembly Reaches Compromise on Constitutional Oath," FBIS-EEU-91-137, July 17, 1991, p. 3.

7. Daily Report, East Europe, "Zhelev Addresses Nation on Elections," FBIS-EEU-91-138, July 18, 1991, p. 3.

8. Daily Report, East Europe, "Zhelev Defends New Constitution," FBIS-EEU-91-140, July 22, 1991, p. 3.

9. Center for the Study of Democracy, *Constitutional Drafts Discussed in Bulgarian Parliament* (Sofia, Bulgaria: Center for the Study of Democracy, 1991), 4–5.

10. Ibid, 8–9.

11. Martin V. Pundeff, *Bulgaria in American Perspective: Political and Cultural Issues* (Sofia, Bulgaria: St. Kliment Ohridski University Press), 185.

12. Daily Report, East Europe, "Princess Meets Supporters," FBIS-EEU-91-089, May 8, 1991, p. 4.

13. Constitution of the Republic of Bulgaria (1991), Articles 62–91.

14. Tony Verheijen, *Constitutional Pillars for New Democracies: The Cases of Bulgaria and Romania* (The Netherlands: DSWO Press, Leiden University, 1995), 124.

15. Ibid.

16. Ibid., 31, 128.

17. Daily Report, East Europe, "Background Information on President, Semerdjiev" [Semerjiev], FBIS-EEU-90-149, August 2, 1990, pp. 4–5.

18. Andrew Nagorski, "With Allies Like These: Bulgaria's New Leaders Turn on Each Other," *Newsweek,* July 12, 1993, p. 34.

19. Maria Yordanova, "President: Resigns or Rules?" *Insider,* January 1992, p. 4; Fred W. Riggs, "Fragility of the Third World's Regimes," *International Social Science Journal* 45 (May 1993): 215.

20. Georgi Bliznashki, "Functions of the Presidential Institution in Bulgaria" (in Bulgarian), *Pravna Misal* (1992): 3–11.

21. Kjell Engelbrekt, "Bulgarian Parliament Adopts Controversial Law on Judiciary," *Radio Free Europe/Radio Liberty,* No. 114, June 17, 1994.

22. BTA, "UDF Challenges Constitutionality of the Land Act," *Bulletin of News from Bulgaria,* May 19, 1995, on Internet.

23. Stefan Krause, "Bulgarian President and Premier Clash Over NATO Membership," *OMRI Daily Digest* 77, pt. 2 (April 19, 1995), on Internet.

24. [Bulgaria] *State Gazette,* "Law on the Judiciary," no. 59/1994, July 22, 1994.

25. [Bulgaria] *State Gazette,* "Decision #8 on Constitutional Case," September 15, 1994; see chapter 9 of this volume for elaboration on this point.

26. Martin Shapiro and Alec Stone, "The New Constitutional Politics of Europe," *Comparative Political Studies* 26 (January 1994): 397–561.

27. Albert P. Melone and Carol E. Hays, "The Judicial Role in Bulgaria's Struggle for Human Rights," *Judicature* 77 (March–April 1994): 249.

28. Daily Report, East Europe, "International Civil Rights Protocol Ratified," FBIS-EEU-89-244, December 12, 1991, p. 14.

29. Decision #7 on Constitutional Case #6/92, in Bulgarian Academy of Science, *Decisions and Definitions of the Constitutional Court of the Republic of Bulgaria 1991–1992* (Sofia, Bulgaria: Bulgarian Academy of Science, 1993).

30. Duncan M. Perry, "Bulgaria: A New Constitution and Free Elections," *Eastern Europe: RFE/RL Research Report,* vol. 1, no. 1 (January 3, 1992): 80.

31. Melone and Hays, "Judicial Role," 252–53.

32. On December 19, 1996, the Constitutional Court rejected a petition of ninety-four MPs asking that the MRF be declared a political party in

violation of the Constitution. The court cited its previous opinion on the question. BTA, "Petition to Rule Ethnic Turks' Movement as Anticonstitutional Rejected," *Bulletin of News from Bulgaria,* December 20–27, 1996, on Internet.

33. BTA, "UDF Challenges Constitutionality of Land Act," *Bulletin of News from Bulgaria,* May 19, 1995, on Internet.

Chapter 7

1. Interview with Ginio Ganev, leader of the Fatherland's Union, Fatherland's Union Headquarters, 18 Vitosha Boulevard, Sofia, Bulgaria, October 5, 1993. Ganev was born in the city of Bourgas on March 2, 1928. He completed his higher education degree in state and legal studies at the St. Kliment Ohridski University in Sofia. He speaks French and Russian. He is a political independent.

From 1953 to 1976, Ganev worked as the chief legal consultant and the chief secretary of the Ministry of Energy. In 1977, he became a member of the Bureau of the Patriotic Front's National Council, and from June 1982 to December 1989, he worked as the council's secretary. From December 21, 1989, to February 15, 1990, Ganev was the council's vice chair, and from February 15 to April 1, 1990, he served as its chair. He was a people's representative in the Seventh, Eighth, and Ninth National Assemblies. In the Ninth National Assembly, Ganev was the secretary of the Legislative Commission. From June 17, 1986, to 1989, he was a member of the State Council of the People's Republic of Bulgaria.

On April 1, 1990, he was appointed chair of the presidency of the Patriotic Union's National Council.

Ganev worked as a coordinator in the contact group of the National Roundtable and as the chair of its secretariat. On April 11, 1990, he was appointed coordinator of the State and Social Commission for the National Question.

In the Seventh Grand National Assembly, Ganev was a deputy from the Patriotic Union. From July 18, 1990, to July 12, 1991, he served as the vice chairperson of the Grand National Assembly. Elected on July 26, 1990, he also became the chair of the Commission for Drafting the Procedural Rules of the Grand National Assembly, and the Commission for Drafting the Constitution of Bulgaria. After Andrey Lukanov's resignation as prime minister, Ganev declined the proposal to take Lukanov's place.

Ganev served as chair of the Coordination Council of the Independent Social Committee on National Issues. He is a member of the board of trustees of the National Academic Foundation. Ganev is also the president of the Bulgarian Sports Foundation, and the chair of the Franco-Bulgarian Association of Lawyers. Since September 1994, Ganev has been the chair of the Union for the Fatherland Party. Beginning on February 6, 1995, he has served as president of the Agency for the Bulgarians Living Outside Bulgaria. Since March 1996, Ganev has been chair of the Bureau of the Constitutionalism and Democracy Association.

2. Ganev is referring to the repeal of paragraphs 2 and 3 of Article 1 of the then existing constitution in early 1990. Those provisions declared Bulgaria a socialist state headed by the working class, meaning the Communist Party.

3. Interview with Petko Simeonov, leader of the Bulgarian Party Liberals, at Party Headquarters, 3 Alabin Street, Sofia, Bulgaria, October 4, 1993.

4. Interview with Stefan Gaitanjiev, secretary of the Bulgarian Democratic Center and former member of Parliament in the Grand National Assembly, at BDC Headquarters, 12 A Narodno Subranie Square, Sofia, Bulgaria, October 13, 1993.

5. Interview with Jordan Vasilev, leading activist of the UDF and former editor-in-chief of the *Democracy* newspaper at the Institute of Literature, Academy of Sciences, 37 Chapaev Street, Sofia, Bulgaria, October 7, 1993. Born on September 26, 1935, in the city of Radomir, Jordan Vasilev is a graduate of the St. Kliment Ohridski University in Sofia. His degree is in Bulgarian philology. He is an assistant professor of philology and a senior research associate. Vasilev has a working knowledge of Russian and German. He is the husband of Blaga Dimitrova, the former vice president of Bulgaria; she resigned in protest against the direction taken by President Zhelev.

Vasilev is the president and a founding member of the Democracy Clubs Federation. He is the initiator and first editor-in-chief of the *Demokratsiya* (Democracy) newspaper. In the Seventh Grand National Assembly, he was a representative from the UDF's party list and was elected from a constituency located in the city of Trojan. His tenure in the Grand National Assembly was directed toward securing a mechanism for accomplishing privatization and the transition to a market economy. He appealed for the creation of a strong and professional military force and for provisions guaranteeing minimum social security allowances for retired citizens and the unemployed. In the sphere of national education and culture, he supports the idea of reforming the educational system and sending capable young people to study in the developed countries. Vasilev is the author of the idea behind and the declaration of the thirty-nine deputies who expressed their protest against the adoption of the constitution by leaving Parliament. He was a deputy in the Thirty-sixth National Assembly and was chairperson of the Commission for National Security. Vasilev resigned twice from parliament: the first time in November 1990, and the second in May 1992. He is the author of several books.

6. Interview with Ivan Glushkov, leader of the Christian-Agrarian Party at Party Headquarters, 18 Vitosha Boulevard, Sofia, Bulgaria, October 6,

1993. Born in Sofia on January 17, 1937, Ivan Glushkov studied at a French college. His university degree is in philological education. In 1971, he started work in the *Zemedelsko Zname* (Agricultural Banner) newspaper as a journalist, later rising to the position of editor in chief. At the Agricultural Party's Thirty-sixth Extraordinary Congress, he was elected a member of the leadership council. At the council's session on April 6, 1990, Glushkov was elected a permanent member of the party.

In the Seventh Grand National Assembly, he was a deputy from the Agricultural Party, and on July 18, 1990, Glushkov was elected vice chairman of that body. He was also a member of the Commission for Drafting the Constitution. After the elections in October 1991, Glushkov abandoned the leadership of the Agricultural Party. On August 10, 1992, he was appointed permanent representative of the Republic of Bulgaria at the Geneva headquarters of the UN and other international organizations. But he refused the honor. Glushkov led an exploratory committee for creating the Christian Agrarian Party, and at the party's founding conference, on December 19, 1992, he was elected the party leader.

In the Thirty-seventh National Assembly, Glushkov served as a UDF deputy. He has also served as the vice chair of UDF's parliamentary group, a member of the permanent parliamentary delegation to the European Union's Assembly, and as a member of the Commission for National Security. Since September 1995, he has also worked as a political coordinator of the United Democratic Opposition in Sofia.

7. There were only twenty-three actual hunger strikers.

8. BTA Reference Service/VM, *The Seventh Grand National Assembly* (Sofia, Bulgaria: Bulgarian Telegraph Agency, 1993), 5–6.

9. Ibid.

10. Ibid.

11. Ibid.

12. Interview with Petar Dertliev, leader of the Social Democratic Party at Party Headquarters, 37 Exzarh Josif Street, Sofia, Bulgaria, October 6, 1993. Born on April 7, 1916, in the village of Pissarevo, Lovech district, Dertliev is the son of teachers and a graduate of the Medical Academy in Sofia. Beginning in 1943, he worked as an assistant professor at the medical department.

He was fifteen years old when he became an active member of the Social Democratic Party. While a student, he was the secretary of the Social Democratic Youth Club at the medical department. During the period 1934–40, he participated in strikes and other activities organized by progressive-minded students. He was arrested on multiple occasions and in 1938 was prosecuted for publishing Social Democratic literature. In 1946, he became the secretary of the Social Democratic Youth Union. In October 1946, he was elected a deputy to the Sixth Grand National Assembly with the list of the United Bulgarian Social Democratic Labor Party. On July 1948, he was arrested and sentenced to prison for ten years. Dertliev was kept in custody at two labor camps: Venchan and Belene. Released in 1958, he worked as a physician until his retirement. In November 1989, Dertliev led the resuscitated Social Democratic Labor Party, which was renamed the Bulgarian Social Democratic Party in January 1990. At the party's Thirty-eighth Congress in May 1991, Dertliev was elected the party leader. In June 1990, he entered the Seventh Grand National Assembly as a deputy from the UDF coalition. He took part in drafting and adopting Bulgaria's new Constitution. Dertliev is married and has two daughters who live in North America.

13. Dertliev is alluding to fascism when he uses the words *national-socialism.*

14. Readers may want to compare Dertliev's view of a middle class with Andrey Lukanov's interpretation in chapter 5, pp. 115–16.

Chapter 8

1. Howard J. Wiarda, *Introduction to Comparative Politics: Concepts and Processes* (Belmont, Calif.: Wadsworth, 1993), 119.

2. Adam Przeworski, *Democracy and the Market: Political and Economic Reforms in Eastern Europe and Latin America* (Cambridge: Cambridge University Press, 1991), 189.

3. Samuel P. Huntington, *The Third Wave: Democratization in the Late Twentieth Century* (Norman: University of Oklahoma Press, 1993), 208.

4. Giuseppe Di Palma, *To Craft Democracies: An Essay on Democratic Transitions* (Berkeley and Los Angeles: University of California Press, 1990), 137–55.

5. Ibid., 21.

6. Ibid., 151.

7. BTA, "Parliament Today Also Amends Its Rules of Procedures," *Bulletin of News from Bulgaria,* December 15, 1995, on Internet.

8. [Bulgaria] *State Gazette, Rules of Organization and Procedure of the National Assembly,* Promulgated State Gazette No. 105 of December 19, 1991, amended SG No. 1 of 1992, amended No. 4 of 1992, and SG No. 6 of 1992, amended No. 44 of 1992.

9. The number of standing committees has changed over time.

10. Charles A. Moser, *Theory and History of the Bulgarian Transition* (Sofia: Free Initiative Foundation, 1994), 245.

11. Albert P. Melone, "Bulgaria's National Roundtable Talks and the Politics of Accommodation," *International Political Science Review* 15 (1994): 259, 265–67.

12. Interview with Nora Ananieva, leader of the parliamentary group and member of the Supreme Council of the Bulgarian Socialist Party, former deputy prime minister of Bulgaria, at the National Assembly, 1 Narodno Subranie Square, Sofia, Bulgaria, October 14, 1993. Nora Ananieva was born on March 30, 1938, in the city of Lovech. After finishing a foreign language high school, she majored in law at the St. Kliment Ohridski University in Sofia. Ananieva earned her doctor of philosophy degree in 1986 and has worked as a professor ever since. Her scholarly research has been in the fields of constitutional law, political theory, and comparative political systems. She speaks German, English, and Russian.

A member of the Bulgarian Communist Party since 1960, she was the secretary of the Executive Committees of the People's Lenin Council in Sofia and the Sofia City Council. In 1971, she began work as a scholar in the Institute for Contemporary Social Theories at the Presidium of the Bulgarian Academy of Science (BAS). In 1989, she became the institute's vice chairperson. By 1986, she was appointed chair of the International Relations Department at the Karl Marx Higher Economic Institute (currently known as the National and World Economy University). At the National Roundtable Talks, Ananieva represented the Democratic Women's Union. From February 8, 1990 to December 20, 1990, she served as the vice chair of the Cabinet of Ministers. On February 2, 1990, Ananieva was elected a member of the Supreme Council of the Bulgarian Socialist Party. Beginning on December 20, 1991, she served as a member of the Executive Bureau of BSP's Supreme Council. In June 1990, she was elected a deputy to the Seventh Grand National Assembly, where she was a leading member of the Commission for Drafting the Constitution. Ananieva was elected as a deputy to the Thirty-Sixth National Assembly, where she was elected chair of the parliamentary group of the BSP's Primary Elections Union. She also served as a deputy at the Thirty-seventh National Assembly. In January 1995, she was elected vice chairperson of the Thirty-seventh National Assembly. She was among the founders of the Interbalkan Women's Cooperation Association that was formed under the initiative of the Women's Democratic Union. Ananieva has also been active in the International Political Science Association, serving as cochair of the Research Committee on Women in Politics.

13. Daily Report, East Europe, "List of Parties, Groups Registered for Elections," FBIS-EEU-90-094, May 15, 1990, pp. 18–19.

14. See chapter 5 for details.

15. Emilia Droumeva, "A New and Original Election System in Bulgaria—June 1990," in *Law in a Fast-Changing Society,* edited by Silvy Chernev (Sofia, Bulgaria: St. Kliment Ohridski University Press, 1994), 28–29.

16. Daily Report, East Europe, "Further on One-Party Cabinet," FBIS-EEU-90-183, September 20, 1990, pp. 3–4.

17. Daily Report, East Europe, "SDS Leader Dimitrov Wants May Elections," FBIS-EEU-91-020, January 30, 1991, p. 9.

18. Rumyana Kolarova and Dimitr Dimitrov, "Electoral Laws in Eastern Europe: Bulgaria," *East European Constitutional Review* 3 (Spring 1994): 54.

19. Albert P. Melone and Carol E. Hays, "The Judicial Role in Bulgaria's Struggle for Human Rights," *Judicature* 77 (1994): 252–53.

20. Interview with Stefan Savov, floor leader of the UDF and leader of the Democratic Party, formerly chairman of the National Assembly, at the Parliament building, 1 Narodno Subranie Square, Sofia, Bulgaria, October 11, 1993. Born on January 8, 1924, in Sofia, Stefan Savov is a son of the businessman, industrialist, financier, and publicist Dimitur Savov, who was the minister of finance in Ivan Bagryanov's government (1944). Stefan Savov served a sentence in a labor camp after the Communist takeover on September 9, 1944. Stefan's grandfather participated in the National Liberation Movement of 1872–78.

Stefan Savov completed his university degree in law at the St. Kliment Ohridski University in Sofia. He speaks Spanish, French, and German. He worked as a translator until November 10, 1989. He has translated more than thirty books from Spanish into Bulgarian and has twice received awards for outstanding translation. He is the first Bulgarian awarded the Spanish Knight Cross. Savov is the president of the Bulgarian Spanishists Association and a member of Rotary Club International.

Savov was elected the leader of the Democratic Party at the party's Thirteenth Congress on December 16, 1990.

He was a deputy at the Seventh Grand National Assembly. From August 1990, to February 1991, Savov was the vice chairman of the Permanent Commission for Foreign Policy at the Grand National Assembly. He was a leading UDF deputy in the Assembly but he became a leader of a hunger strike in protest to the adoption of the new Constitution. He returned to the Parliament on July 23, 1991, after the Constitution had been adopted. From May 31 to November 4, 1991, he was one of two chairpersons of the parliamentary group of the National Movement UDF.

Savov joined the Thirty-sixth National Assembly as part of the UDF's party list. On November 4, 1991, he was elected chairman of the Thirty-sixth National Assembly. On July 23, 1992, upon the demand of the opposition, the Parliament failed by one vote to relieve him of his duties before the expiration of his term: of the 230 present deputies, 115 voted for and 112 against.

Savov served as chairman of the Parliament until September 24, 1992. From March 17, 1993, to October 13, 1994, he was the chair of the UDF's parliamentary group. On October 13, 1994, he became the chair of the newly formed parliamentary group of the Democratic Party. He is a leader of the National Union coalition between the Agricultural Party, led by Anastasia Moser, and the Democratic Party. Savov is also the director of a newspaper. In the Thirty-seventh National Assembly, he was a deputy from the National Union coalition and cochair of the coalition's parliamentary group. He is also a member of the Commission for Foreign Policy and of the permanent parliamentary delegation to the European Union's Assembly.

21. Daily Report, East Europe, "Government Survives No-Confidence Vote," FBIS-EEU-92-143, July 24, 1992, p. 2.

22. Daily Report, East Europe, "Parliament Votes on Dismissal of Assembly Chairman," FBIS-EEU-92-143, July 24, 1992, pp. 2–3.

23. Daily Report, East Europe, "Zhelev Justifies Criticism of SDS, Policies," FBIS-EEU-92-189, September 29, 1992, pp. 3–4.

24. Interview with Philip Dimitrov, leader of the Union of Democratic Forces and former prime minister, at UDF Headquarters, 134 Rakovsky Street, Sofia, Bulgaria, October 12, 1993. Philip Dimitrov was born in Sofia on March 31, 1955. He graduated from an English language high school and completed his higher education degree in law at the St. Kliment Ohridski University in Sofia. He has considerable experience as a lawyer in the Second Attorney Collective in Sofia. Before November 10, 1989, he had not participated in political organizations. He was never a member of the BCP. Dimitrov is among the founders of the Green Party in 1989. From 1990 to 1991, he was the vice chairperson of the same party. Strongly religious, during the initial years of change in Bulgaria, he was a member of the Committee for Defending Religious Rights led by Father Christofor Sabev. Dimitrov was also among the founders of the first monarchical association in Bulgaria, the Democracy Foundation, and the National Security Foundation. From July 6 to December 1990, he was the vice chairperson of the Coordination Council of the Union of Democratic Forces. On December 11, 1990, he became the council's chairperson. From May to December 1991, Dimitrov was also the chair of UDF's Central Elections Club. He was elected a deputy to the Thirty-sixth National Assembly. On November 8, 1991, with a vote of 131 representatives for and 94 against, Philip Dimitrov was elected the forty-second prime minister of the Republic of Bulgaria. After a no-confidence vote on October 29, 1992, he resigned. On November 19, 1992, President Zhelev commissioned Philip Dimitrov to form the new cabinet, and proposed Dimitrov's reelection to the Thirty-sixth National Assembly. The National Assembly, however, did not give Philip Dimitrov the support he needed to form a cabinet. He remained

prime minister in resignation until December 30, 1992. From June 1 to December 30, 1992, Dimitrov served as chairperson of the Governmental Commission for Regulation and Control Over the Regime for Production and Trade with Military and Specialized Products. On October 23, 1993, he was elected chairperson of the political chamber in the Conservative Ecological Party. He was a member of the board of directors of the Atlantic Club until March 1994. In the Thirty-seventh National Assembly, he worked as a UDF affiliated deputy. At the end of 1994, he resigned as the leader of UDF. In February 1995, Dimitrov became a member of the Foreign Policy Commission in the National Assembly and joined the Bulgarian Parliamentary Delegation for Relations with the European Parliament.

25. Charles Moser, *Theory and History of the Bulgarian Transition* (Sofia: Free Initiative Foundation, 1994), 86–93.

26. Ibid., 87.

27. Ibid., 88.

28. Daily Report, East Europe, "DPS Proposes Berov for Prime Minister," FBIS-EEU-92-247, December 23, 1992, p. 3.

29. Daily Report, East Europe, "Maneuvering Over Berov Candidacy Continues," FBIS-EEU-92-251, December 30, 1992, p. 4.

30. Daily Report, East Europe, "Berov Presents Government Program to Assembly," FBIS-EEU-92-252, December 31, 1992, p. 2; Daily Report, East Europe, "Berov Says Cabinet to Implement SDS Program," FBIS-EEU-93-003, January 6, 1993, p. 9.

31. Daily Report, East Europe, "SDS to Act as 'Stiff Opposition' in Parliament," FBIS-EEU-93-003, January 6, 1992, pp. 9–10.

32. Daily Report, East Europe, "Parliament Debates SDS No-Confidence Motion," FBIS-EEU-93-101, May 27, 1993, p. 2.

33. Daily Report, East Europe, "Parliament Approves New Cabinet," FBIS-EEU-93-120, June 24, 1993, p. 5.

34. Daily Report, East Europe, "Savov Explains SDS Parliamentary Group," FBIS-EEU-93-122, June 28, 1993, p. 5.

35. Daily Report, East Europe, "Zhelev Regrets SDS Boycott of Parliament," FBIS-EEU-93-122, June 28, 1993, p. 5.

36. Daily Report, East Europe, "SDS to Ask Parliament to Call Elections," FBIS-EEU-93-128, July 7, 1993, p. 13.

37. Daily Report, East Europe, "DPS Leader Dogan 'Tired' of 'Balancing Force' Role," FBIS-EEU-93-172, September 8, 1993, p. 5.

38. Kjell Engelbrekt, "Bulgarian Parliament Approves Government Resignation," *RFE/RL Daily Report,* no. 179 (September 9, 1994), on Internet.

39. Stan Markotich, "Bulgarian Socialist Party Declines to Form Government," *RFE/RL Daily Report,* no. 177 (September 16, 1994), on Internet.

40. Jiri Pehe, "Socialist Party Ahead in Bulgaria? " *RFE/RL Daily Report* no. 188 (October 4, 1994), on Internet.

41. Kjell Engelbrekt, "Bulgarian Opposition Refuses to Form New Government," *RFE/RL Daily Report* no. 180 (September 21, 1994), on Internet.

42. Jiri Pehe, "Bulgarian Prime Minister Proposed, " *RFE/RL Daily Report* no. 186 (September 29, 1994), on Internet.

43. BTA, "Parliament Passes 82 Laws in Its First Six Months," *Bulletin of News from Bulgaria,* August 7, 1995, on Internet.

44. Jiri Pehe, "Former Communists Gain Absolute Majority in Bulgaria," *RFE/RL Daily Report* no. 239 (December 20, 1994), on Internet.

45. BTA, "Leader Zhan Videnov Elected PM-Designate," *Bulletin of News from Bulgaria,* January 16, 1995, on Internet.

46. BTA, "Parliament Passes 82 Laws in Its First Six Months," *Bulletin of News from Bulgaria,* August 7, 1995, on Internet.

47. Stefan Krause, "Bulgarian Government Survives No Confidence Vote," *OMRI Daily Digest* 8, pt. 2 (January 11, 1996), on Internet.

48. Ekaterina Kazassova, "Sendov Remains Head of Parliament," *Bulletin of News from Bulgaria,* February 8, 1996, on Internet.

49. BTA, "Parliament to Take Vote on Change in Government," *Bulletin of News from Bulgaria,* May 9, 1996, on Internet.

50. BTA, "Opposition Decides Against No-Confidence Vote," *Bulletin of News from Bulgaria,* May 16, 1996, on Internet.

51. BTA, "Trust in Institutions Wanes," *Bulletin of News from Bulgaria,* May 16, 1996, on Internet.

52. Stefan Krause, "Bulgarian President Calls for Stronger Presidency," *OMRI Daily Digest* 102, pt. 2 (May 27, 1996), on Internet.

53. Stefan Krause, "Bulgarian President Calls for Presidential Republic," *OMRI Daily Digest* 134, pt. 2 (July 12, 1996), on Internet.

54. Stefan Krause, "Bulgarian Government Reshuffle: Videnov's Last Straw," *OMRI Analytical Brief* 1, no. 156 (June 10, 1996), on Internet.

55. Stefan Krause, "Bulgarian Cabinet Reshuffle: Too Little Too Late," *OMRI Daily Digest* 113, pt. 2 (June 11, 1996), on Internet.

56. Stefan Krause, "Attacks on Bulgarian Government Continue," *OMRI Daily Digest* 103, pt. 2 (May 28, 1996), on Internet; Stefan Krause, "While Protests against Austerity Measures Start," *OMRI Daily Digest* 105, pt. 2 (May 30, 1996), on Internet.

57. Evgenia Droumeva, "Parliament Debates No-Confidence Vote," *Bulletin of News from Bulgaria,* June 11, 1996, on Internet.

58. Stefan Krause, "Bulgarian President Defeated in Primaries," *OMRI Daily Digest* 107, pt. 2 (June 3, 1996), on Internet.

59. Stefan Krause, "Bulgarian Socialists Pick New Presidential Candidate," *OMRI Daily Digest* 171, pt. 2 (September 4, 1996), on Internet.

60. Stefan Krause, "Socialist Reactions to Stoyanov's Victory," *OMRI Daily Digest* 213, pt. 2 (November 4, 1996), on Internet.

61. Stefan Krause, "Bulgarian Socialists Meet to Decide Fate of Premier," *OMRI Daily Digest* 219, pt. 2 (November 12, 1996), on Internet; Stefan Krause, "Bulgarian Premier Survives Party Confidence Vote," *OMRI Daily Digest* 220, pt. 2 (November 13, 1996), on Internet.

62. BTA, "Purvanov—New Socialist Party Leader," *Bulletin of News from Bulgaria,* December 24, 1996, on Internet.

63. BTA, "Parliament Debates Opposition's Draft Declaration on National Salvation," *Bulletin of News from Bulgaria,* January 4, 1996, on Internet.

64. BTA, "United Opposition Stages Protest Rally in Sofia," *Bulletin of News from Bulgaria,* January 4, 1997, on Internet.

65. BTA, "Consultations on New Bulgarian Government," *Bulletin of News from Bulgaria,* January 6, 1996, on Internet.

66. Maria Koinova, "Will a Wave of Protests in Sofia Overflow Bulgaria?" *OMRI Daily Digest* 4, pt. 2 (January 7, 1997).

67. Alison Smale, "Ex-Communists Besieged in Balkans," *St. Louis Post-Dispatch,* January 14, 1997, p. 11B.

68. "Bulgaria Gets Tense," *Southern Illinoisan,* January 12, 1997, p. 11A.

69. Jane Perlez, "To Quiet Protests, Party in Bulgaria Offers Talks," *New York Times,* January 14, 1997, p. A6.

70. BTA, "Parliament Opens Winter Session," *Bulletin of News from Bulgaria,* January 16, 1996, on Internet.

71. BTA, "President Zhelev Starts Consultations," *Bulletin of News from Bulgaria,* January 16, 1997, on Internet.

72. Stefan Krause, "Bulgarian President Calls on Socialists, Opposition to Reach Compromise," *OMRI Daily Digest* 19, pt. 2 (January 28, 1997), on Internet.

73. BTA, "Flash: Dobrev Returns Mandate: Agreement on Early Elections Reached," *Bulletin of News from Bulgaria,* February 4, 1997, on Internet.

74. Fred W. Riggs, "Presidentialism versus Parliamentarism: Implications for Representativeness and Legitimacy," *International Political Science Review* 18 (July 1997): 253–78.

75. BTA, "Constitutional Court Invalidates Land Act Amendments," *Bulletin of News from Bulgaria,* June 20, 1995, on Internet.

76. BTA, "President Zhelev Calls for Accord," *Bulletin of News from Bulgaria,* May 15, 1995, on Internet.

77. BTA, "I Will Not Allow Repoliticization of the Army," *Bulletin of News from Bulgaria,* August 5, 1995, on Internet.

78. Stefan Krause, "Bulgarian President Defends Constitution, Criticizes Socialists," *OMRI Daily Digest* 135, pt. 2 (July 13, 1995), on Internet.

79. Stefan Krause, "Bulgarian Premier Attacks President, Constitutional Court," *OMRI Daily Digest* 147, pt. 2 (July 31, 1995, on Internet.

80. BTA, "President has the Right to Political Statements," *Bulletin of News from Bulgaria,* December 21, 1995, on Internet.

81. Georgi Karasimeonov, "The Legislature in Post-Communist Bulgaria," in *The New Parliaments of Central and Eastern Europe,* edited by David M. Olson and Philip Norton (London and Portland, Ore.: Frank Cass, 1996), 50.

82. Stefan Krause, "Socialists Lead After First Round of Bulgarian Local Elections," *OMRI Daily Digest,* October 30, 1995, on Internet.

83. Stefan Krause, "Bulgarian Opposition Prepares for Cooperation in Local Elections," *OMRI Daily Digest* 213, pt. 2 (November 1, 1995), on Internet; BTA, "Opposition Forces Unite for Run-Off," *Bulletin of News from Bulgaria,* November 1, 1995, on Internet.

84. Huntington, *Third Wave,* 266–67.

Chapter 9

1. Carl F. Pinkele, "Emerging in the Transitions: The Case for Assessing the Private Law Arena Within a Civil Society Focus" (paper prepared for the Santa Fe Conference of the IPSA Research Committee on Comparative Judicial Studies, 1993), 4.

2. Alexis de Tocqueville, *Democracy in America* (New York: Knopf, 1945), 280.

3. Torbjorn Vallinder, "The Judicialization of Politics—A World-wide Phenomenon: Introduction," *International Political Science Review* 15 (April 1994): 91–99.

4. In this chapter I do not reveal the names of the persons I interviewed during October 1993. Although I have permission to reveal their names, I chose not to do so because of the tensions that exist between Parliament and the judiciary. My knowledge of the problems in the judiciary is supplemented by extensive interviews I conducted in 1992 with fifteen Bulgarian jurists visiting the United States as part of a USIA grant and by informal contacts with many Bulgarian legal professionals.

5. Albert P. Melone and Carol E. Hays, "The Judicial Role in Bulgaria's Struggle for Human Rights," *Judicature* 77 (March–April 1994): 251.

6. Ibid., 251–52. My thanks to Judge Kina Choutourkova for providing me with these data.

7. Ibid., 252.

8. "Decision #12 on Constitutional Case," [Bulgaria] *State Gazette,* July 30, 1992.

9. "Decision #3 on Constitutional Case," [Bulgaria] *State Gazette,* April 3, 1992.

10. BTA, "New Cases," *Bulletin of News from Bulgaria,* July 26, 1995, on Internet.

11. Stefan Krause, "Bulgarian Constitutional Court Invalidates Another Law," *OMRI Daily Digest* 193, pt. 2 (October 4, 1995), on Internet.

12. Daily Report, East Europe, "Possibility of Zhelev Vetoes Examined," FBIS-EEU-94-119, June 21, 1994, p. 2.

13. Kjell Engelbrekt, "Bulgarian Parliament Adopts Controversial Law on Judiciary," *Radio Free Europe/Radio Liberty,* No. 114, June 17, 1994.

14. Kjell Engelbrekt, "Bulgaria's Communist Legacy: Settling Old Scores," *RFE/RL Research Report* 1 (July 10, 1992): 6–10.

15. Daily Report, East Europe, "Former Prime Minister Atanasov Taken to Prison" and "BSP Issues Protest," FBIS-EEU-93-170, September 3, 1993, p. 3.

16. BTA, "Prosecutor General Will Continue Criminal Prosecutions Against Three Socialist MPS," *Bulletin of News from Bulgaria,* January 17, 1995, on Internet.

17. "Decision #10 on Constitutional Case," [Bulgaria] *State Gazette,* July 29, 1992.

18. BTA, "European Human Rights Commission Says Prosecution Violated Loukanov's Rights," *Bulletin of News from Bulgaria,* November 19, 1996, on Internet.

19. Panaiot Denev, "UDF Has No Reason to Give Up Parliamentary Boycott," *Demokratsiya,* June 1994.

20. Kjell Engelbrekt, "Council of Europe Memorandum Stirs Controversy in Bulgaria," *Radio Free Europe/Radio Liberty,* No. 119, June 24, 1994.

21. "Decision #8 on Constitutional Case," [Bulgaria] *State Gazette,* September 15, 1994.

22. "Decision #3 on Constitutional Case," [Bulgaria] *State Gazette,* April 3, 1992.

23. Stefan Krause, "Bulgarian Constitutional Court Invalidates Another Law," *OMRI Daily Digest* 193, pt. 2 (October 4, 1995), on Internet.

24. BTA, "Constitutional Court Invalidates Land Act Amendments," *Bulletin of News from Bulgaria,* June 20, 1995, on Internet.

25. BTA, "Farmers Unrest," *Bulletin of News from Bulgaria,* June 27, 1995, on Internet.

26. BTA, "Arguments Over Land Act Continue," *Bulletin of News from Bulgaria,* June 28, 1995, on Internet.

27. Stefan Krause, "Bulgarian President Defends Constitution, Criticizes

Socialists," *OMRI Daily Digest* 135, pt. 2 (July 13, 1995), on Internet; Stefan Krause, "Bulgarian Premier Attacks President, Constitutional Court," *OMRI Daily Digest* 147, pt. 2 (July 31, 1995), on Internet.

28. Stefan Krause, "Bulgarian Government Evicts Constitutional Court," *OMRI Daily Digest* 151, pt. 2 (August 4, 1995), on Internet.

29. BTA, "Tuesday News Briefs," *Bulletin of News from Bulgaria,* August 9, 1995, on Internet.

30. BTA, "Tuesday News Briefs," *Bulletin of News from Bulgaria,* September 13, 1995, on Internet.

31. BTA, "Supreme Judicial Council Elects Heads of Two Courts," *Bulletin of News from Bulgaria,* June 27, 1996, on Internet.

32. BTA, "President Zhelev Addresses the Nation," *Bulletin of News From Bulgaria,* July 17, 1996, on Internet.

33. Stefan Krause, "Bulgarian President, Socialists Clash Again," *OMRI Daily Digest* 137, pt. 2 (July 17, 1996), on Internet.

34. BTA, "President Zhelev Addresses the Nation," *Bulletin of News From Bulgaria,* July 17, 1996, on Internet.

35. BTA, "Ruling of Constitutional Court Inconclusive on the Appointment of Presidents of Supreme Administrative Court and Supreme Court of Cassation," *Bulletin of News from Bulgaria,* July 26, 1996, on Internet.

36. Ibid.

37. "Constitution Watch: Bulgaria," *East European Constitutional Review* 5 (Spring 1996): 6.

38. BTA, "Parliament Amends Bulgarian Citizenship Act," *Bulletin of News from Bulgaria,* June 1, 1996, on Internet.

39. BTA, "Constitutional Court Rules on the Issue of Citizenship by Birth," *Bulletin of News from Bulgaria,* July 24, 1996, on Internet.

40. BTA, "Disputes Impede Presidential Elections in Bulgaria," *Bulletin of News from Bulgaria,* July 30, 1996, on Internet.

41. BTA, "Major Presidential Candidates Denied Registration," *Bulletin of News from Bulgaria,* August 28, 1996, on Internet.

42. BTA, "Opposition's Presidential Candidate Will be Registered, Ruling Left's New Presidential Candidate Gives First News Conference," *Bulletin of News from Bulgaria,* September 5, 1996, on Internet.

43. Stefan Krause, "Bulgarian Socialists Pick New Presidential Candidate," *OMRI Daily Digest* 171, pt. 2 (September 4, 1996), on Internet.

44. BTA, "Culture Minister Ivan Marazov Named New Socialist Presidential Candidate," *Bulletin of News from Bulgaria,* September 5, 1996, on Internet.

45. Stefan Krause, "Opposition Candidate Wins Bulgarian Presidential Elections," *OMRI Daily Digest,* 213, pt. 2 (November 4, 1996), on Internet.

46. Stefan Krause, "Bulgarian Premier Attacks President, Constitutional Court," *OMRI Daily Digest* 147, pt. 2 (July 31, 1995), on Internet.

47. Stanley Bach and Susan Benda, "Parliamentary Rules and Judicial Review in Romania," *East European Constitutional Review* 4 (Summer 1995): 49–53; Spencer Zifcak, "The Battle Over Presidential Power in Slovakia," *East European Constitutional Review* 4 (Summer 1995): 61–65.

Chapter 10

1. This was not only true of Bulgaria but was the case for the entire region. See Stephen White, "Eastern Europe After Communism," in *Developments in East Europe European Politics,* edited by Stephen White, Judy Batt, and Paul G. Lewis (Durham: Duke University Press, 1993), 8–9.

2. David S. Mason, "Poland," in *Developments in East European Politics,* edited by Stephen White, Judy Batt, and Paul G. Lewis (Durham: Duke University Press, 1993), 37–40.

3. Giuseppe Di Palma, *To Craft Democracies* (Berkeley and Los Angeles: University of California Press, 1990), ch. 3.

4. Georgi Karasimeonov, "Bulgaria's New Party System," in *Stabilising Fragile Democracies,* edited by Geoffrey Pridham and Paul G. Lewis (London and New York: Routledge, 1996), 264; Georgi Karasimeonov, "The Legislature in Post-Communist Bulgaria," in *The New Parliaments of Central and Eastern Europe,* edited by David M. Olson and Philip Norton (London and Portland, Ore.: Frank Cass, 1996).

5. Gerhard Loewenberg and Samuel C. Patterson, *Comparing Legislatures* (Boston: Little, Brown and Company, 1979), 10.

6. Rumyana Kolarova and Dimitr Dimitrov, "Round Table Talks in Bulgaria," (Center for Constitutionalism in Eastern Europe, University of Chicago Law School, 1991), 1.

7. Albert P. Melone and Carol Hays, "The Judicial Role in Bulgaria's Struggle for Human Rights," *Judicature* 77 (March–April 1994): 252.

8. Di Palma, *To Craft Democracies,* 21, 115.

9. United Nations Development Programme, *Bulgaria: Human Development Report 1995* (Sofia: National and Global Development UNDP, 1995).

10. BTA, "Lev Depreciates 600% in 1996," *Bulletin of News from Bulgaria,* January 8, 1996, on Internet.

11. Di Palma, *To Craft Democracies,* 22.

12. Jill Chin, "Political Attitudes in Bulgaria," *RFE/RL Research Report* 2, no. 18 (April 1993): 39–41.

13. Di Palma, *To Craft Democracies,* 145.

14. The economic and political conditions in Spain were very different from those existing in Bulgaria. See Daniel N. Nelson, "The Comparative

Politics of Eastern Europe," in *Developments in East European Politics,* edited by Stephen White, Judy Batt, and Paul G. Lewis (Durham: Duke University Press, 1993), 253–55.

15. *The Europa World Year Book 1995,* s. v. "Bulgaria," p. 648.

16. BTA, "President Zhelev: Communism Cannot Return in Its Classical Form," *Bulletin of News From Bulgaria,* September 25, 1995, on Internet.

17. Ibid.

18. Ibid.

19. Ibid.

20. BTA, "European Human Rights Commission Says Prosecution Violated Loukanov's [Lukanov] Rights," *Bulletin of News from Bulgaria,* November 29, 1996, on Internet.

21. BTA, "Declaration," *Bulletin of News from Bulgaria,* October 2, 1996, on Internet.

22. BTA, "Lukanov: Repercussions," *Bulletin of News from Bulgaria,* October 4, 1996, on Internet.

23. See for example, Aristotle's *Politics:* Book 4, chapters 1, 5, 6, 11; Book 6, chapter 4, and Book 7, chapters 3–7. Also see Plato's *Republic:* Book 7, 544 c–e.

24. Laird Addis, "The Individual and the Marxist Philosophy of History," in *Readings in the Philosophy of Social Sciences,* edited by May Brodbeck (London: Macmillan Company, 1968), 317–35.

25. Karl Deutsch, "Social Mobilization and Political Development," *American Political Science Review* 55 (September 1961): 493–514; Daniel Lerner, *The Passing of Traditional Society* (New York: Free Press, 1958); Seymour Martin Lipset, "Some Social Requisites of Democracy: Economic Development and Political Legitimacy," *American Political Science Review* 53 (March 1959): 69–105; W. W. Rostow, *The Stages of Economic Growth* (New York: Cambridge University Press, 1960).

26. Samuel P. Huntington, *Political Order in Changing Societies* (New Haven: Yale University Press, 1968).

Bibliography

Ananieva, Nora. Interview by author. Sofia, Bulgaria, October 14, 1993.

Avramov, Georgi. Interviewed by author. Sofia, Bulgaria, October 13, 1993.

Bach, Stanley, and Susan Benda. "Parliamentary Rules and Judicial Review in Romania." *East European Constitutional Review* 4 (Summer 1995): 49–53.

Baker, Randall. *Summer in the Balkans: Laughter and Tears After Communism.* West Hartford, Conn.: Kumarian Press, 1994.

Bell, John D. *Peasants in Power: Alexander Stamboliski and the Bulgarian Agrarian National Union, 1899–1923.* Princeton: Princeton University Press, 1977.

———. "'Post Communist' Bulgaria." *Current History* 89 (December 1990): 417–20, 427–29.

Beron, Petar. Interview by author. Sofia, Bulgaria, October 7, 1993.

Bertschi, C. Charles. "Lustration and the Transition to Democracy: The Cases of Poland and Bulgaria." *East European Quarterly* 28 (January 1995): 435–51.

Bliznashki, Georgi. "Functions of the Presidential Institution in Bulgaria." *Pravna Misal* (1992): 3–11.

———. Interview by author. Sofia, Bulgaria, October 8, 1993.

Bova, Russell. "Political Dynamics of the Post-Communist Transition: A Comparative Perspective." *World Politics* 44 (October 1991): 113–38.

Boyadjiev, Vladimir. "Socio-Economic Platform of the Bulgarian Opposition." *Peace Research* 22 (August 1990): 45–51.

Brinton, Crane. *The Anatomy of Revolution.* Revised and Expanded Edition. Englewood Cliffs, N.J.: Prentice Hall, 1939.

Brodbeck, May, ed. *Readings in the Philosophy of Social Sciences.* London: Macmillan, 1968.

Bryant, Christopher G. A., and Edmund Mokrzycki. *The New Great Transformation? Change and Continuity in East-Central Europe.* London and New York: Routledge, 1994.

"Bulgaria Gets Tense." *Southern Illinoisan,* January 12, 1997, 11A.

Bulgarian Academy of Science. *Decisions and Definitions of the Constitutional Court of the Republic of Bulgaria, 1991–1992.* Sofia: Bulgarian Academy of Science, 1993.

Bulgarian Telegraph Agency (BTA). *Bulletin of News from Bulgaria.* Obtained from Bulgaria@Access.Digex.Net and Embassy-Washington@Bulgaria.Com. The BTA is currently preparing a new website; the above e-mail addresses are no longer valid. Subscriptions available directly by mail at Bulgarian Telegraph Agency, 49 Tsarigradskoshosse, 1124 Sofia, Bulgaria.

———. "Leader Zhan Videnov Elected PM-Designate." January 16, 1995. Bulgaria@Access.Digex.Net.

———. "Prosecutor General Will Continue Criminal Prosecutions Against Three Socialist MPS." January 17, 1995. Bulgaria@Access.Digex.Net.

———. "Socialists Elect Zhan Videnov Prime Minister Designate." January 17, 1995. Bulgaria@Access.Digex.Net.

———. "President Zhelev Calls for Accord." May 15, 1995. Bulgaria@Access.Digex.Net.

———. "UDF Challenges Constitutionality of Land Act." May 19, 1995. Bulgaria@Access.Digex.Net.

———. "Constitutional Court Invalidates Land Act Amendments." June 20, 1995. Bulgaria@Access.Digex.Net.

———. "Farmers' Unrest." June 27, 1995. Bulgaria@Access.Digex.Net.

———. "Arguments Over Land Act Continue." June 28, 1995. Bulgaria@Access.Digex.Net.

———. "New Cases." July 26, 1995. Bulgaria@Access.Digex.Net.

———. "I Will Not Allow Repoliticization of the Army." August 5, 1995. Bulgaria@Access.Digex.Net.

———. "Parliament Passes 82 Laws in its First Six Months." August 7, 1995. Bulgaria@Access.Digex.Net.

———. "Tuesday News Briefs." August 9, 1995. Bulgaria@Access.Digex.Net.

———. "Tuesday News Briefs." August 13, 1995. Bulgaria@Access.Digex.Net.

———. "President Zhelev: Communism Cannot Return in Its Classical Form." September 25, 1995. Bulgaria@Access.Digex.Net.

———. "Opposition Forces Unite for Run-Off." November 1, 1995. Bulgaria@Access.Digex.Net.

———. "President Has the Right to Political Statements." December 21, 1995. Bulgaria@Access.Digex.Net.

———. "Parliament to Take Vote on Change in Government." May 9, 1996. Bulgaria@Access.Digex.Net.

———. "Opposition Decides Against No-Confidence Vote." May 16, 1996. Bulgaria@Access.Digex.Net.

———. "Trust in Institutions Wanes." May 16, 1996. Bulgaria@Access.Digex.Net.

———. "Parliament Amends Bulgarian Citizenship Act." June 1, 1996. Embassy-Washington@Bulgaria.Com.

———. “President Zhelev Addresses the Nation.” July 17, 1996. Embassy-Washington@Bulgaria.Com.

———. “Constitutional Court Rules on the Issue of Citizenship by Birth.” July 24, 1996. Embassy-Washington@Bulgaria.Com.

———. “Supreme Judicial Council Elects Heads of Two Courts.” June 27, 1996. Embassy-Washington@Bulgaria.Com.

———. “Ruling of Constitutional Court Inconclusive on the Appointment of Presidents of Supreme Administrative Court and Supreme Court of Cassation.” July 26, 1996. Embassy-Washington@Bulgaria.Com.

———. “Disputes Impede Presidential Elections in Bulgaria.” July 30, 1996. Embassy-Washington@Bulgaria.Com.

———. “Major Presidential Candidates Denied Registration.” August 28, 1996. Embassy-Washington@Bulgaria.Com.

———. “Opposition’s Presidential Candidate Will be Registered, Ruling Left’s New Presidential Candidate Gives First News Conference.” September 5, 1996. Embassy-Washington@ Bulgaria.Com.

———. “Culture Minister Ivan Marazov Named New Socialist Presidential Candidate.” September 5, 1996. Embassy-Washington@Bulgaria.Com.

———. “Declaration.” October 2, 1996. Embassy-Washington@Bulgaria.Com.

———. “Loukanov [Lukanov]: Repercussions.” October 4, 1996. Embassy-Washington@Bulgaria.Com.

———. “European Human Rights Commission Says Prosecution Violated Loukanov’s [Lukanov] Rights.” November 29, 1996. Embassy-Washington@Bulgaria.Com.

———. “Purvanov—New Socialist Party Leader.” December 20–27, 1996. Embassy-Washington@Bulgaria.Com.

———. “Petition to Rule Ethnic Turks’ Movement as Anticonstitutional Rejected.” December 20–27, 1996. Embassy-Washington@Bulgaria.Com.

———. “Parliament Debates Opposition’s Draft Declaration on National Salvation.” January 4, 1997. Embassy-Washington@Bulgaria.Com.

———. “United Opposition Stages Protest Rally in Sofia.” January 4, 1997. Embassy-Washington@Bulgaria.Com.

———. “Consultations on New Bulgarian Government.” January 6, 1997. Embassy-Washington@Bulgaria.Com.

———. “Parliament Opens Winter Session.” January 16, 1997. Embassy-Washington@Bulgaria.Com.

———. “President Zhelev Starts Consultations.” January 16, 1997. Embassy-Washington@Bulgaria.Com.

———. “Flash: Dobrev Returns Mandate: Agreement on Early Elections Reached.” February 4, 1997. Embassy-Washington@Bulgaria.Com.

Bulgarian Telegraph Agency (BTA) Reference Service/NM. *The National Roundtable.* Sofia, Bulgaria: Bulgarian Telegraph Agency, 1993.

Bulgarian Telegraph Agency/VM. *The Seventh Grand National Assembly.* Sofia, Bulgaria: Bulgarian Telegraph Agency, 1993.

Cantori, Louis J., and Andrew H. Ziegler, Jr. *Comparative Politics in the Post-Behavioral Era.* Boulder: Lynne Rienner, 1988.

Center for the Study of Democracy. *Constitutional Drafts Discussed in Bulgarian Parliament.* Sofia, Bulgaria: Center for the Study of Democracy, 1991.

Chernev, Silvy, ed. and trans. *Law in a Fast-Changing Society.* Sofia, Bulgaria: St. Kliment Ohridski University Press, 1994.

Chilcote, Ronald H. *Theories of Comparative Politics: The Search for a Paradigm Reconsidered.* Boulder: Westview, 1994.

Chin, Jill. "Political Attitudes in Bulgaria." *RFE/RL Research Report* 2, no. 18 (April 30, 1993): 39–41.

Constitution of the Republic of Bulgaria. July 1991.

Crampton, R. J. *Bulgaria, 1878–1918: A History.* New York: Columbia University Press, 1983.

———. *A Short History of Modern Bulgaria.* Cambridge: Cambridge University Press, 1987.

Dahl, Robert A. *Polyarchy: Participation and Opposition.* New Haven: Yale University Press, 1971.

Dahrendorf, Ralph. *Reflections on the Revolution in Europe.* London: Chatto and Windus, 1990.

Daily Report, East Europe. "Sofia Lawyers Seek End to Party's Leading Role." FBIS-EEU-89–241. December 18, 1989.

———. "Democratic Union Delegation." FBIS-EEU-90-003. January 4, 1990.

———. "Preliminary Talks Begin." FBIS-EEU-90-003. January 4, 1990.

———. "Preparations Under Way for Roundtable Talks ." FBIS-EEU-90-003. January 4, 1990.

———. "Procedures Discussed." FBIS-EEU-90-003. January 4, 1990.

———. "Bulgarian Roundtable Discussion Moving Ahead." FBIS-SOV-90-004. January 5, 1990.

———. "Further on Talks." FBIS-EEU-90-004. January 5, 1990.

———. "Roundtable Expresses Views on Ethnic Issue." FBIS-EEU-90-004. January 5, 1990.

———. "Roundtable Talks Scheduled for 16 January." FBIS-EEU-90-004. January 5, 1990.

———. "Amendments Considered." FBIS-EEU-90-010. January 16, 1990.

———. "Assembly Session Opens; Article 1 Repealed." FBIS-EEU-90-010. January 16, 1990.

———. "Opposition Spokesman Discusses Roundtable." FBIS-EEU-90-010. January 16, 1990.

———. "Thousands Attend Rally on Nationality Issue." FBIS-EEU-90-010. January 16, 1990.

———. "BTA Reports Results." FBIS-EEU-90-011. January 17, 1990.

———. "Preliminary Roundtable Talks Open 16 January." FBIS-EEU-90-011. January 17, 1990.

———. "UDF Presents Demands at Roundtable 13 January." FBIS-EEU-90-011. January 17, 1990.

———. "Union Demands Listed." FBIS-EEU-90-011. January 17, 1990.

———. "Lukanov Speech at National Assembly Session." FBIS-EEU-90-012. January 18, 1990.

———. "Roundtable Talks Resume 18 January." FBIS-EEU-90-012. January 18, 1990.

———. "Walkout Threatened." FBIS-EEU-90-012. January 18, 1990.

———. "Bokov Statement on Reports." FBIS-EEU-90-015. January 23, 1990.

———. "Zhelev on Beginning of Roundtable Talks." FBIS-EEU-90-015. January 23, 1990.

———. "BCP, Opposition Hold Roundtable Talks." FBIS-EEU-90-016. January 24, 1990.

———. "Politburo Orders Dissolution of Army BCP Bodies." FBIS-EEU-90-019. January 29, 1990.

———. "Relay of Sofia Roundtable Talks." FBIS-EEU-90-019. January 29, 1990.

———. "Further on Discussions at Roundtable Talks." FBIS-EEU-90-026. February 7, 1990.

———. "Semerdjiev [Semerjiev] Speaks." FBIS-EEU-90-026. February 7, 1990.

———. "Roundtable Negotiations 'Going Slowly'." FBIS-EEU-90-027. February 8, 1990.

———. "Roundtable Contact Group Holds Sessions." FBIS-EEU-90-032. February 15, 1990.

———. "Commissions on Constitution." FBIS-EEU-90-040. February 28, 1990.

———. "BCP Daily Denounces UDF Declaration." FBIS-EEU-90-044. March 6, 1990.

———. "Democrats State Views on Elections, Roundtable." FBIS-EEU-90-044. March 6, 1990.

———. "Roundtable Draft Documents Published." FBIS-EEU-90-044. March 6, 1990.

———. "Further on Agreements." FBIS-EEU-90-049. March 13, 1990.

———. "Lilov Opens Roundtable Talks." FBIS-EEU-90-049. March 13, 1990.

———. "Declaration on Roundtable Role, Status." FBIS-EEU-90-051. March 15, 1990.

———. "On Transition to Democracy." FBIS-EEU-90-051. March 15, 1990.

———. "List of Roundtable Agreements Signatories." FBIS-EEU-90-052. March 16, 1990.

———. "Lukanov Speaks at Roundtable." FBIS-EEU-90-052. March 16, 1990.

———. "Roundtable Discusses Market Reform." FBIS-EEU-90-052. March 16, 1990.

———. "BTA on Continuation of Roundtable." FBIS-EEU-90-061. March 29, 1990.

———. "Elections 10, 17 June." FBIS-EEU-90-063. April 2, 1990.

———. "Roundtable Agrees on Mladenov as President." FBIS-EEU-90-063. April 2, 1990.

———. "Roundtable's Agreement on Amendments." FBIS-EEU-90-064. April 3, 1990.

———. "UDF: Contradictory Assembly, Roundtable Rulings." FBIS-EEU-90-101. April 5, 1990.

———. "List of Parties, Groups Registered For Elections." FBIS-EEU-90-094. May 15, 1990.

———. "Roundtable Ethics Code for Elections." FBIS-EEU-90-066. May 24, 1990.

———. "President Mladenov Denies SDS Charges." FBIS-EEU-90-116. June 15, 1990.

———. "Background Information on President, Semerdjiev [Semerjiev]." FBIS-EEU-90-149. August 2, 1990.

———. "Further on One-Party Cabinet." FBIS-EEU-90-183. September 20, 1990.

———. "SDS Leader Dimitrov Wants May Elections." FBIS-EEU-91-020. January 30, 1991.

———. "Princess Meets Supporters." FBIS-EEU-91-089. May 8, 1991.

———. "Constitution Passed, 'Virtual Split of SDS'." FBIS-EEU-91-132. July 10, 1991.

———. "Rally, Hunger Strike Reported." FBIS-EEU-91-133. July 11, 1991.

———. "SDS Council Issues Declaration." FBIS-EEU-91-133. July 11, 1991.

———. "National Assembly Adopts New Constitution." FBIS-EEU-91-135. July 15, 1991.

———. "Poll on Constitution, Elections Reported." FBIS-EEU-91-135. July 15, 1991.

———. "Reaction to Zhelev Meeting with Hunger Strikers." FBIS-EEU-91-136. July 16, 1991.

———. "Assembly Reaches Compromise on Constitutional Oath." FBIS-EEU-91-137. July 17, 1991.

———. "Podkrepa Demands Referendum on New Constitution." FBIS-EEU-91-137. July 17, 1991.

———. "DUMA Praises Newly Adopted Constitution." FBIS-EEU-91-138. July 18, 1991.

———. "Zhelev Addresses Nation on Elections." FBIS-EEU-91-138. July 18, 1991.

———. "Zhelev Defends New Constitution." FBIS-EEU-91-140. July 22, 1991.

———. "International Civil Rights Protocol Ratified." FBIS-EEU-89–244. December 12, 1991.

———. "SDS to Act as 'Stiff Opposition' in Parliament." FBIS-EEU-93-003. January 6, 1992.

———. "Government Survives No-Confidence Vote." FBIS-EEU-92-143. July 24, 1992.

———. "Parliament Votes on Dismissal of Assembly Chairman." FBIS-EEU-92-143. July 24, 1992.

———. "Zhelev Justifies Criticism of SDS, Policies." FBIS-EEU-92-189. September 29, 1992.

———. "DPS Proposes Berov for Prime Minister." FBIS-EEU-92-247. December 23, 1992.

———. "Maneuvering Over Berov Candidacy Continues." FBIS-EEU-92-251. December 30, 1992.

———. "Berov Presents Government Program to Assembly." FBIS-EEU-92-252. December 31, 1992.

———. "Berov Says Cabinet to Implement SDS Program." FBIS-EEU-92-003. January 6, 1993. (Incorrectly listed on Micro-Fiche as January 8, 1992.)

———. "Parliament Debates SDS No-Confidence Motion." FBIS-EEU-93-101. May 27, 1993.

———. "Parliament Approves New Cabinet." FBIS-EEU-93-120. June 24, 1993.

———. "Savov Explains SDS Parliamentary Group." FBIS-EEU-93-122. June 28, 1993.

———. "Zhelev Regrets SDS Boycott of Parliament." FBIS-EEU-93-122. June 28, 1993.

———. "SDS to Ask Parliament to Call Elections." FBIS-EEU-93-128. July 7, 1993.

———. "Former Prime Minister Atanasov Taken to Prison"; "BSP Issues Protest." FBIS-EEU-93-170. September 3, 1993.

———. "DPS Leader Dogan 'Tired' of 'Balancing Force' Role." FBIS-EEU-93-172. September 8, 1993.

———. "Possibility of Zhelev Vetoes Examined." FBIS-EEU-94-119. June 21, 1994.

Daily Report, Soviet Union. "Bulgarian Roundtable Discussion Moving Ahead." FBIS-EEU-90-004. January 5, 1990.

"Decision #3 on Constitutional Case." (Bulgaria) *State Gazette,* April 3, 1992.

"Decision #7 on Constitutional Case #6/92." Decisions and Definitions of the Constitutional Court of the Republic of Bulgaria, 1991–1992. Bulgarian Academy of Science, Sofia, Bulgaria.

"Decision #8 on Constitutional Case." [Bulgaria] *State Gazette,* September 15, 1994.

"Decision #10 on Constitutional Case." [Bulgaria] *State Gazette,* July 29, 1992.

"Decision #12 on Constitutional Case." [Bulgaria] *State Gazette,* July 30, 1992.

Denev, Panaiot. "UDF Has No Reason to Give Up Parliamentary Boycott." *Demokratsiya,* June 1994.

Dertliev, Petar. Interview by author. Sofia, Bulgaria, October 6, 1993.

Deutsch, Karl. "Social Mobilization and Political Development." *American Political Science Review* 55 (September 1961): 493–514.

Dimitrov, Philip. Interview by author. Sofia, Bulgaria, October 12, 1993.

Di Palma, Giuseppe. *To Craft Democracies: An Essay on Democratic Transitions.* Berkeley and Los Angeles: University of California Press, 1990.

Droumeva, Emilia A. "A New and Original Election System in Bulgaria." Paper presented at the Bulgarian/American Law Days Conference, Varna, Bulgaria, May 29–June 3, 1991.

Droumeva, Evgeniya. "Parliament Debates No-Confidence Vote." *Bulletin of News from Bulgaria,* June 11, 1996. Embassy-Washington@Bulgaria.Com.

East European Constitutional Review. "Constitution Watch: Bulgaria." *East European Constitutional Review* 5 (Spring 1996): 6.

Elster, Jon. "Constitution-Making in Eastern Europe: Rebuilding the Boat in the Open Sea." *Public Administration* 71 (Spring/Summer 1993): 169–218.

Engelbrekt, Kjell. "Bulgarian Parliament Adopts Controversial Law on Judiciary." No. 114, Radio Free Europe/Radio Liberty, June 17, 1994.

———. "Bulgaria's Communist Legacy: Settling Old Scores." *RFE/RL Research Report* 1, no. 28 (July 10, 1992): 6–10.

———. "Bulgarian Opposition Refuses to Form New Government." No. 180, Radio Free Europe/Radio Liberty, September 21, 1994.

———. "Bulgarian Parliament Approves Government Resignation." No. 179, Radio Free Europe/Radio Liberty, September 9, 1994.

———. "Council of Europe Memorandum Stirs Controversy in Bulgaria." No. 119, Radio Free Europe/Radio Liberty, June 24, 1994.

The Europa World Year Book 1995. s. v. "Bulgaria."

Gaitanjiev, Stefan. Interview by author. Sofia, Bulgaria, October 13, 1993.

Ganev, Ginio. Interview by author. Sofia, Bulgaria, October 5, 1993.

Glushkov, Ivan. Interview by author. Sofia, Bulgaria, October 6, 1993.

Hastings, Elizabeth Han, and Philip K. Hastings. *Index to International Public Opinion, 1993–1994.* Westport, Conn.: Greenwood Press, 1995.

Huntington, Samuel P. *Political Order in Changing Societies.* New Haven: Yale University Press, 1968.

———. *The Third Wave: Democratization in the Late Twentieth Century.* Norman: University of Oklahoma Press, 1991.

———. "Will More Countries Become Democratic?" *Political Science Quarterly* 99 (Summer 1984): 193–218.

Karakachanov, Alexander. Interview by author. Sofia, Bulgaria, October 4, 1993.

Kazassova, Ekaterina. "Sendov Remains Head of Parliament." *Bulletin of News from Bulgaria.* February 8, 1996. Embassy-Washington@Bulgaria. Com.

King, Gary, Robert O. Keohane, and Sidney Verba. *Designing Social Inquiry: Scientific Inference in Qualitative Research.* Princeton: Princeton University Press, 1994.

Koinova, Maria. "Will a Wave of Protests in Sofia Overflow Bulgaria?" *OMRI Daily Digest* 4, pt. 2 (January 3, 1997).

Kolarova, Rumyana, and Dimitr Dimitrov. "Roundtable Talks in Bulgaria." Center for Constitutionalism in Eastern Europe, University of Chicago Law School, 1991.

———. "Electoral Laws in Eastern Europe: Bulgaria." *East European Constitutional Review* 3 (Spring 1994): 50–55.

Krause, Stefan. "Bulgarian President and Premier Clash Over NATO Membership." *OMRI Daily Digest* 77, pt. 2 (April 19, 1995).

———. "Bulgarian President Defends Constitution, Criticizes Socialists." *OMRI Daily Digest* 135, pt. 2 (July 13, 1995).

———. "Bulgarian Premier Attacks President, Constitutional Court." *OMRI Daily Digest* 147, pt. 2 (July 31, 1995).

———. "Bulgarian Government Evicts Constitutional Court." *OMRI Daily Digest* 151, pt. 2 (August 4, 1995).

———. "Bulgarian Constitutional Court Invalidates Another Law." *OMRI Daily Digest* 193, pt. 2 (October 4, 1995).

———. "Socialists Lead After First Round of Bulgarian Local Elections." *OMRI Daily Digest* 211, pt. 2 (October 30, 1995).

———. "Bulgarian Opposition Prepares for Cooperation in Local Elections." *OMRI Daily Digest* 213, pt. 2 (November 1, 1995).

———. "Bulgarian Government Survives No Confidence Vote." *OMRI Daily Digest* 8, pt. 2 (January 11, 1996).

———. "Bulgarian President Calls for Stronger Presidency." *OMRI Daily Digest* 102, pt. 2 (May 27, 1996).

———. "Attacks on Bulgarian Government Continue." *OMRI Daily Digest* 103, pt. 2 (May 28, 1996).

———. "While Protests Against Austerity Measures Start." *OMRI Daily Digest* 105, pt. 2 (May 30, 1996).

———. "Bulgarian President Defeated in Primaries." *OMRI Daily Digest* 107, pt. 2 (June 3, 1996).

———. "Bulgarian Government Reshuffle: Videnov's Last Straw." *OMRI Analytical Brief* 1, no. 156 (June 10, 1996).

———. "Bulgarian Cabinet Reshuffle: Too Little Too Late." *OMRI Daily Digest* 113, pt. 2 (June 11, 1996).

———. "Bulgarian President Calls for Presidential Republic." *OMRI Daily Digest* 134, pt. 2 (July 12, 1996).

———. "Bulgarian President, Socialists Clash Again." *OMRI Daily Digest* 137, pt. 2 (July 17, 1996). (omri.cz/Publications/Digests/9607/Digest.960717.)

———. "Bulgarian Socialists Pick New Presidential Candidate." *OMRI Daily Digest* 171, pt. 2 (September 4, 1996). (omri.cz/Publications/Digests/9609/Digest.96094.)

———. "Socialist Reactions to Stoyanov's Victory." *OMRI Daily Digest* 213, pt. 2 (November 4, 1996).

———. "Opposition Candidate Wins Bulgarian Presidential Elections." *OMRI Daily Digest* 213, pt. 2 (November 4, 1996).

———. "Bulgarian Socialists Meet to Decide Fate of Premier." *OMRI Daily Digest* 219, pt. 2 (November 12, 1996).

———. "Bulgarian Premier Survives Party Confidence Vote." *OMRI Daily Digest* 220, pt. 2 (November 13, 1996).

———. "Bulgarian President Calls on Socialists, Opposition to Reach Compromise." *OMRI Daily Digest* 19, pt. 2 (January 28, 1997).

Kurian, George Thomas. *The New Book of World Rankings.* 3rd ed. New York: Facts on File, 1991.

"Law on the Judiciary." [Bulgaria] *State Gazette,* July 22, 1994.

Lerner, Daniel. *The Passing of Traditional Society.* New York: Free Press, 1958.

Liebert, Ulrike, and Maurizio Cotta, eds. *Parliaments and Democratic Consolidation in Southern Europe.* London: Pinter, 1990.

Lipset, Martin Seymour. "Some Social Requisites of Democracy: Economic

Development and Political Legitimacy." *American Political Science Review* 53 (March 1959): 69–105.

Loewenberg, Gerhard, and Samuel C. Patterson. *Comparing Legislatures.* Boston: Little, Brown, 1979.

Lukanov, Andrey. Interview by author. Sofia, Bulgaria, October 14, 1993.

Markotich, Stan. "Bulgarian Socialist Party Declines to Form Government." No. 177, Radio Free Europe/Radio Liberty, September 16, 1994.

McIntyre, Robert J. *Bulgaria: Politics, Economics, and Society.* London and New York: Pinter, 1988.

Melone, Albert P. "Bulgaria," in *World Encyclopedia of Parliaments and Legislatures,* edited by George T. Kurian. Washington D.C.: Congressional Quarterly Press, 1998.

———. "Bulgaria's National Roundtable Talks and the Politics of Accommodation." *International Political Science Review* 15 (1994): 257–73.

———. "Judicial Independence and Constitutional Politics in Bulgaria." *Judicature* 80 (1997): 280–85.

———. "The Struggle for Judicial Independence and the Transition Toward Democracy in Bulgaria." *Communist and Post-Communist Studies* 29 (1996): 231–43.

Melone, Albert P., and Carol E. Hays. "The Judicial Role in Bulgaria's Struggle for Human Rights." *Judicature* 77 (1994): 248–53.

Mezey, Michael L. *Comparative Legislatures.* Durham, N.C.: Duke University Press, 1979.

Mishler, William, and Richard Rose. "Support for Parliaments and Regimes in the Transition Toward Democracy in Eastern Europe." *Legislative Studies Quarterly* 19 (1994): 5–32.

Moser, Charles A. *Theory and History of the Bulgarian Transition.* Sofia, Bulgaria: Free Initiative Foundation, 1994.

Nagorski, Andrew. "With Allies Like These: Bulgaria's New Leaders Turn on Each Other." *Newsweek,* July 12, 1993, 34–35.

O'Donnell, Guillermo, Philippe C. Schmitter, and Laurence Whitehead, eds. *Transitions From Authoritarian Rule: Prospects for Democracy.* Baltimore: Johns Hopkins University Press, 1986.

Olson, David M., and Philip Norton. *The New Parliaments of Central and Eastern Europe.* London and Portland, Ore.: Frank Cass, 1996.

Open Media Research Institute's Daily Digest. Available from omri.cz/OMRI.

Oren, Nissan. *Bulgarian Communism: The Road to Power, 1934–1944.* New York: Columbia University Press, 1971.

Organization for Economic Co-Operation and Development. *Bulgaria: An Economic Assessment.* Washington, D.C.: OECD Publications and Information Center, Distributor, 1992.

Packenham, Robert. *Liberal America and the Third World: Political Develop-*

ment Ideas in Foreign Aid and Social Science. Princeton, N.J.: Princeton University Press, 1973.

Pehe, Jiri. "Bulgarian Prime Minister Proposed." No. 186, Radio Free Europe/Radio Liberty, September 29, 1994.

———. "Socialist Party Ahead in Bulgaria." No. 186, Radio Free Europe/Radio Liberty, September 29, 1994.

———. "Former Communists Gain Absolute Majority in Bulgaria." No. 239, Radio Free Europe/Radio Liberty, December 20, 1994.

Perlez, Jane. "To Quiet Protests, Party in Bulgaria Offers Talks." *New York Times,* January 14, 1997, A6.

Perry, Duncan M. "Bulgaria: A New Constitution and Free Elections." *RFE/RL Research Report* 1, no. 1 (January 3, 1992): 78–82.

Pinkele, Carl F. "Emerging in the Transitions: The Case for Assessing the Private Law Arena Within a Civil Society Focus." Paper prepared for the Santa Fe Conference of the IPSA Research Committee on Comparative Judicial Studies, Santa Fe, N. M., August 1993.

Pridham, Geoffrey, ed. *Securing Democracy: Political Parties and Democratic Consolidation in Southern Europe.* London and New York: Routledge, 1990.

Pridham, Geoffrey, and Paul G. Lewis. *Stabilising Fragile Democracies: Comparing New Party Systems in Southern and Eastern Europe.* London and New York: Routledge, 1996.

Przeworski, Adam. *Democracy and the Market: Political and Economic Reforms in Eastern Europe and Latin America.* Cambridge: Cambridge University Press, 1991.

Pundeff, Martin V. *Bulgaria in American Perspective: Political and Cultural Issues.* Sofia, Bulgaria: St. Kliment Ohridski University Press, 1993.

Riggs, Fred W. "Fragility of the Third World's Regimes." *International Social Science Journal* 45 (May 1993): 199–243.

———. "Presidentialism versus Parliamentarism: Implications for Representativeness and Legitimacy." *International Political Science Review* 18 (July 1997): 253–78.

Rostow, W. W. *The Stages of Economic Growth.* New York: Cambridge University Press, 1960.

"Rules of Organization and Procedure of the National Assembly." [Bulgaria] *State Gazette,* December 19, 1991.

Savov, Stefan. Interview by author. Sofia, Bulgaria, October 11, 1993.

Schmidhauser, John R., ed., *Comparative Judicial Systems: Challenging Frontiers in Conceptual and Empirical Analysis.* London: Butterworths, 1987.

Semerjiev, Attanas. Interview by author. Sofia, Bulgaria, October 11, 1995.

Shapiro, Ian. "Democratic Innovation: South Africa in Comparative Context." *World Politics* 46 (October 1993): 121–50.

Shapiro, Martin. *Courts: A Comparative and Political Analysis.* Chicago: University of Chicago Press, 1981.

Shapiro, Martin, and Alec Stone. "The New Constitutional Politics of Europe." *Comparative Political Studies* 26 (January 1994): 397–420.

Shklar, Judith N. *Legalism.* Cambridge, Mass.: Harvard University Press, 1964.

Simeonov, Petko. Interview by author. Sofia, Bulgaria, October 4, 1993.

Smale, Alison. "Ex-Communists Besieged in Balkans." *St. Louis Post-Dispatch,* January 14, 1997, 11B.

"A Surprise at the Top." *Time,* August 13, 1990, 28.

Szablowski, George J., and Hans-Ulrich Derlien. "East European Transitions, Elites, Bureaucracies, and the European Community." *Governance* 6 (July 1993): 304–24.

Tocqueville, Alexis de. *Democracy in America.* New York: Knopf, 1945.

Trenchev, Konstantin. Interview by author. Sofia, Bulgaria, October 19, 1993.

Troxel, Luan. "Bulgaria: Stable Ground in the Balkans?" *Current History* (November 1993): 386–89.

Tzvetkov, Plaman S. "The Politics of Transition in Bulgaria: Back to the Future?" *Problems of Communism* (May–June 1992): 34–43.

United Nations Development Programme. *Bulgaria: Human Development Report, 1995.* Sofia, Bulgaria: National and Global Development UNDP, 1995.

Vallinder, Torbjorn. "The Judicialization of Politics—A World-wide Phenomenon: Introduction." *International Political Science Review* 15 (April 1994): 91–99.

Vasilev, Jordan. Interview by author. Sofia, Bulgaria, October 7, 1993.

Verheijen, Tony. *Constitutional Pillars for New Democracies: The Cases of Bulgaria and Romania.* Leiden, The Netherlands: DSWO Press, Leiden University, 1995.

Wallerstein, Immanuel. *The Capitalist World Economy.* Cambridge: Cambridge University Press, 1979.

Weber, Max. *The Theory of Social and Economic Organization.* Glencoe, Ill.: Free Press, 1947.

White, Stephen, Judy Batt, and Paul G. Lewis, eds. *Developments in East European Politics.* Durham, N.C.: Duke University Press, 1993.

Wiarda, Howard J. *Introduction to Comparative Politics: Concepts and Processes.* Belmont, Calif.: Wadsworth, 1995.

———. *Latin American Politics: A New World of Possibility.* Belmont, Calif.: Wadsworth, 1995.

Wightman, Gordon, ed. *Party Formation in East-Central Europe: Post-Communist Politics in Czechoslovakia, Hungary, Poland and Bulgaria.* Brookfield, VT: Edward Elgar, 1995.

Yin, Robert K. *Case Study Research: Design and Methods.* Beverly Hills: Sage, 1984.

Yordanova, Maria. “President: Resigns or Rules?” *Insider* (January 1992): 4–5.

Zifcak, Spencer. “The Battle Over Presidential Power in Slovakia.” *East European Constitutional Review* 4 (Summer 1995): 61–65.

Index